Let's Ask the Cook

Let's Ask the Cook

by NAN WILEY

Cowles Book Company, Inc.

NEW YORK

Dedication

It gives me so much pleasure to dedicate this book to Erma Young, former editor of women's news for the *Kansas City Star,* who patiently guided me through the early pitfalls of columning—and to all those other unsung heroines, newspaper food editors everywhere. They are the ones who take it on the chin when a printed recipe fouls up, even when it isn't their fault.

Love and kisses for my husband, too. He is not only constantly encouraging but eats anything I put on the table, defrosts the freezer for me, and is fun to be with.

Contents

1 / Introduction

I devote a big part of my time and energy to dealing with food, and I can't imagine anything else half as fascinating. It all developed as a chain reaction.

I was happily engaged in doing a type of radio show on which I could talk about anything and everything to my heart's content. Then a call came from a much larger radio station in a much larger city to do a show totally devoted to food. I wasn't at all sure I wanted to be "typed" into a single category, but I finally tossed my hat over the moon and signed the contract. The program director of my new, larger assignment explained to me ever so smoothly, "Now, 'Happy Kitchen' is not just a program. It is a service as well."

This was the beginning of my real education in foods. Without realizing it, I was gaining knowledge of that part of the business I couldn't have obtained in any other way. One after another, all day and every day, the questions went like this:

Can I use honey in place of sugar in my cake? How much?

I have run out of bar chocolate for my cookies. Can I use cocoa instead?

My home-canned green beans look funny. Are they all right?

There were some heart-tearing moments, too. Every day we gave a new recipe over the air and offered it in printed form, if the listener would send in a stamped, self-addressed envelope.

One day I spotted a very familiar address in the mail stack. But this time, when I started reading, my eyes popped. "I don't know what recipe you gave yesterday. My husband died just before your broadcast and I wasn't able to listen, but will you send it anyway?"

Good heavens! How callous can you get? But then I read on. "You may think this a strange request but, you see, the only way I can get through all this and hang onto my sanity until my son gets here tonight from California is to try to do everything just the way I've done it every day. I have always listened to your program and I have always sent for the recipes so I just have to do it today, too."

I still gulp every time I think of that pathetic letter. If you don't feel terribly small and humble and grateful at the sudden realization that you have really become a part of someone's family, then you are a lot tougher than I will ever be.

I spent several years conducting daily radio cooking shows, plus another long stint as food consultant for a large supermarket chain. It convinced me there was a crying need for some sort of clearinghouse column that would answer all the questions many cookbooks never do. And it inspired me to create "Let's Ask the Cook."

When a recipe flops, for goodness knows what reason, the frustrated home cook usually can't find an immediate answer in the cookbook. I could own mink-lined cupboards if I had a dime for every letter that says, "Here is my recipe and here is what I did with it. What did I do wrong?"

I try to keep every column as down-to-earth as I can make it and do not airily assume that champagne and truffles are standard items in every kitchen cupboard. It is quite possible to live nicely without either.

Since I work from my own kitchen at home, I am in small danger of taking the "shining white laboratory" approach. I appreciate the tremendous research done in professional test kitchens, but sometimes their recipes must have been figured out with a slide rule rather than through actual performance. In home kitchens results are not always the same.

And while I have given the approximate number of servings per recipe in this book, it is just that—approximate. It is impossible to determine how far any dish will stretch because we are all so different in our needs and eating habits. One of my readers put it best: "When a cookbook tells me a recipe will make 4 servings I automatically double it. Then maybe it will be enough for the six of us. Just maybe." Me, too. There is a long-standing cookbook axiom that 4 ounces of meat constitutes a serving. At our house that is considered little more than a good mouthful. The day I can't polish off an 8-ounce steak it is time to take my temperature.

I have tried many a cookie recipe that assures me it will make 6 dozen. It just never does for me. I am lucky if I wind up with 4 dozen. And not very big cookies, at that.

It is foolish to suppose the man engaged in active labor is going to be happy with what a sedentary worker finds adequate. Small tots usually want small portions. By the time they hit junior high they are bottomless pits. Elderly people may be very light eaters. You know your family's intake better than I do. I tried to dodge this how-many angle, but the editors insisted it had to be included, so send any I-am-mad-at-you letters on this score to them.

"Just what is it you have to do to get to be a columnist?" That's the one curious question any columnist hears over and over again.

Well, it helps if you're a bit schizophrenic to begin with, but don't let the lack of a mental quirk stop you. You'll be half-crazy in no time, anyway. There will come days when you will moodily doubt your sanity in ever having gotten involved in the first place.

Doing a regular column on any subject at all has been compared to digging a daily grave for yourself. You have to be prepared to remain calm through family births, deaths, and similar traumatic experiences. Columnists do not live in ivory towers. They have family fights, tax problems, hangovers, and runny noses the same as anyone else. And you can never call up the boss to say, "Sorry, I don't feel like working today." But will you find any of us parting with our hard-won by-lines without a bit of shin kicking and eye gouging? Not on your sweet life. It's a habit harder to kick than eating.

How do you get to be a columnist? First, you decide there is some subject about which you think you know at least a little more than the average person. You won't know it all. Practice learning to be a master diplomat, psychologist, and sympathizer with human nature, but remain gutsy enough to take issue with popular opinion when you think you are right.

If you are a free-lancer—working on your own when the columning bug bites you—you head for the nearest newspaper, large or small, fight your way in to see the editor, and confess your intentions. If his ulcers are not kicking up too badly that day, he may say, "Okay, make up ten sample columns and we'll take a look." He hopes you will never come back. But you do and sometimes you're in.

From there on out, you are hooked. In all probability you will not get rich overnight—despite the common belief that all columnists, especially syndicated ones, drive chartreuse Cadillacs and that lady columnists sleep on satin sheets and own a collection of hand-tied lavender wigs.

One other requisite. You must not be the sensitive type. Unfortunately I am very thin-skinned. I still bleed from even an occasional pan letter; I glow with every bit of praise or appreciation.

I am a great one to encourage experimentation in cooking. How else would I have discovered that adding a healthy pinch of powdered pizza seasoning to cooked green beans will have the whole family sniffing kitchenward, "What smells so good?"

A reader from Saginaw, Michigan, asked, "What does a person have to do to get into your column? I have sent in two questions which haven't been answered. How do you choose what you use?"

I agonize, that's what I do! Only those close to me know how much fretting and hand-wringing I do when it's zero hour for getting the next batch of columns in the mail. Mostly, I try to use what I think will be of most interest to the greatest number of people; now and then I use a column so completely offbeat it is either fascinating or funny. Sometimes a subject seems so basic that I wonder why I ever thought it should be included. That's when I am most apt to get surprised by the number of people who write saying, "That's something I always wanted to know!" Often a question is seasonal and must be held for another year before it can be answered.

There are people who don't mind seeing their names in print; there are others who request, "No name, please." And still others say, "It was fun once but not again. I was busy with phone-answering and neighbors running in for days afterward. Everybody in town called to say, 'Hey, you made headlines.' I even heard from distant relatives I would just as soon got lost permanently."

Every now and then, some earnest lady or even a research group will ask, "Do you have your own panel of experts for cross-section sampling of the foods you write about?"

Oh, yes, by all means. Of course, my "panel" might be a little different from what you would imagine. Nevertheless I consider its members experts. That panel consists of half a dozen lads at the corner service station, the postman, the man who picks up my cleaning, and a couple of neighbors. I figure you just can't get more of a cross section than that. What's more, they can be brutally frank on the comparative merits of any given pie, cake, or cookie. Not that they ever pass up a chance at the next batch!

2/Kitchen mechanics

In my high school days I wasted forty-five minutes a day for a mandatory two years of math trying to master algebra and geometry. It was a total loss.

Better I should have spent that valuable time learning elementary household repair—how to fix a drippy faucet, a leaking toilet tank float bulb, a broken light switch, a clogged lint trap in a clothes dryer, a balky sink drain, to name a few. All relatively simple jobs if you just know the rudiments.

Now I, like every other woman, am at the mercy of His Highness the Appliance Repair Artist. He may or may not come the next day to cope with the emergency. By the time he does arrive, I am so glad to see him that my hand hardly shakes at all as I write out the astronomical check for ten minutes' work.

So our only line of defense now is to take as good care of our pampered mechanical darlings as possible. Save the guarantee; reread the instruction sheets from time to time. Watch what the service person does when he is called. You might learn something. Even so, all of that doesn't always help.

FIRE EXTINGUISHER

The most valuable nonelectrical gadget in my kitchen is my little heavy-duty plastic squeeze-type fire extinguisher. Our house might have gone up in flames one night, or at least considerably more damage could have occurred, if we had not owned one. Just one-fourth inch of grease in a skillet caught fire while I went to answer the doorbell. As I dashed to call the fire department, my husband grabbed the extinguisher from a side cabinet where it had been, unused, for three years. He put the flames out in a short time.

The type of extinguisher I recommend is no larger than a spray can of starch, is filled with a nontoxic powdered chemical, and fits the hand perfectly. All you do is whip off the cap and start spraying. You will find these, under various trade names, at hardware stores and lumberyards. When you get yours —and I hope you do—see to it that every member of the family knows where it is.

Lacking a fire extinguisher, baking soda makes a handy substitute and should be ready for use at all times. In case of a stove fire, try to keep your head long enough to turn off the burner. Then stand back and toss the soda at the base of the flames. It doesn't do much good on deep fat, but for a skillet blaze it's okay. Don't toss flour on a fire. It can explode.

COOKBOOKS

Dear Nan: What sort of cookbook should I buy for a bride who has never cooked before? —LORAIN, OHIO.

Never mind the fancy French or gourmet cookbooks. You'll only scare the wits out of the beginner and she'll never get past TV dinners. More elaborate books can come later. For a starter, I would recommend a good big basic book of long-standing reputation. Newer editions of these keep up to date with revisions and don't sacrifice the good old basics.

RECIPE FILE

Dear Nan: I collect recipes and would appreciate any suggestions on how to keep them neat. —OGDEN, UTAH.

You can paste clippings in a separate scrapbook for each category. You don't have to spend a lot of money on this thing. Loose-leaf pages in a ring binder are ideal; it's easy to add more as you go along. Or, if you have finally tried some recipe that sounded great but didn't appeal to you, it's a simple matter to remove it without messing things up. There are some all-time favorite recipes and I would have an absolute fit if I lost them. Those are the ones I copy into one special loose-leaf notebook. Many is the time I have been glad I did!

REFRIGERATOR

Here comes the voice of expensive experience again. With the outdoor temperature a soaring 95 degrees, my three-year-old refrigerator-freezer started throwing fits. I started throwing the same, especially when all I could get out of service companies was, "Maybe tomorrow—we're stacked with calls." Oh, fine!

The bottom part of my freezer was icing up something awful with thick frost all over everything. At the same time, the temperature was upping from its proper zero reading. I checked the top part and found the temperature was not holding at its accustomed 38 degrees. Nothing seemed to be working except the refrig lights.

Finally, one serviceman diagnosed the trouble, on the phone, as "back frost" and instructed me to pull the plug at once or I might burn out the motor.

The first thing the repairman did on arrival was remove the plate at the bottom, the one that covers the works in my particular model. "Here is your problem. Dust collects in not only the first coil, but in the second set, which you can't possibly see. When you get enough of a buildup, it is like trying to drive your car with a blanket tossed over the engine."

He recommended using the blower attachment of a vacuum sweeper every now and then to clean the coils. Turn the refrig off while you are doing this brief chore.

Any refrig must be absolutely level to perform correctly.

It is also handy to keep portable thermometers in both sections of your refrigerator. That way, you know precisely what is happening to the temperatures.

SINK DRAINS

Even persnickety clean people who have dustcloths for their dustcloths run into a smelly sink-drain problem now and then. Our automatic garbage disposers are just great, but those little wheels in the mechanism do collect a bit of crud in their daily chunk-and-chew job. It's almost impossible to reach down to do much about it. The bad part is that you can't use commercial cleaners on them without doing more harm than good. Such cleaners nullify the sewage action.

There is an answer, though. Just pour hot salt water through the disposer unit once or twice a week. That's okay for the other side of a divided sink, too, because salt water doesn't harm the pipes.

TOASTER

Dear Nan: My sister's toaster doesn't always pop the toast the way it should, so she reaches down into it with a fork to pick up the bread. This makes me nervous as I have heard you can get a bad shock that way. —CHARDON, OHIO.

You surely can. Sis has just been lucky this far. If she hits one of those glowing little wires with a metal fork before the toaster clicks off, she may get a jolt she will remember. Or, worse still, if the toaster is really faulty, she may never remember anything again. If she thinks she just has to use that fork, she had better unplug the toaster first.

How long since she has cleaned the toaster? It may be jammed with a load of crumbs, especially if she butters the bread before toasting—something it isn't wise to do. Tell her to upend the toaster and unscrew the bottom plate for cleaning. She may be surprised at the mess of goop she finds there.

ELECTRIC DEEP FRYER

A young friend of mine remarked that she didn't think it worthwhile to own an electric deep fryer because she made French fries only occasionally.

My goodness, a "deep fryer" is really a deep cooker all by itself because it is ideal for so many dishes. I discovered that years ago when I had to wait for a serviceman to make a small but important repair on my range. Soups, stews, pot roasts, navy beans, stewed fruits, stewed chicken, spaghetti are just a few of the items and suggested temperatures listed on the front of mine.

In most cases, you would lift out the fry basket for the uses I have mentioned, except for spaghetti. For that, leave the basket in. When the spaghetti is done, it is perfectly drained without fuss or muss as you lift the basket from the water.

CAN OPENER

When I was doing a daily radio show, I asked, "Ladies, what would you say is the dirtiest appliance in your kitchen? Guess again. It's probably your can opener. It's so easy just to toss it back in the drawer without a thorough scalding, maybe not even a cold-water rinse."

At the time, I was talking about a manually operated opener, but it holds just as true today for our nice little electric helpers. It is awfully hard to do a thorough cleaning job on the small cutter mechanism unless you take the whole thing apart. Day by day, almost unnoticed in our hurry-up schedules, the goop surrounding the can cutter builds up until, all of a sudden, it is visible to the naked eye.

OVEN THERMOMETERS

Dear Nan: Do you think it is worthwhile to have one of those little portable oven thermometers? What's the use when all ranges come equipped with thermostatic controls these days?
— HAMLIN, TEXAS.

I wouldn't be without mine. As wonderful as today's ranges are, they can still get off kilter once in a while. I like my portable thermometer as a double check. It has paid off more than once, even though my oven control is the kind you can lift off to correct a faulty setting. You can't know just how far off the setting is without the portable checker.

SPACE

Dear Nan: You say you cook from a small kitchen right in your own home, so what do you do with all the pans you must need and all your canned stuff? Where do you cool batches of cookies when the sink space is all taken up with mixing bowl mess? Don't tell me on the kitchen table. I don't have room for one. — COLUMBIA, MISSOURI.

Neither do I. My beloved little antique commode is full of pans. For cookie cooling I set up the ironing board or a card table temporarily. Lightweight pans and gadgets that I use most often hang on the wall over my range. They are suspended from hooks latched into a strip made for the purpose that you can buy at hardware stores or lumberyards.

We turned the broom closet into the handiest canned goods cupboard I have ever owned by lining the back wall with shelves just large enough for one-can depth. Now I can see at a glance what I have without having to lunge into a floor cupboard. I put my less-used pans there. I should mention, in that closet there is still room for the broom by hanging it on the door. A top shelf holds the dustpan and a sack of clean rags. My string sack of paper bags sits on the floor. Every inch is used to best advantage.

You might check on how many battered old pans you've been hoarding without having used them in years. Donate them to the rummage sale. The newer nested pans are space savers in themselves.

SALAD BOWLS

Dear Nan: I washed my new wooden salad bowls in good suds and set them on a sunny windowsill to dry, and my mother about flipped. She said that was all wrong, but couldn't give me any reason why. What do you say?

—MADISON, NEW JERSEY.

I side completely with the method of just wiping the bowls with paper toweling when I have used a vinegar-oil dressing. It conditions and preserves such bowls as nothing else can. One noted gourmet so treasured the big wooden salad bowl he had so treated for a long period of years that he willed it to his best friend as his most cherished possession. He wanted to make sure it would continue to be well cared for.

Some people claim unwashed bowls eventually develop cracks and a rancid taste. I have had my uncoated wooden bowls for thirty years, and they have done neither. I just make sure they are not nested away damp and that there are small squares of waxed paper or clear plastic wrap between each one.

To my way of thinking, constant laundering of the bowls is much more apt to cause a soapy taste and aroma. Detergents are simply murder on coated wooden bowls. They'll eat through that supposedly good-forever coating in no time.

Never set wooden salad bowls in direct sunlight or other heat to dry. That encourages splits or cracks like crazy. Never, never let them soak in water.

CUTLERY

Dear Nan: Why can't we buy paring knives that stay sharp or can be sharpened? I have tried all kinds of knives and right now the best ones I have are the steak knives I got last winter in laundry soap boxes. I have just one butcher knife I can sharpen after almost twenty years of use.
—MINNEAPOLIS, MINNESOTA.

My pet paring knife is the slotted kind, not stainless steel. It isn't very pretty, but it does a good job, and it seems to be self-sharpening. I have some stainless steel cutlery, too, including small serrated knives. When it comes to larger knives, I still prefer two nonstainless monsters I have had for years.

I still get a beautiful edge on my knives by giving them an occasional run-through on one of those little handled sharpeners where you whisk the blade between two wheels. What is even better, when necessary, is my electric knife-and-scissors sharpener that is part of my automatic can opener.

I know there are authorities who insist it is easier to get a good cutting edge on a stainless blade. However, beyond even my own experience, I have talked to many a professional meatcutter, and they wouldn't dream of using anything but the nonstainless knives. It is a good investment to buy the best quality you can find, stainless or nonstainless. Then take good care. Keep the knives racked, not tossed in a kitchen drawer. Sharpen well before they get so dull they won't even cut butter.

I heard a man on a TV cooking show say every kitchen ought to have a chef's knife, but he didn't show one, and those of us who watched have no idea what he was talking about. I'm sure you do.
—TARENTUM, PENNSYLVANIA.

That item is also called a French knife. Almost any housewares department stocks them. The blade is rather broad at the base, and is used for chopping or dicing vegetables on a cutting board with a rocking motion of blade against board, one hand on the handle right below the base of the blade, the other on the dull portion of the blade tip. The chef who showed me how to use one cautioned me to keep my thumb folded back into my palm, or it would shortly be among the missing.

MEAT LIFTER

Dear Nan: What do you consider the most useful gadget in your kitchen? —RALEIGH, NORTH CAROLINA.

That's a toughie! I guess, aside from my fire extinguisher and small electrical appliances, it just has to be my meat lifter. It looks like an oversized, fan-shaped pancake turner. If that was the last one in the world, I would guard it with a pair of ornery lions leashed to the cupboard.

That thing not only lifts roasts (what it was meant for) but gets hand-molded meat loaves out of the pan in one piece, even when they are on the juicy side. It helps lift turkeys onto the platter without having them skid to the kitchen floor. (That happened to me once.) It is great for scooping several cookies from the baking sheet at one time.

COOKWARE

Dear Nan: Maybe sometime you can say something about skillets. I can't get along at all with my stainless steel one. I know you like cast iron and I have a small one, but it has a "hot spot." Plain aluminum goes out of shape. How about heavy aluminum? I want to buy a really good skillet but hesitate. —KANSAS CITY, MISSOURI.

If I were skillet shopping tomorrow, I know my vote would go for a good, heavy, cast-aluminum one, if you can find such a thing. Some of the best are not sold in stores but by house salesmen. Anytime you burn food in aluminum, just boil water in the pan until the particles soften enough to scoop out with a plastic scraper.

No one material has all the advantages, but some have more than others. Aluminum heats quickly and evenly—that means a lot—but if it is too thin, it dents and warps. Heavy aluminum is practically indestructible.

Stainless steel is durable and easy to take care of, but a great deal of it is a poor conductor of heat. Uneven heat can cause sticking and burning of thick foods. Very high cooking temperatures may discolor stainless steel permanently. I notice that if a pan boils over on a new set I got not long ago, the watermarks on the outside remain. I have used everything, including remedies suggested by the manufacturer, but these spots are still there. A utilities test kitchen says it is having the same trouble. There are some superior brands of stainless steel ware that do a good job. Unfortunately, most of these, too, are not available at stores but are sold through individual salesmen.

Cast iron is especially good for long, slow cooking, but I use mine for anything. You do have to watch any soaking of these pans in dishwater these days, because detergents take off the "seasoning." But they're easy to reseason. Just coat the inside of the pan with unsalted fat or oil, heat in a 200- to 250-degree oven for 2 or 3 hours. You can now find cast-iron cookware coated with colorful ceramic. It is exceptionally durable.

Heat-resistant glass for top-of-the-range cooking looks nice and heats slowly but evenly. It is easy to see what's cooking, but glass cracks with sudden temperature changes or can break outright if you let it boil dry. On an electric range, use a small wire grid under the pans when cooking on high.

The ceramic glass utensils—the kind you take directly from freezer to oven—have a lot going for them. They don't discolor and don't break if they boil dry, but they can break if dropped onto a hard surface. The cost is high for general use, but I notice some of the prices are now coming down.

TEFLON COOKWARE

Dear Nan: I bought a whole new set of Teflon-lined pans. They are very pretty and colorful but now the nonstick part gets a sort of spotty white film on it that I can't get off. And food still sticks no matter how much they claim it won't! It isn't scratchproof. I'm mad! —UTICA, NEW YORK.

Before you get teed off any further, go take another look at the instruction book that, I am sure, must have come with your set. While it is true that newer Teflon-lined pans are a lot better than those first thin-coated ones, they still won't stand a lot of abuse.

There are certain rules for their care. That "white film" you speak of probably comes from an accumulation of minerals in the water. There is nothing wrong with the Teflon. You can get it off safely with a solution of equal parts water and vinegar or lemon juice in the pan. Let soak for about 10 minutes. If there is any film on the inside of the cover, dip a soft cloth in a little of the solution and rub. Of course, you must then recondition, as instructions tell you to do, before you use the pans again. That's a step a lot of people just don't bother with when they should pay strict heed. You are supposed to wash every pot and pan thoroughly with hot soapy water to remove any lingering of manufacturing oil. Rinse with hot water and dry. Then wipe a teaspoon of vegetable oil with a paper towel over the nonstick part. If you don't, you can't be sure that you won't have a sticking problem. You may also use special Teflon cleaners, being careful to recondition. Most Teflon pans are dishwasher safe, but again you have to recondition. Since they clean so easily anyway, I see no reason to put them in the machine.

Your guarantee undoubtedly says "scratch resistant," but that's not the same thing as "scratchproof." While it is now considered safe to use smooth metal spoons and spatulas on hard-coated Teflon, you are still cautioned not to use rotary beaters, metal mashers, or knives.

Here are some other rules to follow: Use just low to medium heat for top-of-the-range cooking, never the highest heat.

Don't overheat empty pans when a dish calls for preheating. Don't put Teflon-coated ware under a broiler! Never pour cold water into a hot pan.

CAKE PANS

Dear Nan: I am buying new cake pans. Is there any special kind you would recommend?   —FOND DU LAC, WISCONSIN.

Get one of two kinds, and you'll never get stuck with stuck cake layers. The ones I like best are those that have an attached metal strip running from the center of the pan to the rim with a little handle attached. When the cake is cool, all you do is whack that handle around, and it's a breeze to get the cake out.

Then there are the two-piece pans with removable bottoms. Run a knife around the edge, push the pan bottom with your hand, and out comes the layer for further cooling.

FOIL

Dear Nan: Which side of the foil should be on the outside— the shiny or the dull?   —BEREA, KENTUCKY.

One aluminum foil manufacturer states: "It really doesn't matter which side you use. In the rolling process, one side of the foil becomes shiny; the other—not in contact with the heavy roller—comes out with a mat finish."

Another reader asks: "I just hate to clean my broiler. Is it okay to lay a sheet of foil across the rack when I am broiling steak? A neighbor says I shouldn't do this because foil can catch fire."

No, foil does not catch fire. If you are broiling steaks or

chops with quite a lot of fat to them, the melted fat collects on the foil and gets very hot. It is the grease that catches fire, not the foil. Same thing can happen if you try to use a shallow foil-lined pan for broiling. Best not to risk it. When you use your regular broiler rack arrangement, without foil, the grease drips down into the pan below, usually out of danger.

FOOD STORAGE

Dear Nan: What sort of containers do you find satisfactory for storing rice, macaroni, and the like? When a person leaves them in their original boxes or bags it makes for such a messy looking cupboard. —EUGENE, OREGON.

Sometimes we do get quite a jumble of various-sized packages. I know I used to get plenty mad at myself when I'd knock over an opened box and the contents would be all over the place! Ever try to find that last grain of spilled rice?

I have some attractive canisters I keep right on a counter top for things like flour and sugar. For my cupboard, I like to transfer items into saved-up glass jars with screw tops, large or small. I always store brown sugar, raisins, nuts, and similar items that way. They not only stay fresher, but I can see at a glance just how much I have left.

There is something else I do: transfer opened boxes of baking soda into a jar right after I've used it the first time. I label this so I won't mistake it for a look-alike.

3 / Seasoning for all seasons

A neighbor once confided to me, "My wife is not an imaginative cook. She just salts and peppers everything, including the Sunday roast. As soon as she takes off for church, I add a few herbs and spices on my own. She hasn't caught on, even now, that this is what makes the meat taste so good."

In recent years a good many cooks have just caught on to what their pioneer ancestors knew all the time. Many a Conestoga wagon going west carried carefully nurtured herb cuttings for future gardens. They knew those herbs would perk up otherwise monotonous meals.

What puzzles beginners is, what herb goes where? There really is no hard and fast rule. While I regret I can't take up scarce space in this book for a complete listing, you would probably forget anyway without frequent reference. Your best bet is a good-sized herb chart hung right in the kitchen. You can find them in housewares departments, gourmet and gift shops, even some mail order catalogs. After a while, you'll be an old pro at the game.

Don't be disappointed if you don't love every herb flavor. Few people do. Don't make the mistake of thinking "if a little is good, a lot would be better." That can be disastrous. Play it slow and easy. Don't have more than one herbed dish a meal.

DRIED VEGETABLE FLAKES

Dear Nan: Could you tell me how to make my own dehydrated flakes from celery leaves, parsley, and green pepper? I think I remember reading that they were baked in a slow oven overnight. —OGDEN, UTAH.

You can do any of them in the oven, but I wouldn't try it overnight. I like to keep an eye on these things because timing cannot be exact. There can be a difference in moisture content of these items. I dry the celery leaves and parsley by spreading them out on a cookie sheet in a 200-degree oven till they crumble in my fingers. Bottle the flakes perfectly dry or they become moldy in the bottle.

I do the green peppers in a 170-degree oven to be on the safe side. You don't want to scorch them before they are dry inside. I dice the peppers into about ¼-inch pieces, strew them around on the cookie sheet, close the oven door, and take a check-look now and then. It takes about 3 hours. Every now and then during this time I swish the pepper bits around with my fingers for even drying. Allow them to sit in an open shallow dish and shrink them still further before storing.

You can also sun-dry parsley and celery leaves, as well as just about any herb in your garden, by washing well, stemming, and then spreading them out on cheesecloth or any porous material on a cookie sheet placed in a warm, sunny, protected spot. It helps if you turn them every so often. If it is at all breezy, you will have to cover them with another layer of the material or they might get blown into the next county. It may take as long as three days for complete drying. It is possible to dry some types of whole peppers by hanging them in the sun, especially if they are the long narrow kind.

MINT LEAVES

Dear Nan: Here's my method for drying fresh mint leaves to be used in stews, etc., and for making mint sauce. I wash the mint leaves, then put them in paper bags and tie them to the clothesline, letting them dry for several days till they are crisp. Then I put the dried leaves in my blender and buzz them around until they are just green dust. Bottle for use. My husband is an Englishman and insists on having mint sauce with lamb. After the fresh mint is finished, we use the dried. —OTTAWA, ONTARIO, CANADA.

Blenderizing the dried mint is a great idea. An easy way to make mint sauce is to scald ½ cup of vinegar and stir in anywhere from 1 to 2 tablespoons sugar till it dissolves. That done, add about ¼ cup shredded fresh mint leaves and be sure to let the sauce stand for an hour or more before using, so you will get the full infusion.

My family likes chopped mint in melted butter on whole cooked carrots. Chives, the same way. The mint, especially, gives the carrots an unusual flavor. One year I raised dill and put sprays in plastic bags to freeze. Then I used those pieces of dill in melted butter to put on small heated canned potatoes. Dill and butter are used on potatoes in Sweden at nearly every meal. This freshens the canned potatoes with a nice touch. —ST. PAUL, MINNESOTA.

TARRAGON

Dear Nan: I have a friend whose husband is on a salt-free diet. To vary this she plans to bake a chicken, brushing same with a mixture of ginger and oil and adding minced tarragon. My dictionary defines that herb as a European plant. Where can this be obtained? —TOPEKA, KANSAS.

Tarragon is found in dried form in any good spice and herb section of your store. With any luck at all, it can also be grown in the garden, although a hot dry summer might burn it out.

It has a very distinctive taste—something of a licorice flavor—so it's best to go easy until you see if it's liked. And marinate the dried tarragon in the ginger-oil blend for a few minutes before using.

SEA SALT

Dear Nan: One of my cookbooks has a recipe calling for sea salt, but where do you get it? My grocery doesn't have it. What's the advantage of it, anyway? —LINCOLN, NEBRASKA.

You can find sea salt at food specialty shops and some health food stores. But I warn you, once you become acquainted with it you may never settle for anything else as a table salt. It is more coarse than regular salt and comes in several grinds. You don't need as much of it in most instances.

BAY LEAF

It's amazing how many people don't know about bay leaf uses. Have you ever tried adding a leaf to a pot of potatoes you are boiling for "butter potatoes"? Please do. You'll be surprised.

JACK TOBIN'S MUSTARD SAUCE

Dear Nan: While driving through the Middle West on a Saturday morning, I happened to tune in on a radio show and heard a recipe for a mustard sauce that sounded pretty good. —PATERSON, NEW JERSEY.

You were undoubtedly listening to the Jack Tobin "Jack of All Trades" show emanating out of WDAF, Kansas City, Missouri. That mustard sauce can't be anything but his. It goes like this:

Mix 1 cup white vinegar with 1 cup dry mustard and let it set overnight. Next morning stir in 2 well-beaten eggs, 1 cup sugar, and a pinch of salt. Bring that to a slow boil and cook till it coats the spoon, stirring continuously. Cool and refrigerate.

This mustard sauce is an awfully good base for sauces on vegetables. Fish, too, but you certainly won't need any other seasonings. If you like any of the condensed cream soups as vegetable dressings, it won't be a bit amiss to add 1 or 2 spoon-fuls of this—if you like mustard, that is.

NOTE: The "1 cup dry mustard" is by volume, not weight. It takes only about 3 to 4 ounces dry mustard to fill your 8-ounce measuring cup. In jars or cans, dry mustard packs down some-what, fluffs up when you spoon it out.

PAPRIKA

Dear Nan: Could you tell me if paprika is hot or not? I have never used any because I cannot eat highly seasoned foods.
—DEER PARK, NEW YORK.

Oh, my, I would be lost without my paprika shaker. Most of the paprika we get in this country is very mild, but some food specialty shops have several gradations right on up to what is called for in real Hungarian dishes such as paprikash. It is pungent rather than hot. The brighter the color, usually, the better the grade.

Do you like plain boiled noodles? Paprika sprinkled over the buttered noodles gives a lot more appeal. And I can't imagine deviled eggs without a dash of paprika over the golden filling. I like to give a dash on all sides of little boiled potatoes when I butter-brown them in a skillet. Gives them a lovely rosy glow.

I really don't think paprika would upset your digestion if you get the mild kind.

GARLIC

Dear Nan: My mother grows garlic and gives me a good sup-ply every year, but it always dries out before I can use maybe half a dozen of the buds. It stays fresh in the stores, so what do they do that I'm not? —CHERRYVALE, KANSAS.

There are several solutions to your problem. One lady who raises her own garlic separates and cleans the garlic buds just as you would for ordinary use. Then she slips them into a jar with a tight-fitting lid and covers the buds with ordinary salad oil. You do have to refrigerate the jar. If you like the taste of garlic in a vinegar-oil salad dressing, you can use a little of the garlic oil in that.

You can also freeze the garlic. Pull it apart into the separate cloves but don't peel them. Store in tightly capped baby-food jars or something about that size. The garlic may be a little soft on thawing but the flavor is still fine.

POTPOURRI

I doubt if any of us makes as much use of all our fine seasonings as we might. Ever tried a touch of nutmeg with green beans, cabbage, cauliflower, meatballs, fried bananas, or berries with cream?

A little chili powder puts zip in scrambled eggs.

Ginger is fine on melon, summer squash, canned peaches, pears, apricots, or applesauce.

You'll be living it up with a touch of mace in chocolate dishes, fish sauces, broiled grapefruit, whipped cream for cake or pudding topping.

French fries, beets, and cabbage wedges are all improved with caraway seed. Nice blended with cheese spreads, too.

I would be lost without celery seed for soups, stews, slaw, fish, tomato, or potato dishes.

I do like the blended pumpkin pie spice, a mixture of ginger, cinnamon, nutmeg, allspice, mace, and cloves. It not only makes a terrific pumpkin pie, but I use it for apple and other pies as a change, and sometimes in cookies or cakes that may call for just cinnamon or ginger. About pumpkin pie, it's funny that so many of us relegate it solely to the holidays. It's good any old time. One restaurant in my locality advertises, "Pumpkin pie 365 days of the year!" It sells, too.

4 / Meats: the meal maker

Let's face it. Just about any kind of meat is costly today. Some just aren't as expensive as others, so we'll concentrate on those. You won't find any thick steaks here.

It isn't enough that a dish be relatively inexpensive. (1) It has to taste good. (2) It has to look good. (3) It should contain a decent amount of protein, one way or another.

Choose meat with the least waste to it. Chuck steaks may seem a lot cheaper than flank steak, but not when you consider that flank is all meat and chucks often have a lot of fat, bone, and gristle. Buy lean chuck roasts when you can. Cube the meat yourself. There is a whale of a price difference between the two. The chuck often makes a more flavorful dish.

Packaged "lunch meats" are not inexpensive. Look at those little 6- or 8-ounce packages and figure up what you're paying per pound. Most frankfurters have an awfully high percent of fat included.

SALISBURY STEAK

Dear Nan: Please tell me how to prepare Salisbury steak.
— REDDING, CALIFORNIA.

It is a problem to give an exact version of Salisbury steak. Salisbury is an overgrown hamburger on the thick side, smothered in the sauce, whatever it might be. Could be brown gravy sauce, a thick creole tomato sauce with green pepper and celery tossed in, even a sour cream or mushroom sauce with a touch of curry.

Don't pack the meat down hard when you shape it into the patties. There is usually some added moisture like water or milk. If you'll fork-toss the mixture, it will stay on the fluffy side. One of the best versions I ever tasted included a small amount of finely chopped raw salt pork or bacon mixed in with the beef. That does give good additional flavor. But here is a favorite recipe:

Salisbury Steak Deluxe

You can serve this when company comes and never feel apologetic. It's the seasoning that counts.

1 can condensed golden mushroom soup	1 egg, slightly beaten
1 tablespoon prepared mustard	¼ cup fine dry bread crumbs
2 teaspoons Worcestershire sauce	¼ cup chopped onion
1 teaspoon horseradish	½ teaspoon salt
1½ pounds ground beef	Pepper to taste
	½ cup water
	2 tablespoons chopped parsley

Blend soup, mustard, Worcestershire, and horseradish. Combine beef with ¼ cup of this mixture. Then add the egg, crumbs, onion, salt, and pepper. Shape into 6 patties. Brown in a skillet, pour off any excess fat, stir in the rest of the mixture, water, and parsley. Cover and cook over low heat for about 20 minutes, stirring sauce occasionally. Serve with mashed potatoes or rice. A big electric skillet is ideal for this. *Makes 4 to 6 servings.*

HAMBURGERS

Dear Nan: Could you help me out? My husband is on an ulcer diet so his hamburgers must be broiled, but I can't fix

> *them that way without having them wind up hard and crusty. His have to be on the soft side. Is there something I could mix with the hamburger?*—GRAVOIS MILLS, MISSOURI.

You can add about ½ cup of milk-soaked cracker crumbs or uncooked oatmeal to the meat or—if he is permitted to have it —1 or 2 tablespoons of mayonnaise, worked into the mixture. Most ulcer people are allowed some fats or oils, as long as they aren't used for frying. Check his diet list.

I am inclined to think you simply have those patties too close to the broiler heat. Try moving the rack down another notch. They'll take a little longer to get done, but you won't have that hard crust.

Most beef is ground fine by the butcher. That's okay for meat loaves and such, but it isn't so hot for broiled burgers. When you shape the patties, try to do them sort of looselike. And don't whop them with the turner when you do the other side. That presses juices out.

> *Has the lady ever tried baking her hamburgers? I always cook my ground beef patties that way and find them so much nicer than fried or broiled. I always add mayonnaise to the meat for extra moistness, just as you do, but I also add a little lemon juice. That's still better taste.* —SALINA, KANSAS.

I have my own ideas about hamburgers but, since burgers often seem to taste better at drive-ins than they do at home, I checked with an obliging cook at a good drive-in. He recommends cooking the hamburgers rapidly on a barely greased grill set at 350 degrees, no higher. Nor does he salt the burgers till they are ready to go into the buns because, as with so many meats, this draws out the juices.

MEAT LOAF

> *Dear Nan: I can't make a meat loaf to satisfy my husband. He does not like cooked onions, and what is a meat loaf with-*

out onions? Is there any certain way to make a good one?
—NEW KENSINGTON, PENNSYLVANIA.

The day they take away my onions and garlic, I'm a dead duck in the cooking department. Does he really not like onion because it talks back to him, digestively speaking, or does he have a thing about it?

I know one man who sat at the table laboriously picking out all the onion and green pepper bits—something else he wouldn't eat. Then his wife hit on the idea of tossing the onion, celery, and green pepper into the blender. It came out so liquefied that nothing was identifiable. It got added to the meat and he never knew the difference.

I count on celery as a tremendously good natural seasoning. A mixed-seasoning salt is a possible solution for you. There is also more than one kind of special meat loaf seasoning on the market.

I have yet to see my problem dealt with: meat loaf that falls apart on slicing. It seems no matter what I add, it becomes a crumbly mess. —DAVIS, CALIFORNIA.

I can't know what you are doing wrong but "crumbly" sounds like dryness. Could be that so simple a thing as letting the meat loaf stand for 10 minutes after it is out of the oven is your answer. Adding ¼ pound of fresh pork to a pound of beef hamburger makes an ideal combination. Good-grade hamburger is better than ground chuck because it is usually juicier.

Nan Wiley's Meat Loaf

There are jillions of recipes, but mine calls for 1½ pounds of meat, a couple of good dollops of catsup right from the bottle mixed into 1 or 2 fork-beaten eggs in a cup, whatever diced onion, celery, and green pepper suits my whim of the moment, salt and freshly ground pepper. Then I hold about 3 or 4 slices of sandwich bread, toasted dry, under the water faucet, squeeze them good to get rid of all the water, and add to mixture. You do have to mix well or you may get bready spots, but it helps make a moist loaf that still slices okay.

I hand-shape my loaf in my cast-iron skillet, pour half-way diluted cream of mushroom or tomato soup over, bake uncovered at 325 to 350 degrees for an hour or so. Baste occasionally. Use a broad meat lifter to get it from the pan. *Makes 4 to 6 servings.*

> *What causes meat to shrink? Could it be that the ground beef has too much fat in it?* —LANCASTER, PENNSYLVANIA.

Any time ground beef has too high a fat content, your meat loaf or hamburgers will shrink out of all proportion. A little shrinkage is normal. So, although ground meat like that may be cheaper per pound to start with, you aren't saving anything because you don't get as many servings. Crackers or bread crumbs mixed in with the meat will absorb some of the fat, but you still can't overdo it.

> *What do you do with leftover meat loaf? My family just won't eat it the second day. They say it tastes stale.*
> —SAN DIEGO, CALIFORNIA.

Oh, my! I always make extra so we'll have some left for sandwiches the next day. It does sometimes take some dressing up, maybe, to lift the flavor, but that's easy. Pickle relish, sliced dills, sweet onion rings, or mayonnaise and crisp lettuce. On occasion I have steamed it, over low heat, just in the covered skillet with ever so little water or bouillon added.

I hope you remember that, any time you dash in the house too late to get a whole meat loaf fixed in time, you can always bake individual servings in large muffin tins or those cute little miniature bread pans. I have sometimes resorted to that trick when I got caught flat-footed with unexpected company and nothing very dressy to serve on practically a moment's notice. Yes, that happens to me, too, sometimes.

A platterful of these individual meat loaves looks very

attractive if you crisscross the tops with thin strips of pimento, centered with a slice of bread-and-butter pickle or some thinly sliced gherkins. You do this after the loaves are out of the oven.

Ever try glazing meat loaf for something different? About 20 minutes before it's due out of the oven, spread it with a mixture of 2 to 3 tablespoons prepared mustard mixed with a scant cup of cranberry or currant jelly. Bake the rest of the way.

Potato-frosted meat loaf is another thing that looks very festive, but people are always asking how to get the coating of mashed potato brown on the sides as well as the top. It takes around 4 cups of well-seasoned mashed potatoes to completely frost a 1 or 1½ pound loaf, and you need them a bit more firm than usual to stay in place. Sometimes I add maybe ½ cup of grated cheese to the potatoes for a change.

When your loaf is within 20 minutes of being done, haul it out and frost evenly with the potato mixture. Dollop the top lightly with the back of a spoon so you have little peaks. Dot with butter and put back in the oven. Boost the temperature to around 400 degrees during the last 5 minutes of cooking to brown coating.

Instead of using only butter, mix 1 tablespoon of it, melted, with some slightly crushed cornflakes and sprinkle on top of meat loaf. If you are careful, you can even pat a little of that mixture on the sides without disturbing the potato coating, but don't boost the temperature on this one or the buttered flakes can scorch.

FLANK STEAK

Dear Nan: How do you cook a flank steak? A meat cutter told me just to drop it in hot fat on a grill or skillet and cook 5 minutes to the side but everyone else says it should be cooked longer. —SOUTHGATE, CALIFORNIA.

It has been my experience that it takes an unusually good quality and grade of flank to get away with frying. It does a lot better if it is simmered or oven-braised for a while. It should always be run through the scoring machine first, of course, to break up the outer fiber. Then dip pieces in seasoned flour, brown it, and add water or tomato juice from time to time as it cooks down. Cook and simmer, covered, over very low heat till tender. That could be anywhere from 30 to 60 minutes.

My favorite way is the following recipe:

Superduper Flank Roll

All meat, no waste, and what a flavor! Have your meat department run the flank through a tenderizing machine to break up that thin outer skin.

1 flank steak	1 can condensed tomato
Salt and pepper	soup, diluted with 1
2 tablespoons chopped	can water
parsley	1 teaspoon vinegar
1 clove chopped garlic	1 teaspoon crushed
½ cup grated Parmesan	oregano
cheese	
2 to 3 tablespoons	
shortening	

Sprinkle one side of steak with salt, pepper, parsley, garlic, and cheese. Roll tightly, jelly roll fashion. Tie in 2 or 3 places with heavy string. Brown on all sides in a Dutch oven or chicken-fry skillet. Combine soup with rest of ingredients. Pour over rolled steak. Simmer, covered, 1½ to 2 hours or till tender. Nice served with spaghetti. *Makes 4 servings.*

NOTE· Sometimes, instead, I spread the steak with about ½ inch well-seasoned bread stuffing and use cream of mushroom or celery soup. Proceed the same.

Honest-to-goodness London broil is made with a whole flank steak. Again, it should be top quality, machine scored on both sides. Then, brush with salad oil. If you like garlic flavor, rub the meat with a cut clove of it before oiling. Broil the meat about five minutes to the side on a preheated broiler.

Put the meat on a hot platter, slather with butter or margarine, and slice it diagonally across the grain, in very thin slices. It takes a good sharp carving knife to accomplish this.

A good way to tenderize any cheaper cut of meat is to marinate it in a vinegar-and-oil salad dressing for a couple of hours. Commercial tenderizers are popular and quite all right in their place, but I find any leftover tenderized steak, no matter how I cook it, has a mushy texture by the next day.

SWISS STEAK

Dear Nan: Could you suggest something different than mashed or baked potatoes to serve with the tomato-sauce Swiss steak? —BOULDER, COLORADO.

I use noodles with mine. I used to cook them partway first until I happened on a better way. I put my "steak" in the roaster in one piece, pour a large-size can of tomatoes over it, along with an onion cut in half. About 45 minutes before the meat is due to come out of the oven, I just pour in raw egg noodles, arranging them around the meat. They soak up the combined meat juices and tomato just great, far more than if you had parboiled them first. You will probably have to add some tomato juice toward the end—or some water-diluted catsup—but it's worth it.

CORNED BEEF

Dear Nan: I guess I just don't know how to boil corned beef. I get the kind that is already spiced and packaged. Everybody else says it is so good, but mine always turns out tough and stringy. —EDMONTON, ALBERTA, CANADA.

I'm sure corned beef is just about one of the most misunderstood meats there is. The trouble lies mostly with that word "boiled." That is exactly what shouldn't happen. Here's what the professional chefs do.

Put the meat in cold water and turn burner to simmer. Hold at a gentle simmer until it's fork tender. Takes about 1 hour to the pound, and you just can't rush it. If you plan to serve it hot, it is ready. If you are planning to slice it down cold sometime later (as for those marvelous Reuben sandwiches), then let it cool right in its own liquid before draining and refrigerating. You can move the pot to a moderately cool place to hasten things, but no sharp temperature changes, please.

Correct slicing plays an important part, too. Corned beef, hot or cold, should always be sliced diagonally, across the grain, and on the thin side. There are still types of corned beef that may need to be soaked in cold water for an hour before cooking in fresh water. If you are in doubt and the label doesn't say, ask at the counter where you buy it.

If you are planning on a New England boiled dinner, don't put the cabbage wedges in till about the last 15 minutes. Other vegetables can go in about 45 minutes before the finish.

For a real dinger of a dinner, try cornmeal dumplings dropped into the simmering corned beef pot liquor for about 15 minutes. For dumpling recipe, see page 144.

LAMB

Why do so many people dislike lamb? Probably because it was never served at home when they were growing up and forming their tastes. It seems to be a regional thing. Or maybe because they don't know how to cook it properly.

Thick broiled lamb chops are terrific. Lamb makes a very fine, rich stew. Just use lamb where you've been using beef. And talk about braised lamb shanks! It was always a treat when my mother fixed those, so tender, so flavorsome. And then there are sandwiches made with the remains of thinly sliced cold lamb, spread with good mustard. That's one thing a lot of people don't understand. Lamb must be served very hot or very cold. If it's lukewarm, it can be rather tasteless.

BRINGING HOME THE BACON

At best, bacon is the most expensive meat you can buy because so much of that pound you pay for never hits the table. Fry the fat out of it and what do you have left? You might really be paying anywhere from two to four dollars per pound for the edible part. But who wants to give up bacon entirely? Not me. I love it, at least for Sunday breakfast.

> *Dear Nan: Is there anything you can do with bacon that is was too salty? I bought some the other day and we just can't eat it!* —PHOENIX, ARIZONA.

When I have been absolutely stuck with salty bacon, I have used it to season green beans in the same manner I would use salt pork—cut up raw and fried and crumbled. Then you don't salt the beans as much. It can also be used in a sweet-sour dressing for wilted lettuce or other greens. Fried bacon bits may be mixed in with scrambled eggs, or added (well drained) to biscuit dough or muffin batter, or mixed with mayonnaise for a sandwich filling. You can even sprinkle some over a tossed salad for a change of pace.

> *Please don't throw that salty bacon away! Soak slices 15 to 20 minutes in warm water, then roll in cornmeal or flour. (I prefer flour.) Fry rather slowly till crisp. Drain and you'll love it. Wonderful with baked potato or potato salad.* —INDIANAPOLIS, INDIANA.

BAKED BACON

> *I eat at a cafeteria where the bacon is heaped up in warming pans, all ready to go. It is always so crisp, I asked the girls how they did it. They said they baked it slowly whenever their ovens weren't in use otherwise. But exactly how?* —FORT WORTH, TEXAS.

Place the bacon strips on a large cold cookie sheet, the kind with a rim, so there won't be any chance of grease overflowing, whether you use a rack or not. Set the oven at 300 degrees.

Turn the bacon as needed, using kitchen tongs. You will probably have to do this just once unless you have very thick slices. You have to open the oven door for an occasional peek-check, but it beats standing over a skillet. There is no spattering, either. You can use your broiler rack and pan for baking, which makes for an even drier bacon, but I find the cookie sheets easier to clean in the long run.

You can also broil bacon satisfactorily, but you can do only one load at a time. You have to keep it on the lowest rack for best results. It has to be watched constantly or it spatters.

IRENE CLEETON'S PORK CHOPS

Here's a pork chop dish I think is just fine. It doesn't make any difference whether the chops are the good-looking ones or the poor relations. Here's just the way Irene Cleeton told me to do them:

Spread the chops with mustard on one side and coat that side with flour. While the chop lies in the flour, coat the top side with mustard, turn to flour. They can rest awhile on waxed paper till you finish the whole batch or they can be put right into fairly hot fat in a skillet. A cast-iron one is perfect.

Sprinkle with salt right about here. Do use a pancake turner to run under them before turning so they don't lose all that good coating. Brown the second side, lay them in a shallow pan. When all are browned, pour over them a can of undiluted —and be sure it is undiluted—chicken-with-rice soup. Then add about ¾ cup of water to the pan so you'll have enough liquid. Place in a 325-degree oven, let bake for 1 to 1½ hours. Or, if things are going to be delayed for a while, turn the heat back to 300 degrees or a little lower. Put a sheet of foil over them if the rice part is getting too crisp and they'll wait for quite a spell. With baked spuds and a green salad, you've got yourself quite a meal. *Makes 3 to 4 servings.*

For more than 6 or 7 chops, use 2 cans of the soup, and water accordingly. You don't want them covered with liquid. Just enough to make good pan gravy. You might substitute tomato soup with rice for a change.

PROSCIUTTO

Dear Nan: What is prosciutto ham and what do you do with it? —PROVO, UTAH.

It is best known as an Italian specialty, but now such hams are also prepared in this country. Prosciutto is darker in color than ordinary hams, rather thin slabbed but with a marvelous flavor. It is used in many Italian dishes, but here we run into it more often as something of an appetizer, sliced paper-thin and wrapped around melon wedges, usually casaba or honeydew. It's good around fresh figs, too. At superior delicatessens all over the country, you can buy only as many wafered slices as you need.

GLAZED BAKED HAM

Dear Nan: How do you get a really beautiful crusty sort of glaze on a whole ham? —SPOKANE, WASHINGTON.

I don't know what kind of glaze you like, but it doesn't make much difference, if you'll let your broiler into the act right at the last. Try this recipe for ham baked in a brown paper bag and follow the suggestions that will give your ham a beautiful glaze.

This method makes for a juicier ham with no basting, but glazing, if any, must wait until the final step. Many people skip the glazing entirely, preferring the ham as it comes right from the sack.

Most hams today have complete time and temperature

charts on the wrappers or cans. However, here is a time chart, if your ham wrapper has none.

325-Degree Oven Used Throughout

Whole uncooked ham (10-14 pounds) 22-25 minutes per pound depending on size
Half of uncooked ham (5-7 pounds) 22-25 minutes per pound
Picnic ham (shoulder) 30-35 minutes per pound
Ready-to-eat types (10-12 pounds) about 10 minutes per pound
Canned hams, any weight—15 minutes per pound or as can directs

Place the ham in a heavy brown paper sack. Twist the end shut and tie with string. Place it on the rack over the broiler pan in a 325-degree oven. If an uncooked ham is used, place it fat side up. When cooking time is completed, tear away the sack. Remove the rind. Score the remaining layer of fat in diamond shapes. Stud with cloves if desired. Brown sugar mixed with a variety of jams, jellies, juices, honey, or just some of the ham drippings makes an ideal broiled glaze. Even canned hams may be scored.

Whichever you use, mix sugar with just enough of any of these to make a fairly thick pastelike topping. Pat it on the scored ham. Place the ham under turned-on broiler as far away from the heat as possible. Watch carefully. It can take only ½ minute or so for sugar mix to start bubbling and browning. Remove the ham from the oven. When the ham has set a few minutes, the mixture is a beautifully semicaramelized glaze.

Suggested Glazes

1. Brown Sugar-Jelly or Jam Glaze: Mix sugar with just enough peach or apricot jam to make a fairly thick paste. Two tablespoons ham drippings may be substituted for part of the jam. Apple butter or any red jelly also works well.

2. Brown Sugar-Pineapple Glaze: Mix sugar with canned crushed pineapple. If necessary, add a bit of the juice for proper consistency—enough to hold in place, not slide off the ham.

3. Brown Sugar-Orange Glaze: Mix sugar with enough

orange juice to moisten, add 1 teaspoon dry mustard. Apple cider is also nice in place of orange juice.

NOTE: If you like a spicier taste to a glaze, add 1 teaspoon prepared mustard or horseradish. They blend amazingly well with even the jelly or jam preparation.

LIVER

Dear Nan: Would you please tell me how to fry pork liver or beef liver so it will be tender without using a tenderizer?
—KINGSTON, TENNESSEE.

Would you please tell me how to do beef liver so it isn't so chewy? —SHARON, PENNSYLVANIA.

These two questions are so representative of the many queries on liver that I know a lot of you have trouble. I just wouldn't use a tenderizer on liver at all. Makes it mushy. Most of the trouble comes from cooking too long in too much shortening. Overcooking will toughen even the nicest liver so it comes out akin to leather. Some liver is simply sliced too thin or unevenly.

Here's the best tip I ever got for making beef liver taste like the more expensive calf's liver. Marinate the slices, for at least 1 hour, in any vinegar-and-oil salad dressing that does not contain sugar. Or make your own—3 parts oil, 1 part vinegar or lemon juice, salt and pepper to taste, a shake of garlic or onion salt. Then go ahead and cook any way you like, even broiled. It's magic.

Never overcook liver.

Liver Stroganoff

1 pound liver thinly sliced
1 tablespoon butter, margarine, or bacon drippings
⅔ cup water

1 envelope dry onion soup mix
1 cup dairy sour cream
Parsley noodles

Cut the liver slices into 2-inch squares on a floured board. Brown quickly in the fat. Stir in water and soup mix. Cover and simmer for about 5 minutes, or until the liver loses its pink color, just barely. Remove from heat, stir in sour cream, serve at once. Combine noodles with plenty of butter, chopped parsley, and freshly ground pepper. *Makes 4 servings.*

Another way: Brown liver slices. Remove. Sauté a diced onion and a stalk of celery, cut in chunks, in pan fat. Combine a pint of dairy sour cream and a can of condensed cream soup with water to make it like thick gravy. Pour in pan, add liver, cover and simmer till tender. Do not boil.

BEEF ROAST

Dear Nan: The only thing hotter than the roast beef around our house is the arguments on how to cook it. How do I get the meat rare to medium-rare without an absolutely raw core? We always preseason, and I do top whatever type roast I am doing with butter or margarine. I'm frustrated!

—NASHVILLE, TENNESSEE.

Anyone with your problem should run right out and buy a first-rate meat thermometer. It is the only absolutely accurate way to tell. It will have a chart and directions. Just make sure, when you insert the thermometer in the meat, that it is not touching bone, gristle, or the bottom of the pan. Those things can mislead you with a higher reading than what the meat is really getting.

You aren't going to use the same timing for a standing rib roast as you are for one of the more economical cuts. For the latter type I never use a temperature over 325 degrees for 45 minutes per pound or thereabouts. I may even swing it down to 300 degrees and cook for 1 hour per pound. That means covered, of course, and with a little liquid in the pan. I know that is called "braising," rather than roasting as you would for an uncovered prime rib roast or any other meat of very high quality, a better cut, but I still call mine a roast and I think most people do.

High-heat searing and cooking is pretty much out except for some professional chefs who know how to handle it. The higher the temperature, the greater the shrinkage. The 300-to-325-degree temperature throughout makes for a more tender, juicy, and flavorsome roast. There is no hard crust to cut through and the interior part holds together better for slicing.

I see no reason for topping your roast with butter or other shortening, if there is a reasonable amount of natural fat. The National Livestock and Meat Board gives the go-ahead on salting and peppering the meat either before, after, or during cooking. The salt doesn't penetrate much more than ¼ inch, anyway.

Personally, I never salt my roasts until they are almost due to come out of the oven, or even just as I bring them to the table. Of course, this salting business is for roasts only. When you are broiling or frying a steak, you will surely draw out some of those nice juices if you season raw meat.

One more item: Roasts keep right on cooking from their own heat after they are out of the oven and they are easier to carve if they "set" for 20 minutes. That could take care of that "raw core" you experience with a rib roast. In that case, take the meat from the oven when the thermometer registers 5 to 10 degrees below doneness, depending on cut.

> *I would like to know how to cook a roast in the oven so it will not dry out. I do mine in a Dutch oven, very little water, but it still dries out, isn't juicy.* —EMMET, IDAHO.

I have always said, only half in fun, you can cook an old boot to fork tenderness if you will just cook it slow enough and long enough. It's the prime success factor when you are doing the less expensive cuts. And before every purist in the country rushes in to tell all of us that when you use moist heat, as here, it is not really roasting, it is braising, I know. I still call mine a roast and I am sure I have lots of company on that score.

I have often set the oven right at 300 degrees. Sometimes I even use 275 degrees, but never higher than 325 degrees.

It is impossible to give exact timing because of meat age, weight, thickness and grade, but a 3-to-5-pound roast can take around 3 to 4 hours. It's one of those things you eventually learn by instinct and experience. First time you try it, allow plenty of time. If the meat seems to be getting done before meal-time, you can always keep it warm at your very lowest setting.

Very lean meat just isn't going to be as juicy as some with a little fat to it. There, a small piece of suet added to the pan will at least make for better browning and gravy. It's about the only way you can get accompanying potatoes nicely browned, too.

Are you searing the roast first? You might be overdoing that—to the point of dryness before it ever hits the oven. I gave up searing years ago when one of the family could have nothing remotely fried. I was surprised the meat browned quite nicely anyway—not as much as with heavy searing, but plenty good enough. Now this is being touted by meat authorities as "a new method." I've been doing it for thirty years. It is also better if you don't salt the meat at the start. You'll be surprised at how much natural salt is in the meat if you taste the unthickened pan gravy at the last.

You say you add very little water. That could be another trouble. You don't want to drown your roast or make a stew out of it, but have about ¼ inch liquid in the pan at the start, maybe more as you go along.

BROWNING MEATS

Dear Nan: Why, why, why, after twenty-eight years of cooking and no problems do I now have trouble browning meats for stews, roasts, and especially round steak?

—MINNEAPOLIS, MINNESOTA.

I got in touch with the National Livestock and Meat Board at Chicago. This is what I learned: When meat has not been aged long enough, there can be this problem of moisture retention when browning. Trouble is, with constantly increased demand, frequently meat is marketed before there is time for much aging. Another thing pointed out by Reba Staggs, director of home economics for NLMB, would be the cooking of frozen meats that had been handled improperly—the way you wrap, freeze, or store them. Meat should always be wrapped in completely moisture- and vapor-proof wrapping, frozen quickly (below zero), and stored at zero degrees or under.

> *I had trouble browning meats, too, especially roasts, until I started using paprika. Now I put my seasonings and spices on the meat, rub them in well, sprinkle with a good deal of paprika, rub that in a little and I get beautifully browned meats.*
> —MINNEAPOLIS, MINNESOTA.

BREADING MEATS

> *Dear Nan: How do you get the breading to stick to chops? I've been trying for thirty-five years and I'm still trying. It all comes off in the pan.* —MADISON, WISCONSIN.

The big thing to watch for in breading just about anything is to see that every bit of the meat is evenly coated with whatever mixture you use. Where there are sparse or bare spots, and they hit the hot fat, it's kaboom! Too, if you will lay the breaded meat on waxed paper to dry for ½ hour, it's a big help in doing away with that "good-bye forever" routine.

Be sure the crumbs—bread or crackers—are finely crushed or they won't stick, either. For most meats I like the double-dip method: Dip quickly into whatever crumbs you are using, then into oil or a combination of oil and a beaten egg—about 2 tablespoons of oil—then back into the very fine crumbs again. One thing about using that egg with the oil is that it seals and keeps the fat from soaking through with indigestible results. It isn't strictly necessary.

Do have the fat just medium hot to start with, not smoking. Brown on both sides, then turn the heat down and brown slowly the rest of the way. You may not have thought of it, but it doesn't always have to be bread or cracker crumbs. How about those broken potato chips, cornflakes, and cheese or cocktail crackers that always wind up at the bottom of the box, anyway?

MEAT WRAPS

Dear Nan: Why isn't it okay to put packaged meats in the refrigerator or freezer just in the tray and wrappings they were in at the store? Surely they wouldn't use anything unclean or harmful. —BISMARCK, NORTH DAKOTA.

It doesn't take long for a lot of good meat juice to saturate a cardboard-type carton completely, as you can tell if you leave the package in the refrigerator for even a day. You find red goo all over the shelf. I prefer to put my meat on a plate, wrap loosely with waxed paper or foil, then refrigerate.

For freezing, a good moisture- and vapor-proof paper is what you want. Wrap meat as closely as possible to seal out all air. Make what I call a "gift box wrap," where you double-seam the long fold, then bring the ends up to lap well. Don't forget to mark poundage so, when the time comes, you won't be all at sea on figuring cooking time.

5/ Are you in a fowl mood?

Once upon a time "chicken every Sunday" was regarded as a state of affluence. Now that, as well as turkey and other poultry, can be year-around best buys. Most people like it, as there are so many ways to fix it. The only chicken dish against which I am dead set is in reference to this next comment:

"I'm with you! I deplore the awful habit of grinding chicken so fine it might be pork, tuna, or who knows. I have eaten chicken salad at some pretty nice places where, even if they had added a few feathers, I still wouldn't have been convinced. Are you old enough to remember the widely advertised etiquette course that used the slogan 'She always ordered chicken salad'? Intimating the poor girl was so socially unsure of herself it was the only dish she felt would be a safe choice. Socially, yes. Gastronomically she could still have been taking a risk."

You bet I remember that slogan! I was sixteen at the time, and my date was "an older man." All of twenty-one. For the evening's after-theater finale he squired me grandly to the old College Inn at Chicago's Hotel Sherman. That frighteningly huge and glittering menu had me in an agony of embarrassment. I *loved* chicken salad, I *wanted* chicken salad, but that horrible full-page ad, then appearing everywhere, was emblazoned on my mind. I just didn't dare. When I became a more sophisticated woman of seventeen, I knew the inn was famous for its chicken à la king. I always ordered that. Definitely in-the-know, y'know.

CHICKEN 'N' STRIP DUMPLINGS

Dear Nan: My husband keeps talking about something called strip dumplings the way his mother fixed them with stewed chicken, but I just don't know what he means. They sound more like broad noodles to me, but he insists they were called dumplings. —DUNNELLON, FLORIDA.

You are both right. They are more noodle than dumpling, but "strip dumplings" are what they have always been called. They are what history says Yankee soldiers plucked with their fingers from outdoor cook pots while racing with General Sherman on his march through Georgia. Here's how the directions go in a small church cookbook, the only place I have ever seen these described.

Cook a reasonably fat hen, cut in pieces, in salted water as for any stewed chicken. There should be enough broth to cover the pieces when the dumplings are added. Simmer the chicken pieces till tender.

Now sift together 2 cups of flour, 1 teaspoon salt, ½ teaspoon baking powder. Cut in 1 rounded tablespoon shortening. Add a scant ⅔ cup milk. Add all the milk at once and mix dumpling batter as for biscuits, to a stiff dough. Divide in 2 portions and roll out like pie crust. Cut in 2-inch-wide strips, stretching the pieces as you add them to the chicken broth.

Place several strips of dough on top of chicken pieces in the broth, which should be on a simmer-boil. Replace the lid and continue boiling till the broth has boiled up over the dumplings. Then add another layer of strips, let boil up and over again. Continue till all are used. Takes 4 or 5 additions of the strips. Allow 20 to 30 minutes from the time the first strips are added. If broth runs low, heat some milk and add as you go, pushing back the dumplings and chicken. Pour the milk into the near side of the kettle.

The broth may be thickened slightly before serving, moving carefully to keep the chicken pieces intact. *Makes 4 servings.*

SOUTHERN FRIED CHICKEN

Dear Nan: How do you make that really crusty fried chicken like they do in the South? —LAS VEGAS, NEVADA.

I had to hit a little southern Missouri town before I found any fried chicken as good as what my mother-in-law's cook used to fry every Sunday years ago! What chicken! Crispy, crusty, served so fast and hot from the pan you had to watch that first mouthful, but not a bit greasy. The proprietor of the little restaurant didn't mind giving me the recipe.

So here's what you do: Shake or roll the chicken pieces in salted and peppered flour. No egg, no milk. Just flour. Set the pieces aside to dry for about 10 minutes. Then flour again and into the pan. Now—and this is important—that chicken isn't going to be just great unless you use enough cooking fat in the pan. Should be a good ½ inch deep, not smoking hot but "hot enough." Brown those pieces on all sides. Then turn down the heat and keep on cooking until the chicken tests tender. Don't cover the pan or you'll lose all the crispiness.

Everything depends on having the frying shortening or oil deep enough and at a just-right temperature. And you do have to stand over it to turn and turn until the chicken is just right. A thermostatically controlled frypan is a big help, but these people were using just big old black skillets, know-how, and fresh chicken.

Half the appeal is the dividend of the glorious cream gravy you can make here. Heavenly over hot biscuits, rice, grits, or just plain bread. Of course, you pour off all but about 2 or 3 tablespoons of the drippings, but be sure you leave all those little brown bits in the pan! Stir in a like amount of flour, then whatever milk or cream you like. About 2 cups are right.

OVEN FRIED CHICKEN

Dear Nan: I have eaten an extra good kind of oven-fried chicken at a friend's house on several occasions but she won't tell any of us how it is done. Her chicken is crisp, a beautiful golden brown all over, but not greasy. —MENTOR, OHIO.

I never expect a professional chef to part with any of his secrets, but I can't understand home cooks who won't share an admired recipe. Your "friend" may have used one of the following methods:

Dip the chicken pieces in undiluted evaporated milk, then in very fine cornflake crumbs seasoned to taste with salt and pepper. Be sure you dip in enough of the milk to cover all over, then in enough crumbs to leave absolutely no bare patches. Place the chicken pieces in a shallow baking pan lined with heavy-duty foil. Chicken should be skin side up and don't crowd the pieces. Bake uncovered in a 350-degree oven for about 1 hour. You don't even need to turn the pieces.

Another way is to dip the chicken pieces in egg beaten with 1 tablespoon or so of water for each egg, season to taste with whatever you prefer, then roll the pieces in dehydrated potato flakes. It has to be the flakes. You won't get the same effect if you use the granular type. Melt ½ stick of butter in a shallow pan. Place the chicken skin side up. Bake about 1 hour at 400 degrees. You do have to turn the pieces midway through the baking period just once.

BAKED CHICKEN

Dear Nan: Here is a way of baking chicken that may be new to you. Cut up a chicken, roll the pieces in biscuit mix, sprinkle with salt and pepper. Place in a greased casserole. Put liberal spoonful of marmalade on each piece. Fill the bottom of the dish with wine. Cover and bake at 350 degrees till tender. —LOS ANGELES, CALIFORNIA.

I would suggest using a dry white wine here. The chicken pieces should not be stacked. Pour the wine in carefully, not over the chicken itself. Start with about ¼ inch of the wine. You can always add more as you go along, if necessary. It takes about

1 hour or so to get the chicken tender. A lot depends on how big a bird you are using. I believe this lady used orange marmalade, but peach or apricot wouldn't be a bit bad either. Fruit flavors team well with chicken.

Terri Tholin's Chicken Enchiladas

Pardon me while I brag! This one comes to me from my granddaughter. It's popular on the army base at Fort Riley, Kansas, where she and her husband often serve it to friends. If you cook the chicken the day before, half the work is done.

Stew a cut-up chicken with an onion and a garlic bud or two for seasoning. Save at least 2 cups broth. Bone the cooled chicken. Either cut up the meat in small pieces or, as Terri does, shred with your fingers.

Sauce

4 tablespoons flour	2 cups broth and more
4 tablespoons salad oil	water as it cooks
2 tablespoons chili powder	Salt and pepper
(more to taste)	1 teaspoon garlic juice

Mix flour and oil in a medium-sized saucepan and simmer 1 minute. Take from heat, gradually stir in broth. Add chili powder and other seasonings. Simmer about ½ hour.

Chop 1 onion. Chop or crumble a 10-ounce package Monterey Jack (or mild Cheddar) cheese. Heat the shredded chicken and onion in about ⅔ stick of butter. Arrange chicken. onion, and cheese on tortillas. (Fills about 18.) Roll and secure with a toothpick. Line up in a large flat pan (no stacking). Put extra cheese on top. Pour the sauce over all. Heat at 350 degrees for 20 to 25 minutes or till cheese melts and all is heated through. *Makes 6 to 8 servings.*

NOTE: Dairy-case tortillas are usually already pliable enough to roll without breaking, but if you use any other kind you will have to heat them in a little oil till soft.

Chicken Maciel

Dear Nan: We used to eat a simply terrific chicken dish at the old Westport Room of the Kansas City Union Station. It had rice and Swiss cheese and some sort of unusual flavoring in a cream sauce. Now that restaurant is no more. I am hoping that recipe isn't lost to us forever.—TOPEKA, KANSAS.

It isn't! You are talking about Chicken Maciel, named for its creator, Joe Maciel. It was such a hit right from the start that it became a house specialty. You do have to like a curry flavor —this calls for a pretty fair amount of that spice blend—and if you are going to worry about calories, it is best to forget the whole thing. It's rich but ever so good. The amount given here is supposed to serve 6, but I have seen it lapped up by just 4.

4 medium-sized chicken breasts	3 cups medium cream sauce
½ cup butter	3 cups saffron rice, cooked
2 tablespoons curry powder	1 cup grated Swiss cheese
¼ cup sherry wine	

Simmer the chicken breasts till tender. Skin and bone them. Cut into 1-inch squares. Melt the butter. Stir in the curry powder and wine, then the chicken. Sauté for 5 minutes. Add the cream sauce and bring to a full simmer so everything is well combined.

Ring a large casserole or chafing dish with the hot rice. Pour the creamed mixture in the center. Top with the grated Swiss cheese and place under a broiler till lightly browned. *Makes 4 servings.*

Saffron Rice for Chicken Maciel

1 cup long grain rice (not quick-type)	1 teaspoon salt
2 cups water	1 pinch saffron

Combine ingredients in a 1½-quart pan. Cook on high till

steam escapes from the lid. Switch heat to low. Simmer for about 30 minutes without removing cover.

Terri's Scalloped Chicken Squares

Makes a marvelous party dish, so easy to fix and serve, and the family will be clamoring for it, too.

4- to 5-pound stewing chicken, cut up	⅛ teaspoon pepper
Salt and pepper	2 cups fresh bread crumbs
½ cup butter	2 egg yolks, beaten
½ cup flour	½ cup chicken broth
2 cups chicken broth	2 egg whites beaten stiff
1½ cups milk	1 can sliced mushrooms, drained
½ teaspoon salt	2 tablespoons butter

Simmer chicken till tender, bone and cut up. Then, 1½ hours before serving time, heat oven to 325 degrees. Arrange chicken meat in greased 13x9x2-inch baking dish. Sprinkle lightly with salt and pepper. In pan melt ½ cup butter, stir in flour, then add 2 cups broth and the milk. Cook till thick. Remove from heat, cool slightly, stir in ½ teaspoon salt, the pepper, crumbs, beaten egg yolks, and ½ cup chicken broth. Fold in whipped egg whites. Pour over chicken. Bake 1 hour. When almost done, sauté mushrooms in 2 tablespoons butter. Scatter over chicken before serving. Cut in squares to serve. *Makes 8 to 10 servings.*

CHICKEN SAUTÉ

Really good main dishes that can be tailored to just one serving or a dozen are pretty hard to find, but this one does it! Now that you can easily buy just the breast of chicken, either fresh or frozen, even the live-aloner can eat in style.

Dear Nan: Here is a chicken breast recipe I just love. It is not only delicious, but is so easy to adjust to one or a dozen servings. What's more, it is so well balanced you can consider it a meal-in-one.

> *For each serving allow ½ full chicken breast and ½*
> *cup cooked rice. While the rice is cooking, chop enough*
> *celery to make ½ cup, about ¼ of a green pepper, and 1*
> *small tomato.*
>
> *Slice the chicken meat from the bone in thin slices or*
> *strips. In a hot skillet melt at least 1 tablespoon of butter*
> *or margarine. That is for each serving. Add the raw chicken*
> *strips and brown quickly. Not too long or it dries out. Gets*
> *done much faster than you'd think.*
>
> *To serve, put the hot rice on each plate, cover with*
> *the chopped raw vegetables—celery, green pepper, and to-*
> *mato—then the cooked chicken with any of the pan drip-*
> *pings left. Salt to taste and have your soy sauce bottle on*
> *the table.* —LEXINGTON, MISSOURI.

Very nice! Those raw vegetables give great texture contrast and, between the hot rice below and the hot chicken on top, are not at all cold.

PAPER BAG TURKEY

Dear Nan: Doing turkey in a brown paper bag is one great
idea. My husband was a bit concerned that the bag would
catch fire, and I was apprehensive about browning, but we
all agreed it was the best turkey in years! Drumsticks were
especially good—not too hard or brown. After forty-two
years I say, "No more great big heavy turkey roasters for
me." —ROCHESTER, NEW YORK.

Yours isn't the only roaster that no longer gets the bird. That was one thing I liked so much the first time I tried the stunt about fifteen years ago. I was just as apprehensive about the whole thing the first time as you were. You could have knocked my eyes off with a stick when I tore open that sack and saw that picture book turkey.

There are three things to watch: (1) Be sure the turkey is well thawed. Once I thought mine was, but when I reached into the cavity, I could still feel ice crystals. This would account for the one lady—just one in all these years—who claimed her bird was "raw against the bone." (2) Your oven must be accurate at the 325-degree setting. As a double check on my thermostat, I use a little portable oven thermometer. (3) Note exact weight of your bird before you throw the wrapper away. Then figure 25 minutes per pound for birds around 12 pounds or under—20 minutes per pound for larger birds. I do this with pencil and paper (no guesswork), keep it handy so I won't forget. This timing has always worked fine for me and thousands of others.

No, the bag will not burn—not at 325 degrees.

Prepare the bird exactly as you would for any other method, complete with stuffing. Rub or brush well with butter or other shortening, especially inside the wings. Then slide it into a large, heavy brown paper grocery sack. With a very large bird you may have to have someone to help you. (My husband holds the sack open on the kitchen floor, I lift the turkey into it so it will be breast side up.) Twist the sack shut and tie with strong string. Be sure the sack has no holes. Do not place the bagged bird in a roaster. Set it on a rack over your broiler pan. Place in a 325-degree oven and forget it.

Ideally, you do not peek, poke, or baste till cooking time is up. However, if you get so nervous the first time that you simply cannot stand the suspense, you may untie the sack when timing has just 1 hour to go. Give the bird the "leg test." Reach in carefully and wiggle the drumstick. If it should be starting to "give" easily, then it is possible your bird is done. (This happens only once in a great, great while if you happen to get stuck with a very dry bird, but it has never happened to me.) I have tested time and time again, and my turkey comes out almost to the minute. If the drumstick does not give at this point—very seldom does—just retie the sack. I only truss the legs with a bowknot of string in the first place for easy untying so I won't have a hot knot to deal with. At the finish the turkey will be beautifully browned—with no basting at all.

Now, when turkey is done lift bird, pan and all, to top of the range. Poke a few holes toward the bottom of the sack to let juices run into the drip pan. Some will have seeped through, but usually there is quite a lot left in the sack. Then tear the paper away, slide the turkey to a platter, lift out rack, and make gravy right in that pan. Turkey is always easier to carve if you let it "set" for 20 minutes or more.

TURKEY SOUP

At our house we're big soup-and-salad people, can make a meal on that team. Turkey soup is my specialty and it starts with what a lot of people toss into the garbage—a good big turkey carcass.

Here's what I do with that turkey carcass. I break it up, put it in a big pot, add just enough water to simmer. In go the wings, what's left of the drumsticks, any oddments of skin and gravy. After a couple of hours of slow simmering, you'll be surprised at what's left in that rich broth. Lift out the now bare bones and the pieces of skin. You'll find a healthy amount of turkey scraps you'd swear weren't there in the first place, bits of dressing after you were sure you'd scraped up every last spoonful, and more fine flavor than seemed to be in the bird originally.

When the broth has cooled, I pour it into containers for freezing. Later, when it feels like a good soup day, out comes one of those. What I add then is a matter of inspiration or what's handy. Always I add diced onion and celery, tops and all. From there out it may be some diced raw potato, noodles, or rice, but not so much that it will outdo the heady broth. I still want plenty of that left. Salt, pepper, and a pinch of dried mixed herbs are the seasonings. Maybe even a shake or two of poultry seasoning.

Ladled into big brown earthenware soup bowls and brought steaming to the table, it's perfect with a big tossed salad. Or maybe even a fruit salad. Crackers and cheese on the side.

CHICKEN LIVERS

Dear Nan: Is there any way you can fry chicken livers without having them pop grease at you? We love the things but I have almost given up fixing them because I've had so many small but painful arm burns from them.

—CAMROSE, ALBERTA, CANADA.

I felt just like you do until I learned to pat the livers as dry as possible, and give each one a couple of quick gashes with the tip of my kitchen knife without mangling them altogether. That does help quite a lot, although now and then an extra-contrary one will still do a fair imitation of spontaneous combustion. Too, give them a light dusting of flour before starting to fry them and have the fat just medium hot. You don't want the livers crusty dry on the outside before they are done in the center anyway.

When I am frying a whole chicken, I take the extra precaution of hiding the liver under the biggest back piece. Makes sort of a sheltering cave.

6 / Seafood and other close relatives

I was born and brought up in the Midwest, and it wasn't until we started moving around the country that I began to catch on to all the different fish that existed in other directions. Yes, I knew about trout, crappie, catfish, and the like. I was familiar with finnan haddie because my mother had always fixed it. Smoked fish was popular everywhere in the Chicago area. But that was about all.

You just have to remember that this was long before I ever dreamed I'd wind up in the food business. And that, in my childhood, freezer-style fish hadn't entered the picture on any large scale. Back then, fish that might have been in transit quite a while, no matter how well iced, was something my family viewed with distrust. There was that dreaded word "ptomaine"! My father once nearly died of it.

But eventually, after I had snagged myself a husband and a couple of kids, we moved to Long Beach, California. Oh, that lovely first sight of the Pacific, those lovely flowers, those lovely fish! It did take me awhile to sort everything out, however.

We had scarcely moved into our beachside cottage before a neighbor phoned. "Could you use a bonito?"

Well, now, I hadn't the faintest idea of what that might be, but just never get the notion I was about to admit it. "I'd be delighted! I'll send my little boy right over for it."

When I glanced out the window I was bug-eyed to see poor little six-year-old Johnny staggering home with what looked like a small whale, clutched manfully by the tail. Well, I baked it whole and it was delicious—the first day. Next day we had it creamed. The third day we had it in salad. That was it. Not wanting to hurt anyone's feelings, I waited till dark to sneak out and deposit the rest in the garbage can. That night the yowling of fighting neighborhood cats was something fearful. I might as well have advertised in red neon lighting just what I had done.

Go ahead, Californians, laugh. Now it's pretty funny to me, too.

SALMON LOAF

Dear Nan: Here's a tip for baked salmon loaf. Try adding a 3-ounce package of cream cheese to your favorite recipe and garnish the loaf with a sprinkling of paprika.

—AUSTIN, TEXAS.

It does give extra-nice texture and should surely be the answer to all those people who ask, "How in the world can I make a salmon loaf that won't fall all to pieces when I slice it?" Done in a greased pan, this one works just fine.

Tall can of salmon	¼ cup melted butter
1 cup soft bread crumbs	¼ cup liquid from salmon
3 eggs	2 teaspoons grated onion
2 to 3 teaspoons lemon juice	3 ounce package cream cheese
½ teaspoon salt	

In a big bowl, flake the salmon with a fork. Add well-beaten eggs. Make those bread crumbs a generous cupful and place in a small bowl. Add the lemon juice, salt, butter, salmon liquid, and grated onion. Mix well with a fork. Add the cream cheese, which has been allowed to soften to room temperature. Whip in with the fork. Add to salmon-egg mixture and blend well. Pour into a greased loaf pan. Bake at 325 to 350 degrees for about 1 hour. The loaf should look just faintly golden on top. Turn the loaf out onto a platter. If you have greased the pan enough at the start, the loaf comes out very nicely without breaking. *Makes 4 to 6 servings.*

NOTE: The 3 eggs may sound like too much here, but those eggs are what makes for good holding together and the loaf is still nicely fluffy, not packed.

A salmon loaf is tasty served with a tomato sauce. The platter may be garnished with lemon wedges and parsley.

SALMON CHOWDER

Here's another one that's as easy to get together as it is good.

You'll need a 1-pound can of salmon, 1 chicken bouillon cube, 1 cup boiling water, ¾ cup chopped onion, ½ cup chopped green pepper, 1 finely chopped garlic clove, ¼ cup melted butter, ⅓ cup salmon liquid, 1-pound can of tomatoes, 8-ounce can yellow whole kernel corn, 1 cup sliced okra, ½ teaspoon salt, ¼ teaspoon thyme, 1 whole bay leaf, and a dash of pepper.

Drain the salmon but be sure to save the liquid. Dissolve the bouillon cube in the boiling water. Break the salmon into large chunks. Cook the onion, green pepper, and garlic in butter till tender. Combine all the listed ingredients, cover, and cook for about 15 minutes or until the okra is tender. If you don't like okra, just skip that vegetable.

For a more soupy chowder, there is nothing to stop you from adding some milk. *Makes 4 to 6 servings.*

SHRIMP COOKERY

Dear Nan: How do you cook fresh shrimp in the shell? The box of shrimp-seasoning spice I buy says, "Boil with shrimp for 15 minutes." If I do, it seems to me the shrimp are not as good as when I cook them for no more than 10 minutes. Or do I imagine this? —VAN WERT, OHIO.

No, your imagination is not turning cartwheels. A lot of cookbooks do tell you to cook them for as long as 15 minutes. I never do. I bring the pot of water to a boil. Then I drop the shrimp in, let the water come back to barely boiling, turn the heat off, and let the shrimp stay there until they turn a pretty pink. For me, that is it. I drain them at once, then run cold water over them, and shell as soon as they are cool enough to handle. Or I may park them in the refrigerator for shelling later.

Usually I do not use a spice in the cooking water, because I prefer to dunk unspiced shrimp in my own mixture of catsup, horseradish, and lemon juice. If you want to use that packaged spice mixture, add the mix to the simmering water and continue to cook for a good 5 minutes. Then—and only then—add the shrimp. At most, they then need to be cooked just about 5 minutes. They will be fairly firm.

While we're at it, let's take up the matter of that little black vein that runs down the back of the shrimp. Is there really any great reason why it should be removed? No, none at all, except for the looks of a very few dishes. Yes, I know that black part is the intestinal tract of the shrimp, but it is so minute, so sterilized by the time the shrimp are cooked, it won't hurt you a bit.

You may have to devein shrimp for use in salad or in a creamed dish. Then the shrimp vein can sometimes show up, and it doesn't look nice. How the cookbooks and household hint columns do carry on about the easiest way to devein shrimp. Frankly, I use whatever is handy: the tip of a paring knife, a nutpick, a toothpick, a nail file, a tweezers, etc., etc. The file and tweezers are part of my kitchen equipment, scalded after each use. You'd be surprised how often they come in handy when nothing else will work.

FRIED OYSTERS

Dear Nan: Could you possibly tell me how to fry oysters as they are prepared in restaurants? We have always used a cornmeal mixture but it doesn't equal that of the professionals. —NASHVILLE, TENNESSEE.

While some people will always like cornmeal for oyster coating, I find the majority of chefs prefer very fine bread crumbs or preferably cracker meal. So do I. Most markets carry both.

Pat the oysters dry. Dip first in a mixture of 1 egg beaten with 1 tablespoon of cold water or rich milk. Dip next in the seasoned cracker meal, then in the egg mixture again, lastly in cracker meal once more. If you prefer a thinner coating, use just the first dip in the egg-water and once in the cracker meal.

Some chefs then lay the coated oysters out on waxed paper to dry for about 15 minutes—they feel the coating sticks better that way. Some don't. Either way, fry in about ½ inch of hot oil or lard till brown on one side, turn and brown on the other. If you will add at least a little butter to the other shortening, your oysters will be much more crisply coated and attractively browned. Don't crowd them in the pan.

Really, it takes perfectly fresh oysters, right out of the shell, to do at all well with the cornmeal coating. "Old" oysters don't hold together very well for frying. Then, too, the natural inner juice of washed oysters isn't enough to hold the meal. The oysters must be patted dry before frying, or you will have considerable splattering and, again, a soggy coating. Bacon drippings are a favorite for frying cornmeal oysters in some sections of the country.

OYSTER STEW

Dear Nan: Have you ever heard of putting onions in oyster stew? On a trip to New Orleans I was greatly surprised to

have it served with onions floating generously on top.
—RAYTOWN, MISSOURI.

Yes, in some areas they do use onion in oyster stew, although the onions are usually gently simmered in butter first, just to the limp stage, before adding. Most commonly used is chopped celery, done in the same fashion. As big an onion and celery fan as I am, I prefer such stew without anything except good milk, butter, salt and pepper, and possibly a little celery salt—and the oysters, of course. I don't want anything else to blank out the delicate flavor of the shellfish.

Here's one way to make a good oyster stew. Put the oysters, along with any of their liquor, into the saucepan. Bring to a quick boil but reduce the heat at that point so it is barely simmering. Cook the raw oysters till they curl around the edges, for about 2 minutes. Long cooking makes them tough and destroys some of the flavor. Then add milk, about 1 quart to every pint of oysters. And this is one place I don't spare the butter, no matter what sad news the bathroom scales have given me lately. I use 4 to 5 tablespoons of it for the same amount of oysters. Then season with salt and pepper to taste, and a dash or so of celery salt. The faster you can get this to the table, the better.

There are people who prefer to put the oysters into the soup tureen just as soon as they have plumped with those curly edges. Then the milk is heated separately, butter and seasonings added, and everything brought to barely boiling and poured over the oysters. If you insist on a little zip to your oyster stew, a dash of Worcestershire isn't bad.

ANGELS ON HORSEBACK

Many readers ask, "What are angels on horseback?" They are plump oysters wrapped in half-cooked bacon strips cut cross-wise, just the right size to envelop the oyster and held fast with 2 toothpicks. A little paprika, chopped shallots, and a very few drops of lemon juice season them. Broil them, about 6 inches from the heat, just long enough to crisp the bacon. Don't turn them more than twice or they will get tough. Then each "angel" is placed on a round of white bread that has been fried in butter to a delicate brown. Serve them on a hot platter, toothpicks removed carefully so the bacon stays in place. A little parsley, watercress, or even shredded lettuce dresses things up. This can be used for an appetizer or main course.

FROG LEGS

Dear Nan: My husband says he is going frog hunting one of these days, so I had better learn to clean frog legs! I have never even tasted those things, but I have heard they jump around in the frying pan as though they were still alive. The whole idea gives me the heebie-jeebies.

—MADISON, WISCONSIN.

Keep calm. It's not as bad as you think. Your husband knows good and well he can skin those jumpers, so don't let him kid you. The hind legs of frogs, big or little, are the only part used for eating. Those get cut from the rest of the critter as close to the body as possible, and the skin then strips off as easy as a glove. Chill them well before frying, and they won't hop around in the pan so badly.

You can batter-fry them, if you like, but they're awfully good just dipped in undiluted evaporated milk, then in seasoned flour with a dash of nutmeg added along with the salt and pepper. Fry them slowly in butter until they are golden brown. Fried oysters or scallops in the middle of the platter, surrounded by the frog legs and lemon wedges, are really something to chirp about.

7 / Good gravy!

Gravy does not get thickened by osmosis. It takes flour or corn-starch or arrowroot. There are, of course, the *au jus* or natural meat juices with no thickening at all, but that's something else again. I may make a cream gravy for fried chicken, ham, or some cuts of chops. I certainly do not use it for roasts, nor even for roast turkey. With all the dripped-down juices and short-ening I've used on the bird, and the addition of the cut-up gib-lets and the stock, it is already rich enough.

One sure thing, a lot of good gravy flavoring goes down the drain because most of us won't bother to save and store liquids in which vegetables have been cooked. Or take all those little waste items such as celery tops and skinnings, carrot par-ings, parsley stems, dabs of onion, and the throwaway parts of lots of other vegetables. Simmer those for ½ hour or so in just enough water to cover. These, strained into a jar and added to from day to day (refrigerated, of course), give anemic gravy a flavor hard to match in any other way. A good time to try this is when you are making a big pot of soup or stew and are paring quite a lot of vegetables all at once.

Dear Nan: Have you ever used potato water for gravies? It works best for brown gravies—really good!—and you get your vitamins, too. —TEXARKANA, TEXAS.

A good percentage of gravy lumping can be avoided if you heat the milk or liquid used before stirring it into the mixed drippings and flour. Cold stuff added to the hot paste can really foul things up. Other people have other ideas, bless 'em.

> *For lumpless gravy, the sure way is to stir with a regular fork. Try it next time you're mixing the flour and salt with the fat in the pan. Then add the liquid, ice-cold if you want to, right into the bubbling mixture. Keep right on fork-stirring until it boils to the thickness you desire. Either thick or thin, you will have gravy without lumps.* —MILAN, MISSOURI.

> *Years ago I asked a restaurant cook why his gravy was always so good. He said probably because he cooked his roast beef and pork together. He also added an apple to the roaster. Since then I have done this quite often, especially when I had just one small roast of each but wanted some leftovers. It does make the best gravy to use with either meat. Also, my husband doesn't like hamburgers, but he does like sausage. When I want hamburgers for myself, I cook them with the sausage in the same skillet. It makes better gravy than either one alone.* —GRAVOIS MILLS, MISSOURI.

The presifted flours are popular and just fine for gravy making if you do it right. A lot of cooks keep a large shaker of the flour—like an oversized salt shaker—right near the range, shaking the flour in gradually and stirring like crazy. You have a lot more control of the flour that way, but remember: any flour is going to lump if fat is too hot, and that's that.

Greasy roast gravies occur when the meat is pretty fat. You can remedy this by pouring off all the drippings into a tall metal cup or an empty can. Set the can of drippings in a pan of cold water. The fat will rise to the surface quickly. Skim, leaving only as much as you think wise for richness. Refrigerate the rest. It might come in handy another day when the roast gravy seems to be nothing but watery juice. The liquid left under the chilled fat gets added back to your gravy-making pan. If there isn't enough, you can always make up some nice, quick stock with a bouillon cube.

One of the easiest ways to get rid of excess fat that floats to the top of gravies, soups, or stews is with a bulb-type meat baster. That way, you just siphon it off.

I'd like to tell you how I make good, greaseless gravy. I flour the bottom of the roasting pan and put the meat in after it has been salted and peppered. Do not add water. Cover loosely with foil and bake to the desired doneness. Then remove the roast. Put the pan back in the oven or on the top of the range. (I prefer the latter method because it can be watched better.) Let the flour and meat drippings brown well but be careful they don't burn.

Pour off all the grease, add the desired amount of water, cover, and cook till the mixture is soft and can be scraped from the bottom. This should be done over very low heat. Add a little bottled liquid gravy seasoning and 1 or 2 bouillon cubes, according to how much liquid you have used. Thicken with cornstarch and strain.

—WESTBROOK, MAINE.

BISCUIT-MIX THICKENED GRAVY

Biscuit mix does fine for thickening pan gravy when you're in a hurry or just haven't mastered the technique yet.

Melt 2 tablespoons of fat and 2 tablespoons of the biscuit mix till it's smooth. Cook over low heat, stirring well till bubbly. Slide it from the heat and blend in 1 cup of liquid. That can be water, meat stock, or 1 bouillon cube dissolved in the water first. Bring it to a boil and stir like crazy for 1 full minute. That eliminates any raw taste. Season to suit yourself.

CORNSTARCH THICKENING FOR GRAVY

Dear Nan: Why is cornstarch used only in certain recipes for thickening, such as a few sauces and in Chinese dishes?

I would think gravy made with that clear look would be interesting.   —KANSAS CITY, MISSOURI.

Gravy thickened with cornstarch is much more appetizing in appearance. Surely French and Oriental cooks are among the best in the world. They use cornstarch a great deal and they are masters at sauces. Next time you order chicken chow mein or even beef chop suey, notice the clear look of what holds it together. Wouldn't be nearly as nice if flour had been used in place of cornstarch.

Cornstarch makes the smoothest white sauce ever. Grate a couple of hard-cooked eggs or some cheese into it for a vegetable sauce.

Cornstarch is also the most easily digested of all starches, and it is fine for people who cannot eat flour gravy or who are allergic to wheat. Just one thing to watch for: Always dissolve cornstarch in a little cold water before adding to hot liquids and stir constantly to avoid lumping, just as you would with flour.

Dear Nan: Do you know that dehydrated potato flakes thicken soups and stews to perfection? I had a son-in-law who could not have flour, so I experimented.   —PORTLAND, MAINE.

Yes, it works so well that the potato-flake people have even taken to putting that info on their boxes.

Now, if any of you still can't make good thickened gravy after all this, just lay in a supply of condensed cream soups. For regular gravy, add 1 can of condensed cream of mushroom soup (or the golden mushroom) to 2 or 3 tablespoons of meat drippings. Then all you have to do is stir in enough water to make the thickness you like. Usually takes anywhere from ¼ to ½ cup.

If it's a cream sauce you want, thin cream of celery soup as it comes from the can with ¼ to ½ cup of milk.

CHICKEN GRAVY

Dear Nan: Chicken gravy has me buffaloed! Mine tastes just fine and I never have any trouble getting it smooth, but

it is so pale looking. Not at all like the kind my mother used to make. What do you suppose she did that I am not doing?
—BENTON HARBOR, MICHIGAN.

To begin with, she used part of the chicken stock from a good rich stewing hen as part of the liquid. It wouldn't surprise me, either, if she added a pinch of turmeric. Old-time cooks were hep to the fact that turmeric not only makes for an appetizing color but improved flavor as well. It has something of a ginger-like aroma. Very appetizing.

AU JUS GRAVY

Dear Nan: I would appreciate knowing how to get au jus *juices with a prime rib roast the way they serve it in restaurants. All I ever wind up with is a few brown drippings and a whole lot of grease in the bottom of the pan.*
—LOS ANGELES, CALIFORNIA.

Au jus means "with juice," but the juice from a prime rib cut of meat seldom goes far enough. That beef cut is prime grade with its typical marbling of fat throughout, and you may wind up with excess grease. Pour off most of it.

Scrape the pan well to loosen any browned-on drippings. Then it is perfectly permissible to add a judicious amount of water with a little concentrated beef extract or beef consommé mixed in.

DILL GRAVY

Dear Nan: Do you have a recipe for dill gravy? It is a Czech or Bohemian dish, generally used on boiled beef or roast beef or with dumplings. —BERWYN, ILLINOIS.

Here is one that ought to be similar: Melt 3 tablespoons butter and gradually blend in the same amount of flour over low heat.

Stir in 1 pint of vegetable stock (cooking water from fresh or canned vegetables). Then add 4 tablespoons chopped fresh dill, 1 tablespoon cream, 2 teaspoons sugar, 1 tablespoon vinegar, salt and pepper to taste. Bring to a boil, simmer gently for 10 minutes. When you can't get fresh dill, use just 1 teaspoon of the dried kind or ½ teaspoon dill seed. You may want more. Dill is a marvelous flavoring for any sour-cream sauce over boiled potatoes, green beans, cabbage, cucumbers, broccoli, cauliflower, potato salad, even macaroni and cheese.

RED-EYE GRAVY

Dear Nan: Could you tell me how to make red-eye gravy? I hear southerners use coffee in theirs as a sort of au jus. Here where I live, most people just pour milk into the drippings after they have fried the ham slices and don't do any thickening at all. My interest stems from listening to a friend's reminiscences. He says no one makes it the way he remembers, and thus far my experiments bear him out. And why is it called "red-eye"? —YUMA, ARIZONA.

Your friend's memories probably stem from the fact that it takes real country-cured ham to make this correctly, not the kind we buy in stores today. Generally speaking, the gravy is made by frying the ham slowly and turning it to brown somewhat on both sides, then blending the drippings and scrapings with just enough hot water and stirring well to get all those nice little pan cracklin's.

The little red fat globules you see floating in the gravy are where it gets its name. Yes, many people do use at least part coffee instead of all water. No reason you couldn't use milk but I doubt that it would be called true red-eye.

This is the way you make red-eye. There are tricks to it and it takes practice.

Fry your ham in an iron skillet—it just has to be iron— then remove it from the skillet. Leave ¼ to ½ cup of the ham grease in the pan. Get it smoking hot. Then pour that into a bowl. If there is any extra, save it to cook with cabbage, beans, or turnip greens. Or fry eggs in it later.

Then set the skillet back on the stove. Be sure there is no grease in it, only what sticks after that pouring out. Into the skillet put 1 pinch of salt and 1 teaspoon of sugar. Wiggle the pan around on the fire while the salt and sugar brown, almost burn. It has to melt and be dark brown, almost smoking.

Then have ready about ½ cup of water and ¼ cup of coffee. Both must be hot. Pour that in. Grab the handle, take from the fire, wiggle that all over the bottom of the skillet. Then pour back that ¼ or ½ cup of grease. You have to learn how much to suit your own tastes. It comes out a brown-streaked gravy that is so good.

I doubt it could be done right in anything but an iron skillet. I was raised on this gravy and buttermilk biscuits. The sugar and coffee are the main things. You have to hurry those and the water, use lots of heat and a good shaking around.

A lot of Missouri readers, with plenty of Deep South blood in their veins, even if they are transplanted, go more for the milk version of red-eye gravy.

> *We made the gravy by pouring about 1 pint of mixed milk and cream into the fryings and fat in the skillet. When it was hot we put it in a pitcher and poured it over slices of homemade bread on our plates. This was one of the reasons for having country ham—that luscious gravy! I still make it now but drain off all the fat, use milk only. Still wonderful and still a tradition with our family.*
>
> —NORMAN, OKLAHOMA.

> *I was born and grew up in southern Missouri but I never heard it called red-eye. My mother called it brindle gravy. It was made in the fall when it was cold enough to butcher and was made from fresh, home-killed ham before it was cured. My mother always fried slices slowly and poured coffee into the drippings. It was delicious over hot corn bread crumbled in a bowl with fresh butter. Some people used water instead of coffee but I never heard of using milk.*

*In this day and age, you can have your butcher order a
fresh ham for you just as it comes from the carcass, no salt
or curing to it. Freeze it. You can have it any time you want.*
                                        —ST. LOUIS, MISSOURI.

In addition to pouring red-eye over biscuits and breads, other
enthusiasts say you shouldn't miss pouring it over hominy grits
or plain boiled potatoes. There, the technique is to mash the
potato on your plate, pour on some of the gravy, and mix the
two together.

*When I was a small girl and our dad got Sunday breakfast,
he always served pancakes, fried ham, and cream gravy. He
would fry the ham slices, remove them to a platter, then
pour in cream, season, and let bubble up good to mix with
the ham flavor. This was delicious on pancakes. At that time
we had our own separated cream. Now I use canned milk
instead.*   —BILLINGS, MONTANA.

Yes, the unsweetened evaporated milk will often thicken just
right for any kind of gravy with no additional thickening. Say,
I like that part about dad's getting breakfast! It should happen
more often. (I will now dodge while numerous males toss brick-
bats my way.)

8 / Super hints for stews and casseroles

Many a male columnist has a great time poking fun at casseroles and such. Who can blame them? With every magazine, newspaper, and cookbook striving for something new and different in this line, you find some pretty weird concoctions that could be almost anything. How many times have women complained to me, "But my husband just won't touch any casserole dish!" I know. He pokes it with a dubious, "Yeah. What is it?" There's the clue.

RECIPES TO PLEASE A MAN

Men are naturally suspicious of anything they can't identify with the naked eye; it's a great idea to have casserole ingredients cut only in recognizable pieces, not minced to a fare-thee-well.

Most men relish a good hearty homemade soup. Hearty, that is. Not a limp, watery brew that looks like close kin to dishwater. The same thing goes for stews. There needs to be proper richness, enough meat to make it interesting, some color contrast in the vegetables. That way the whole thing not only looks more appetizing, but tastes that way, too.

Shoot-the-Works Casserole

Years ago unexpected company dropped in, and there I was with no meat in the house except a pound of hamburger! How to stretch it to feed five husky appetites? I just kept adding things. Very flexible. Use whatever amounts you like.

1 pound ground beef (or more)	1 can kidney or pinto beans
1 diced onion	8-ounce package noodles
1 can condensed tomato soup (maybe more)	Salt and pepper to taste
1 large green pepper diced	Catsup or tomato paste
1 cup celery diced	3 teaspoons sugar
	2 to 3 teaspoons chili powder (optional)

Grated fresh cheese (optional)

I lightly brown the hamburger in a very large skillet with chopped onion to suit, but sometimes this dish "grows" so much I have to transfer it to a kettle. Then I stir in a can of condensed tomato soup, diluted with just ½ can of water. Add the celery, green pepper, kidney beans with all their liquid. Add salt, pepper, and sugar. Sometimes I use chili powder, sometimes not. Simmer slowly, covered, for an hour to blend flavors, adding water as needed. Right about here I am apt to toss in a few healthy squirts of catsup, more soup, or tomato paste. Canned pizza sauce would be good, too. Last of all, stir in the cooked noodles. I have been known to dump this into a large casserole, top with grated cheese and pop it into a hot oven till cheese melts. Other times I just serve it in a big bowl. Or you can pile the noodles in the center of a big platter and surround them with the bean-meat mixture. *Makes 4 to 6 servings.*

Liz Taylor's Favorite Chili

The story is that Liz ordered this frequently at Dave Chasen's restaurant in Hollywood, missed it so much when she was filming *Cleopatra* in Rome some years ago that she had Dave ship gallons of it to her via air express, packed in dry ice.

½ pound dry pinto beans	½ cup butter
5 cups canned tomatoes	2½ pounds beef chuck,
1 pound chopped green	coarsely ground
pepper	1 pound ground lean pork
1½ tablespoons salad oil	⅓ cup chili powder
1½ pounds chopped onion	2 tablespoons salt
2 cloves garlic, crushed	1½ teaspoons pepper
½ cup chopped parsley	1½ teaspoons cumin seed

Wash beans, soak overnight in water 2 inches above beans. Simmer, covered, in same water till tender. Add tomatoes and simmer 5 minutes more. Sauté green pepper in salad oil 5 minutes. Add onion, cook until tender, stirring often. Add garlic, parsley.

Melt butter in large skillet and sauté meat 15 minutes. Add meat to onion mixture; stir in chili powder, cook 10 minutes. Add this to beans, add spices. Simmer, covered, for 1 hour. Cook uncovered 30 minutes. Skim any fat from top. Makes 4 quarts. Freezes well!

Sonuvagun Stew

Nobody knows exactly where this old chuck wagon favorite originated, but it is a long-ago ranch specialty of Texas and western states. After a winter of sowbelly and beans, meat-hungry cowboys looked forward to butchering time when this rich, savory stew made its yearly debut. The dish was originally known as SOB stew, but when ladies were present it was either named for a detested enemy or called "district attorney stew." The marrowgut referred to is neither marrow nor gut but the connecting tube between the two stomachs of steer. Ideally it should be from an unweaned calf before the grass-eating stage. It is very tender, tastes like fine marrow, which gives the stew the characteristic flavor and richness. The real thing contained no vegetables whatsoever. Seasoning varied with the cook's imagination.

No strictly western cookbook would dream of skipping it. There is an astonishing modern version that uses white wine, chicken stock, and tripe instead of marrowgut. Other "moderns" do add garlic, celery, tomatoes, peas.

With rare good fortune I have heard from a lady who can give a firsthand account of this stew.

Mrs. Marcus Kroner said, "I have made many a potful of that stew when I cooked for years at several large ranches in the Texas Panhandle, north of the river. It was always a different mixture, depending on what was handy. I am eighty years old now and living at Muskogee, Oklahoma."

Here is a recipe for kitchen-style Sonuvagun Stew, adapted for the average homemaker:

½ pound rendered beef suet	¾ pound calf sweetbreads
¾ pound boneless chuck	1 pound sliced oxtail
1 pound or more of marrowgut	1 set calf brains, membrane removed
About ½ pound liver	

Cook the oxtail slices separately till meat falls off the bone and add to the stew. Some cooks prefer to cook the liver by itself, also, before adding. Render the suet in a Dutch oven or heavy kettle. Cut all meat in small pieces about the size of sugar cubes. Brown lightly in hot fat, stirring to coat. Add just enough water to cover and simmer slowly till very tender, about 3 or 4 hours. Season with any or all of the following: salt, black pepper, a little sage, crushed red pepper, jalapeño peppers, chili powder.

Ham Jambalaya

Here's a way to use up those leftover ham scraps to good advantage. That herb seasoning does wonders but skip it if you don't care for anything like that.

2 cups cooked ham diced	¼ teaspoon paprika
2 onions sliced	2 teaspoons Tabasco sauce
1 diced green pepper	½ cup dry white wine (optional), or substitute water or bouillon
1 garlic clove chopped fine	
¼ cup butter or margarine	
3 cups tomatoes (maybe more)	1 cup regular raw rice (not instant)
½ teaspoon dried thyme	Salt to taste
¼ teaspoon dried basil	

Sauté onions, green pepper, and garlic in fat till limp. Don't brown them. Add the rest of the stuff. Bring to a boil, stirring all the while. Reduce heat. Cover, simmer till rice is tender, about 25 minutes. More salt and pepper to taste. *Makes 4 servings.*

Salmon Casserole Dinner

It has everything. Color, flavor, nutrition. Use a 2-quart casserole with lid. Anything smaller seldom holds it all. Any grade of salmon will do. Red is prettiest but there is little difference in food value. Potatoes should be sliced very thin. I use the slicer side of my 4-sided hand grater.

1 **tall can of salmon** (reserve juice)	1 **large or 2 small eggs**
1 **small can peas** (reserve juice)	1 **cup milk**
2 **large potatoes** (maybe more)	1 **teaspoon salt**
1 **cup shredded raw carrots**	**Pepper**
Chopped onion	**Buttered crumbs** (bread or cracker)

Grease the casserole well. Place two or three layers of the raw sliced potatoes in the bottom. Pepper. Top with half of the salmon. Top the salmon with all of the peas. Then 3 more layers of potatoes, peppered. Now, the rest of the salmon. Finish with the carrot mixed with a bit of onion. Pat down gently with hands.

Mix and heat together ¼ cup juice from peas, ½ cup juice from salmon, 1 cup milk, and a scant teaspoon salt. (The salmon provides some saltiness.) Beat egg well. Stir a little of heated mixture into egg, then pour back into warm liquid and blend thoroughly. Pour over casserole. Put lid on and bake at 350 degrees for 45 to 60 minutes. Remove lid. Top with crumbs dotted with butter. Use brief broiler heat to brown, or up heat to 400 degrees. Don't burn! Serve with "egg gravy" if you like (chopped hard-cooked egg added to medium cream sauce). *Makes 4 to 6 servings.*

VARIATION: Some people prefer a can or more of diluted cream of mushroom or celery soup as the pour-over for the casserole. It does give a different flavor but be sure to use the salmon-peas juice as part of dilution liquid.

Mexicali Corn Casserole

Bless the reader who sent me this quick-and-easy. All from items you can keep stocked on the shelf.

1 **can chili con carne with meat**	1 **package snack-type corn chips**
1 **can whole kernel corn**	1 **large can tamales**
1 **cup corn liquid**	**Thin slices processed cheese**
¼ **cup chopped ripe olives (optional)**	

Mix chili with the corn. If not enough liquid, add water to get that amount. Olives are a nice touch but not necessary. In a greased casserole alternate layers of chili mixture with layers of corn chips. You can stop right there or extend the dish by laying tamales on top, topping each one with a cheese triangle before baking. Bake at 350 degrees for 30 minutes. *Makes 4 servings.*

WILD RICE

Dear Nan: I have a recipe that calls for wild rice. I was planning on preparing it for my family until I discovered the wild rice alone would cost three dollars! Why is it so expensive? Does it taste that much better than regular white rice? Could I substitute regular rice in the same amounts and get similar results? —RAYTOWN, MISSOURI.

Wild rice is expensive because production is limited. It isn't rice but the seed of a wild grass that grows in shallow water close to shorelines of lakes and rivers. It's usually grayish green in color, and the grains may be longer than rice. The area for wild rice is supposed to be around the Upper Great Lakes region in Minnesota and Wisconsin. It has to be harvested largely by hand, another reason for its high cost.

You could probably substitute regular white rice in your recipe but it isn't going to be the same. Wild rice has a marvelous flavor, somewhat nutlike. I have seen recipes suggesting a half-and-half combination of wild and regular rice as a means of stretching an expensive item, but generally the wild takes longer cooking.

Wild rice is wonderful sautéed with mushrooms and onion. Nothing quite matches it as stuffing for game birds or even the little domestic Rock Cornish hens.

Wild Rice and Chicken Livers

With chicken livers wild rice is out of this world. You can do it this way. Sauté 2 or 3 large onions in plenty of butter or margarine—about a cupful. Wash 12 chicken livers and hearts. Pat the livers dry, chop or cut them. Put those in with the onion and add the hearts, tossing all together over moderate heat till well browned. Season with 2 teaspoons salt—more later, if you like—and a little pepper. Add 2 cups raw wild rice and about 6 cups of chicken stock or boiling water. Cover and cook very gently over low heat for about 40 minutes, or until all the liquid is absorbed and the rice is tender. You'll have to stir it occasionally. Serve hot as hot can be. *Makes 6 servings.*

Amy's Green Rice Casserole

A beautiful pastel shade with a "just right" flavor, so easy to put together, so simple to serve. Fine accompaniment for any meat, always calls forth flattering comment.

¾ cup minced young green onions, including tops, or 1 small regular onion, finely diced

1 small clove garlic, minced

3 tablespoons olive oil

1 cup uncooked rice (not instant)

2 cups chicken broth (or dissolve 3 chicken bouillon cubes in 2 cups hot water)

2 to 3 drops green food coloring

½ cup minced green pepper (may be blenderized)

¼ cup diced stuffed olives (optional)

½ cup diced celery

1 cup minced parsley

1 cup freshly grated Cheddar cheese

1 teaspoon salt

¼ teaspoon pepper

Cook onions and garlic in the oil over medium heat till soft but not brown. Add food coloring to chicken broth. Combine all ingredients. Pour into 1½-quart greased casserole. Bake, covered, in 350-degree oven for 45 to 60 minutes or until set. Pass a shaker of prepared dried Parmesan cheese for those who might like a little extra zip. *Makes 6 servings.*

EGG BARLEY OR TARHONYA

Dear Nan: I found a recipe for Hungarian goulash that really appeals to me but it calls for an item that is new to me— egg barley. None of our markets carry such an item or know what I am talking about. Even our university extension department couldn't explain what it is or where to buy it. Is it native to one part of the country or to a foreign country? I need help! —MINNEAPOLIS, MINNESOTA.

I hadn't heard of it either at the time. Then, just hours later, I hit a real luck-in when I picked up one of my foreign cookbooks to look for something else. The book immediately fell open to a page where "egg barley" hit me right in the eye.

Egg Barley

So here is what egg barley is: Mix 1 beaten egg and 1 egg yolk with enough flour to make a stiff ball. Let set in the open for 1 hour or so, then shred it on a coarse grater and spread out on a large platter. When it is completely dry and brittle, it is ready to sprinkle into soup, stew, or goulash. Sort of a kissin' cousin to Pennsylvania Dutch *rivvels*.

If you don't want to go to the trouble of making your own, you can find it at many grocery stores in the section devoted to Jewish specialties. However, it is usually labeled "Farfel" or simply "Egg Drops" with no mention of egg barley except for a small subtitle on some boxes.

> *Your recipe for making egg barley is very accurate. It is easy to make and, once dried, can be stored for long periods of time. In Hungary, we call it* tarhonya.
>
> *The correct way to use* tarhonya *is to brown it first in whatever cooking fat you prefer. Hungarians use lard but I find bacon drippings easier to come by in this country. Butter or margarine is also good to use and may have less cholesterol. After browning, the liquid is added—either broth or gravy or whatever—in the amount of ½ cup* tarhonya *to 1 cup of liquid. It is very absorbent and sometimes needs even more liquid.* —FORT WAYNE, INDIANA.

TIPS FOR SUPERB STEWS

> *Dear Nan: To give boiled beef stew, noodles, etc., the best flavor, just drop a bay leaf into the cooking water. It took me fifteen years to discover that by myself.*
> —GILLIAM, MISSOURI.

Yes, you can win your laurels with this herb, and I do mean laurels literally, because that is what bay leaf really is. There are all sorts of charming legends about bay leaf in Greek mythology, including the ones about all those lads who would rather have appeared without their togas than their laurel wreaths.

People who have trouble with watery stew should let an old kitchen pro give out with a tip that will reduce the excess liquid. Just save some of the beef grease that accumulates in kitchens both domestic and commercial. Heat the grease, strain off the residue, then thicken with flour to the consistency of panroll dough. As the stew enters its final simmering stage, drop in 2 or 3 spoonfuls of this mixture. It will have a marvelous tightening effect and add zest to the culinary triumph that has retained top honors in menu preparation for centuries.

9/Let's hear it for vegetables!

If I could just invent a few new vegetables, I'd be in clover. Since I can't, how about dressing up some oldies? A new look often makes for a new taste.

Water chestnuts, canned mushrooms, and pimento are three things I always try to keep on hand for vegetable perk-ups. Those little flat cans of the chestnuts aren't exactly an economy item but, as thinly sliced as they should be, they go a long way. They're so nice and crunchy.

When I am trying to impress company with something a bit different, I use the Italian green beans from the frozen-food counter if I can't get fresh. I add the sliced water chestnuts along with sliced ripe olives, mushrooms I have sautéed in butter, and some chopped pimento. That last may not do too much more for flavor, but I do like those bits of bright red contrasting with the green, black, and beige stuff. I may even use a small dash of nutmeg with the regular seasonings.

CARROTS

Carrots! They can be the big sticker. How many times have I heard from anxious mamas, "How do I get my kid to eat carrots?" The ideal way to get introduced to carrots is to eat a baby one pulled fresh from the garden. But how many of us have the chance to do that any more? I'll admit cooked carrots can be pretty blah unless they're nicely seasoned or made interesting in some other way. Try these suggestions for a change of pace.

Toss chopped peanuts in melted butter or margarine just till lightly toasted and add to cooked carrot circles. The trick is to chop the peanuts just the right size. You can also buy them already sacked that way at any nut display.

When my youngsters turned up their noses at carrots, I added 2 tablespoons of honey, and whatever melted butter or margarine I chose, to a small skilletful of cooked carrot circles. After they had simmered till syrupy I announced them as "pirate's gold." You have to catch them young for this one, but it works.

You don't want to bother with honey? Add 2 teaspoons of sugar to carrots as they cook. Sugar does as much as or more than salt to bring out the flavor of almost any vegetable.

Stir mashed carrots into whipped white potatoes. Nice color change and taste.

For a fancy trick try Carrot Boats. All you have to do is cook whole, large carrots in salted water till tender. When they have cooled, hollow them out so they look like canoes. You can do this much ahead of time if you like. Comes mealtime, reheat gently in melted butter or whatever and fill with buttered green peas. I've known this one to make a hit at party luncheons.

RUTABAGAS

I had not realized how many vegetables people have never even tasted. As an example, time and time again in supermarket produce sections I have heard one woman say to another, "Rutabagas. I've always wondered what they taste like."

Great day in the morning! Why not live dangerously and

find out? However, if you don't like turnips, you aren't going to like rutabagas. They are close kin and one of those prized "yellow vegetables" supposed to be included in meals several times a week. They can make a fine side dish when cooked properly, perfectly terrible when they are not. I like to include them whenever I am doing a big pot of vegetable soup.

Here's what to do with rutabagas:

Pare them as thinly as possible, dice them, and drop into rapidly boiling water for 15 to 20 minutes or until they pierce easily with a fork. Overcooking is what ruins them. Makes them dark and strong tasting. Drain them, salt to suit, and serve with melted butter with a touch of lemon juice added to it.

Or you can whip cooked rutabagas with a little cream and butter, just as you would potatoes. Make them nice and fluffy.

Still another way, and perhaps the nicest of all: Put the boiled rutabagas—sliced or diced—in a shallow baking dish, pour milk or cream over them, top with buttered bread crumbs or fine cracker crumbs, and bake in a 400-degree oven till the crumbs are a beautiful brown. Some people like to add a little grated onion mixed in with the rutabagas.

> *Dear Nan: In rereading some of your columns I came across your remarks on people wondering about the taste of rutabaga. You said, "Why not live dangerously and find out?" So here goes. I am an old man who lives alone. I watch my calories so I like to cook rutabagas in lieu of potatoes. I cut up about four of them, add a carrot and an apple, both peeled and cut up, cook that all together. When done I mash same and put in a little butter. Sure gives 'em a better taste. Even children like them. So will you.*
>
> —NORTH HOLLYWOOD, CALIFORNIA.

That apple, in particular, sounds like a great idea! Does wonders for flavor. But, now, look, sir, you are not "an old man" when you can still come up with ideas like that and still print so beautifully.

DRY BEANS

Surprise! If you've had the notion that beans—just plain old navy beans, canned or otherwise—are a standby for only people of limited income, hear this. Even people with an annual salary topping $15,000 serve canned beans at least once a week in about one out of three households. People like beans.

Have you ever tried cold leftover baked beans for a sandwich? They're great. Pile them on slices of good rye bread with plenty of catsup and a thin sliver of onion. Or maybe you'd rather have pickle relish. If any of your snooty friends cast a lofty eye at such a concoction, put them in their place with a superior smile and say, "Didn't you know? Beans are such a rich source of vitamins, they're low in fat, they have calcium, phosphorus, even B vitamins. Just loads of iron and energy!" All that in just one little old bean.

> *Dear Nan: Could you give me some hints on how to cook dry beans (lima, navy, or chili beans) so they are more easily digested and do not affect those who eat them? I have tried adding vinegar, soda, or aspirin—all remedies suggested by friends—with no apparent change.* —OGDEN, UTAH.

I should have known better than to reply, "If there is a workable solution to that problem I have yet to see it." Came the mail deluge!

> *My aunt always added one large raw potato to navy or lima beans and let it bake in the pot with them. When she removed the potato, it would still be almost as hard as a rock but the beans were fine. She always said, "It took the snappers out!" And it did.* —MINNEAPOLIS, MINNESOTA.

> *Here's a Texas trick I picked up when I lived near the Rio Grande. Cover the beans with cold water, bring to a boil for just 15 minutes, turn off the heat, and let them stand for an hour. Then start simmering again, gently. When beans are*

about halfway done, add a can of beer and finish cooking. Season any way you like, with meat or otherwise. If anyone is squeamish about the beer, just don't tell 'em. They will just wonder why they can eat pinto beans now when they couldn't before. —ALTAMONT, TENNESSEE.

I took a chef's suggestion. He said to add a good pinch of ginger to cooking beans. It works and you'll never taste the ginger. —NASHVILLE, TENNESSEE.

A lot of you swear by that one, even using as much as a teaspoon of the spice. You really didn't think we were through with the bean subject, did you? All sorts of problems crop up.

Should navy or northern beans be soaked overnight before making baked beans? A friend of mine gave me a good recipe that says just to boil the beans for about 1 hour, then bake them for 1½ hours, but they still seem hard.
—POMONA, CALIFORNIA.

Both dried beans and peas sound so simple, but they can pull as big a prima donna act as the operatic soprano upstaging the basso right in the middle of an aria. A lot depends on where the beans were grown and how old they are when you get them. When in doubt, soak. It can't hurt anything. Of course, there are beans specially treated for quick cooking, but it will say so on the package and give full directions.

As those of you who live in high-altitude areas know, your cooking time may be a lot longer. Another factor is the water in any given area. Soft water shortens cooking time.

BLACK-EYED PEAS

Dear Nan: When we were South we ate some very good black-eyed peas. I bought some and now I find I do not know how to prepare them as they do there. Can you help?
—NEW LONDON, MINNESOTA.

Try this. Wash 2 cups of black-eyed peas and soak them overnight in about 2 quarts of cold water. Or you can soak them in
lukewarm water for no less than 6 hours. Use the same water for
cooking them, adding more if you have to. Then add 1-pound
piece of bacon, salt pork, or pork shoulder, cut in pieces. Some
people fry the bacon or salt pork a little bit first and add it to
the peas along with the drippings. Toss in a quartered onion
and maybe 1 teaspoon salt. If you use the salt pork, you may
not need any salt at all.

Simmer all this, covered, for about 2 hours or till all is
nice and tender. You may have to add a bit more hot water
from time to time, because those peas are pretty absorbent and
a real southern potlikker should never be skimpy. You want a
sizable amount of that rich brew still left when peas are done.
Makes 4 servings.

I know a Virginia cook who adds a whole bay leaf, a
clove of garlic, a few peppercorns, parsley sprigs, and a couple
of whole cloves.

LENTILS

Dear Nan: Every once in a while I run across a recipe calling
for dried lentils. My mother never cooked anything like
that, so I don't even know what they are.
                                        —MAYWOOD, ILLINOIS.

They belong to the dried peas or beans category, have been
known since Biblical times, and are cheap and popular in the
Mediterranean and Orient areas. They are purplish green or
red, depending on variety. In a pinch you can always use any
recipe for dried split peas or beans, but the flavor won't be the
same.

My mother came from France and served lentils often, es-
pecially at Easter with lamb. Cook them when you are hav-
ing a nice roast, whether it's beef, pork, or lamb. Use the

natural meat juices to flavor the lentils. They are even good when reheated by adding a little more liquid.

For 4 servings I use ½ pound dried lentils washed carefully in several waters. Drain, put in a saucepan, cover with water but do not soak them. Boil slowly till tender. Takes about 30 to 45 minutes. If water should cook down add more. If you like, add a bouillon cube, salt, and pepper.
—MOBILE, ALABAMA.

CAULIFLOWER

One day a nicely dressed, well-spoken lady stopped at her supermarket produce section to ask, "Would you please show me what a cauliflower looks like?" She also asked, "Which part of it do you cook—the white part or those green things around the outside?"

She admitted, "My mother never cooked any vegetables except green beans or peas and neither have I. Now the doctor says I have to get a greater variety of vegetables into my family's diet."

I will admit this is an extreme case. But how long has it been since you've served something besides carrots, peas, or green beans?

I just love questions like the next one.

Dear Nan: I would like to know how to French fry cauliflower. —WASHINGTON, D.C.

It's so deliciously different, I don't blame you. Break the cauliflower into flowerets and cook in boiling, lightly salted water till just barely tender. You don't want it the least bit mushy. Drain well, then dip the flowerets in a medium batter made from pancake mix. Or else beat a couple of egg yolks with ½ cup milk, about ¼ teaspoon salt, and approximately ¾ cup flour. Deep fry at about 375 degrees. It's fine just as it is, but you might like to serve it with a sour-cream dressing, or a cheese or creole sauce. But read on for another approach.

Have you ever tried sliced raw cauliflower in a tossed salad? Really good, even though the French might not approve. Their salads are usually greens only, with a vinegar and oil dressing.

Those raw flowerets go over big at cocktail parties arranged around a "dunk bowl" of any sour cream or cheese dip. Teamed up with bright carrot sticks, celery chunks, and healthy-sized green pepper strips, they are colorfully enticing and people do welcome them as a change from limp canapés or all the usual salty snacks.

Any time you cook a whole head of cauliflower, the best way in the world to get it drained well is to upend the head on a couple of pieces of bread. A little lemon juice or sugar added to the cooking water will keep cauliflower snowy white. Just don't overcook it. Go ahead and dress it up with a cheese sauce if you like. I always vote for melted butter and pepper fresh from the grinder.

POTATOES

Poor potatoes! What a walloping they've taken since the get-skinny-quick cult swung into action. Regardless, I will continue to stand up and be counted as one of their staunch defenders. Potatoes are high in food energy and phosphorus. They contain a respectable amount of vitamin A, calcium, and ascorbic acid, with lesser amounts of thiamine and niacin. Yes, they do contain starch, but not as much as rice, peas, and lentils.

> Dear Nan: At our house no meal is complete without potatoes, but I get so tired of fixing them the same old way—fried, boiled, or baked! Could you give me some different ideas? —HUNTSVILLE, ALABAMA.

Here are some of my favorites I hope you'll try and enjoy.

Princess Potatoes

Fry 3 cups of cubed cold boiled potatoes in deep fat until they are a nice golden brown (375 degrees on a deep-fry thermometer). You might be tempted to stop right there but we aren't through with this yet. More to come.

Melt 2 tablespoons butter or margarine in a shallow saucepan. Blend in 1 tablespoon flour and ¼ teaspoon salt with pepper to suit. Blend in 1 cup milk very gradually. An ordinary fork works well here. Get this very smooth and cook over low heat till it's fairly thick. Now add a bouillon cube and stir to dissolve. (That's why we didn't add too much salt.)

Put the fried potato cubes in a serving dish and pour the sauce right over. I like to dust this with paprika. Potato lovers of all ages go wild over these. Sometimes if I have a little left-over cheese roaming around, I grate that over, too. *Makes 3 to 4 servings.*

Baked Potatoes in Spaghetti Sauce

You can juggle proportions to suit yourself, but the basic recipe calls for around 6 medium potatoes peeled and boiled in salted water until partly tender—about halfway. Drain them well and brush them with cooking oil all the way around. Line them up in a shallow pan. Pour a can of meatless spaghetti sauce over them, sprinkle with a clove of shredded garlic, 1 chopped onion, and some chopped parsley. Bake in a 350-degree oven for about an hour or until they test tender. If the sauce seems to be cooking down too much, cover the pan with foil for a while. *Makes 4 to 6 servings.*

Pommes de Terre Soufflées

Antoine's restaurant in New Orleans serves Pommes de Terre Soufflées, which we call inflated French fried potatoes. Can you tell me how these are prepared?

—ST. JOSEPH, MISSOURI.

I don't know exactly how Antoine's does theirs because professional chefs differ in what cooking fats they are devoted to. Each seems to time at a different temperature, but the general technique is the same. Pare Idaho or Burbank potatoes (they "puff" better) and slice them lengthwise just ⅛ inch thick. It is hard to get them even unless you have a potato slicer. You now have flat pieces of potato. They are not cut up like regular French fries, at least not at the places where I have eaten them.

Soak the potato slices in ice water for 15 minutes, then drain and pat very dry on cloth that absorbs well. Thin old linen used to be the ideal, but high-quality paper toweling does a good job. Now comes the double frying. Professional chefs usually use two deep fryers set at different temperatures but you can get by with just one.

Cook just 1 cup of the slices at a time in a combination of oil and regular shortening set at 300 degrees. Turn once for even cooking. Takes about 5 minutes this time, or until slices float to the surface. Remove at once and drain on brown paper or toweling. Let the potatoes cool well before the next step. They may even be placed in the refrigerator. Now set your deep fryer at 425 degrees and plunge the potatoes into that, again just one cup at a time. Crowding ruins things. They ought to start puffing up at once, crisply blistered. Give the fry basket a shake or two to help things along.

These can be tricky and not puff on schedule, but just pop them back into hot fat again if necessary. Drain well and sprinkle with salt. These should be served at once. I agree with that French axiom, "The guests should wait for the potatoes; the potatoes should never wait for the guests."

Baked Shoestring Potatoes

Nobody has asked me but I'd feel I was cheating not to include this one. It's a favorite at our house. Awfully nice for a change and you can do the dish in the oven or out on the grill.

Cut a 48-inch length of foil and fold it in half. Cut about 4 medium-sized potatoes in strips as you would for slim French fries. Put those a little off-center of the foil and dot plentifully with 3 tablespoons butter or margarine. Sprinkle with salt, a generous grinding of pepper, and ½ cup of grated cheese. It looks pretty and gives nice additional flavor if you sprinkle 2 tablespoons of chopped parsley on top, but that's up to you. Sometimes I think we overdo the parsley thing.

Now pull the edges of the foil up to form a pan and pour in ½ cup of light cream or unsweetened canned milk. Fold the whole thing securely so it won't leak, but don't pack it down tight on top of the potatoes or the parsley sticks to the foil. It's wise to leave a little steaming space, anyway, especially for the grill, or you might have a blowup.

For the oven, put the packet in a shallow pan or on a cookie sheet and bake at 400 degrees for 40 to 50 minutes. For the outdoor grill, just place it right on the rack over medium coals. Since you're usually barbecuing meat in the grill's center, it's okay to place the packet to one side, but the potatoes will take longer, so govern yourself accordingly.

Either way, the cream and cheese will be absorbed, the potatoes soft and savory! You don't even have to dirty up a dish when you bring them to the table. Just place the packet in one of those little serving baskets or, for that matter, on a platter. Serve right from the foil, but watch it when you undo the foil! These will be hot, hot, hot. *Makes 4 servings.*

Mashed Potatoes

Is there much of anything you can do with leftover mashed potatoes besides reheating them or making ordinary fried potato cakes? —COLORADO SPRINGS, COLORADO.

Sure thing! Reheat leftover mashed potatoes with just enough milk or cream—and butter—to make them fluffy but not soupy. Mix in 1 beaten egg for every 2 cupfuls or less. Spoon them into a shallow, greased baking dish, fluffing them up into peaks. Dot with butter, sprinkle with paprika, and bake them in a 350-degree oven till browned. Using part of 1 can of creamed condensed soup—something like mushroom or celery—instead of any milk or butter results in a different flavor. You can even sprinkle grated cheese over the top, or mix it right in with the potatoes in the first place.

You can heap individual mounds of hot mashed potatoes onto a greased baking sheet or ovenproof platter, making a good indentation in each mound with the back of a spoon. Drizzle with melted butter and slide that under the broiler to brown. Then fill each indentation with creamed peas or other vegetables.

A really mouth-watering dish is deep-fried mashed potato puffs. Mix 2 cups mashed potato with 2 beaten eggs, 1 teaspoon baking powder, additional salt and pepper if needed, and ⅛ teaspoon paprika. Drop by teaspoonfuls into deep hot fat set at 395 degrees and cook till brown. Drain well on paper toweling placed in a colander. You can do these ahead of time, if you like, and then reheat them in a 425-degree oven.

Another suggestion is to roll balls of the mashed potato mixture in melted butter or an egg white beaten with 2 tablespoons water, then in crushed cornflakes. Bake in a greased pan at 375 degrees.

Hog Potatoes

Recently my husband was served a "hog potato" in an Illinois restaurant. Do you have any idea how these were done?
—COUNCIL BLUFFS, IOWA.

I knew I would be second-guessing if I tried to pinpoint the exact process. So I did what I always do when I'm stumped. I tossed the question to my column readers.

I think I maybe know what the "hog potatoes" are. Of course we raise our own potatoes and use the smaller ones for this. They would be about the size of a medium egg. It takes fresh or new potatoes to do this really right.

I scrape off the peelings, then boil them till they are about half done, and put them in a skillet of hot fat deep enough to come halfway up the potato. Brown on one side, then on the other. They are simply delicious. Soft on the inside, crispy on the other. —BIXBY, OKLAHOMA.

Sweet Potatoes in Orange Sauce

I tasted some sweet potatoes that were flavored with orange gelatin. They were just delicious but I can't find the recipe anywhere. —CHARLOTTE, NORTH CAROLINA.

Search no longer. I have it right here. This makes a well-flavored sauce that really gets syrupy in a perfectly splendid way.

In a skillet heat 1 cup of water until it barely boils. Add a 3-ounce package of orange-flavored gelatin, ⅓ cup brown sugar, a dash of salt. Simmer till that's all well dissolved. Add 2 tablespoons butter and simmer another 5 minutes. Pour this over cooked fresh or canned sweet potato halves in the pan. Don't crowd them because you need basting space. As you cook over medium heat for about 10 minutes, baste the potatoes frequently until the syrup thickens and the sweets have a lovely glaze. *Makes 4 servings.*

CELERY

Dear Nan: There are all sorts of different ways to cook celery. Here is the way my family likes it. I dice it and cook it with seasoned macaroni, butter, and cream.
—KANSAS CITY, MISSOURI.

MUSHROOMS

Dear Nan: What about mushrooms? Are they especially good in reducing diets? Are you supposed to peel them? Are they mainly used in cooking with other foods or can they be cooked separately? —TARENTUM, PENNSYLVANIA.

You mean you've been missing out on cooked mushrooms all this time? They are an excellent low-calorie item, especially the fresh ones. Just about 66 calories to the pound. Since they are such lightweight things, you get quite a few at that weight. Canned mushrooms will rate higher in those dratted calories because some of the water has already been cooked out.

For goodness' sake, don't go trying to peel them. About as futile as trying to peel a grape and totally unnecessary. Don't go scrubbing them either. A lot of the flavor and nutrition roosts on their tops.

You certainly can eat them all by themselves, if you like. Of course, if you add butter or cream that ups the calorie count. I have pretty much whipped that one by starting fresh, sliced ones in a small pan with just a little butter or margarine melted in it, just enough to keep from sticking. Maybe a scant 2 teaspoons or so for as many mushrooms as I can heap into my 7-inch skillet. Then I add just enough water or milk to let them simmer comfortably. They add their own juice as they cook down.

If you are using the absolutely white button type and want them to stay white, simmer them in milk. No butter. Any nice mushroom is also fine sliced raw in a green salad. Or add them to various cooked vegetables for a side dish. Not many people will complain at a whole heap of butter-browned mushrooms topping a broiled steak, either!

RADISHES

Dear Nan: I have heard of a few kooky people spreading butter on radishes for a snack, but now I've heard of something even more wild. Boiled radishes! Whoever heard of cooking a radish? Is somebody putting me on?
—ATLANTA, GEORGIA.

Not at all. While I doubt if anything beats a garden-fresh baby radish crisped in ice water, cooked ones can have an appeal all their own. They really should be fairly young. Big ones can be bitter. Leave them whole, red part and all, or slice them. Then you just cook them tender in a small amount of salted water.

Pretty good served with melted butter and freshly ground pepper! Some people like them in a good cream sauce. It's fun to do something out of the ordinary like this now and then.

But say, now, that buttering raw radishes isn't so bad. Ever try it? And don't tell me you've never tried one of my favorites. A radish sandwich! That's what I said—sandwich. Well-buttered homemade bread with sliced radishes between. That's good! Plenty of salt and pepper.

BEAN SPROUTS

Dear Nan: Could you tell me how to make my own bean sprouts? Do you need special beans or will any kind do?
—NORTH EDGECOMB, MAINE.

Mung beans are regarded as best suited to the purpose, although in some areas of the Orient the people use their native soybeans. Regular grocery stores in some areas of the country—mainly East and West Coast—may carry the mungs in stock, but they are practically a staple item at gourmet or specialty food shops everywhere, or wherever they sell Oriental food supplies.

The grow-it-yourself technique isn't difficult, and the bean sprouts are so superior to the canned variety that there is no comparison. You can spread the beans out in a shallow tray with just about ⅛ inch water. The beans should not be entirely covered with water. You want just enough moisture to make them sprout. I have also heard of people placing them on a bed of tiny pebbles in a pan of water. Either way, they must be kept in a dark place for fast sprouting. A closet or basement would do, but don't forget about them, or they'll start souring with an aroma that is hard to shake.

Sprouting takes about two days or so. Then the sprouts should be refrigerated, but usually not for more than two or three days. They should be well washed and drained before using. Aside from being an ingredient in chop suey and other Oriental dishes, they are awfully good just stir-fried. Toss them in cooking oil in a skillet—along with a little cut-up green onion—for a few minutes. Keep stirring, then add salt to taste. Special dividend: Bean sprouts are low calorie.

> *What can I do with leftover bean sprouts? Sometimes I use only a half can for an Oriental dish, and then I wind up throwing the rest away. I know this is wasteful, but what can I do?* —SACRAMENTO, CALIFORNIA.

Any time you have leftover bean sprouts, try them in a salad, mixing them with sliced mild radishes, cucumbers, green peppers, and diced celery—all tossed with French dressing with possibly a touch of soy sauce. Or use the well-chilled sprouts simply as a salad garnish. At times, when I have had just a few roaming around in the can, I have heated them separately so they wouldn't be overcooked and added them to cooked green beans or peas. They may not add too much by way of flavor, but they make a nice change of taste, texture, and appearance. I just never throw them out.

SNOW PEAS

> *Dear Nan: Do you have any recipes for Chinese foods using snow peas? I have snow peas in my garden now and would like to learn different ways of fixing them.*
> —AUBURN, INDIANA.

They're delicious all by themselves if you toss them quickly in hot oil for a minute or so. Very crisp and tender. The Chinese would use peanut or soya oil. These pods with the peas that don't grow up are added to all sorts of Oriental dishes in combination with bean sprouts, water chestnuts, bamboo shoots, and thinly sliced meats.

In something like that, the peas are often cut in half diagonally before the last 5 minutes of cooking time. Part of the charm of such cookery is that the vegetables are never overcooked and always have something of a crunchy texture without being raw. Many groceries around the country now feature snow peas in their frozen-food cases, but they're never quite as good as fresh.

> *I thought you would like to know how my family likes snow pea pods cooked. I cut them into about half-inch lengths by laying sixteen to eighteen on a board at a time. Just cover the bottom of the pan with water and salt to taste. Bring the pods to a boil and cook covered 3 to 4 minutes or until "crisp tender." I then cream them like ordinary peas.*
> —FORT WAYNE, INDIANA.

SWEET CORN

> *Dear Nan: Settle an argument, please. When you cook sweet corn, are you supposed to salt the water or not? And what is the proper cooking time?* —LOUISVILLE, KENTUCKY.

There is plenty of time to salt the corn when you eat it. Salting the water just toughens the kernels. Instead, add about 1 tablespoon of sugar to each 1 gallon of cooking water. It does much to improve the flavor, especially when corn is not as fresh as it might be. Also, add a little lemon juice to the water. It has a tenderizing effect without any lemony taste.

How long to cook corn? Depends a good deal on variety, kernel size, personal tastes. For most of us, just don't boil the daylights out of it. I changed my corn-cooking methods one day when a potful was just starting to bubble. I had to answer the phone so I flicked off the switch. Took me 15 minutes to get back to the kitchen and that corn was so nice and tender, I didn't have to cook it a lick more. So now I boil for 1 minute, turn off the heat, and let it get its nice little Turkish bath. Even if I am delayed as long as half an hour in getting it to the table, it is still tender.

Foil Corn Bake

I love foil cookery for lots of vegetables—like oven-roasted corn on the cob. I like to do this for dinner guests because, among other things, the individually wrapped corn ears look pretty special heaped on the platter. Too, "seconds" stay piping hot till unwrapped. And what flavor! You just don't lose a bit of it.

Place each cleaned ear on a square of heavy-duty foil, brush with plenty of melted butter or margarine, salt and pepper. If your taste runs to barbecue sauce, you can brush some of that on, too, but mostly I want corn-and-nothing-but. Bring the foil up around the corn ear and seal with a double lap. Twist the ends shut to hold tight. Bake in a 400-degree oven for about 35 minutes.

End-of-the-Month Corn Chowder

I used this one a lot during Depression days when the month and the money weren't coming out even. Our kids liked it, too, and it's still a good little dish. Another of those flexible things where you can vary amounts to suit yourself.

3 to 4 slices bacon	3 to 4 peeled raw potatoes
1 large can yellow whole grain corn	3 to 4 cups milk
1 small onion	Salt and pepper to taste

Fry the bacon, pour off all but about 2 tablespoons of the fat, and break up bacon with a fork right in the pan. Pour in the corn, liquid and all. Add diced potatoes and onion. Season and pour in enough milk to cover. Simmer slowly, covered, for ½ hour or more. Stir to prevent scorching, adding more milk as needed. If you like it soupy, add more milk. Or you can let it cook down quite thick. A little diced pimento makes this look more interesting, but we couldn't afford that frill in our penny-counting days. *Makes 4 servings.*

NOTE: Some people prefer cream-style corn for this. Others like a can of condensed cream soup as part of the liquid. Leftover boiled potatoes may be used, but the raw ones seem to add something.

OKRA

Dear Nan: I would like to know if there is some way to cook okra without it being so slippery! Personally, I don't think I would ever bother with the stuff, but my husband is a southerner and he loves it. —WICHITA, KANSAS.

Oh, come on, now! Once you catch on to how to handle this vegetable, it could be one of your favorites. Of course, okra is a little glue factory to itself, especially as pods get older, but even then you can use it to good advantage in soups, stews, and gumbo because it makes for nice natural thickening. Gives a nice flavor, too.

When you want it boiled, as a side dish, use only young pods. You test by breaking off the tip of a pod. If there are any strings that won't snap easily, the pod is too old for that purpose.

Fried okra is delicious and isn't slippery at all. Cut off the stem ends of young pods, barely cover with boiling water, cook for 5 minutes. Then drain well, pat dry, sprinkle with salt and pepper, roll it in cornmeal, and fry in hot fat till brown. Or maybe you'd rather dip the boiled pods in beaten egg, then in fine cracker crumbs for frying.

One of my southern friends—and they're experts with okra—says it won't ever be sticky if you take care to leave the stems on the pods. Cook them, stems and all, in boiling salted water until they're as tender as a baby's you-know-what. Then it's on with the melted butter or, if your taste runs that way, with a bit of mild vinegar or lemon juice.

Cooking okra with tomatoes is just about foolproof for a nonskid taste, because the tomato acidity counteracts that. There are all sorts of variations for that duo, but see how you like this one.

Okra Mix-up

I don't see how you can beat fresh young okra combined with fresh corn, onion, firm ripe peeled tomatoes—all flavored up with bacon or ham! I start drooling just thinking about that one.

Slice the okra, cut the corn from the cob, quarter the tomatoes, and dice the onion. You're on your own with amounts of whatever. Dice some bacon into a large skillet and let it fry out, or you can use ham bits, but you'll have to brown those lightly in a little additional fat. Add the okra, tomatoes, and onion, and let simmer for 2 minutes. Then in goes the corn.

You do not need water or other liquid. Cover the skillet and the natural vegetable juices will do the trick as the mélange simmers. Then it's time enough to add salt and pepper or even a good mixed-seasoning salt.

JERUSALEM ARTICHOKES

Dear Nan: I would like to know something about Jerusalem artichokes. There are a few growing in the garden of a house I bought and I am wondering if they are worth cultivating. —CRESTON, IOWA.

They're really quite a nice vegetable if they're handled right, but you have to keep an eye on them in the cooking. Too long and they'll get tough.

You don't see them in markets very often because they don't keep well, but they're easily grown in most sections of the country. They aren't the prettiest vegetable in the world—rather knobby and misshapen, even if they do look something like a potato. They aren't a bit like a regular artichoke, and nobody knows what far-out soul tagged them "Jerusalem," because they certainly didn't originate there.

Don't let all that scare you out of trying them when you have the chance, because they do have a very pleasant flavor and they make a nice change from potatoes. Rather fun to grow because they are something of a novelty to a good many people. They are tubers and have to be dug.

When you are lucky enough to have some, choose the ones most alike in size and as smooth as possible. Some people scrape them before cooking, but they're much better if they are done in their jackets. Cook them, in boiling salted water, for anywhere from 15 to 30 minutes, depending on size. It's best to test them with a toothpick after 15 minutes to see what's happening. Remember, you don't want to overcook them or you'll wonder what all this enthusiasm is about. Drain them and strip off the skin. Mash just as you would potatoes, or put them through a ricer. Season with butter, salt, and pepper.

Now that you have mashed Jerusalem artichokes, there are several things you can do with them. Use them as a border for creamed dishes, make them into small flat cakes to fry, or form them into small balls and deep fry.

Chill diced cooked tubers so they can be mixed into a vegetable salad. People eating them for the first time that way might give a quizzical look, but it's ten to one they'll like them.

Slice the peeled cooked tubers into a baking dish with a rich cream sauce between layers, cover with buttered crumbs and cheese, heat in a moderate oven till the cheese melts.

You can even sauté the cooked tubers after they are peeled and sliced, just as you would potatoes.

SALSIFY

Dear Nan: I never see salsify dealt with in your writings. We scrape the vegetable like a carrot (they clean easier but they will still be gray and knotty), boil till tender but not soft, dip pieces in a batter of beaten egg and a little flour. Then French fry till golden brown. This is our favorite vegetable and food fit for the gods. —KANSAS CITY, MISSOURI.

Salsify is a root of the chicory family and is also known as "oyster plant" because it tastes a little like that shellfish after it's cooked.

You can also boil it and mash it with beaten egg and a little flour, along with melted butter and ordinary seasoning, to make a batter stiff enough to form into patties. Roll these in dry bread crumbs, fry in butter or margarine in a heavy skillet, and enjoy another nice dish. Or just boil it, cut it in pieces, and pour melted butter over it.

ZUCCHINI

Dear Nan: Could you tell me how to do stuffed baked zucchini squash boats? What other ways could I fix this vegetable? —CULVER, INDIANA.

The best stuffed zucchini I ever put in my face was nicely tender, not at all overdone as it so often is. This zucchini was just about the longest, narrowest I had ever seen. Not the fat ones we so often see in markets.

Stuffed Baked Zucchini

First, cut off just a bit of the stem end so you get rid of that little scar. Just barely. You do not peel the zucchini. They don't need it unless they are old ones with pretty tough hides, but that isn't what we want here anyway. They can be fairly large, yes, but not granddaddies.

Cook the zucchini, whole, in boiling salted water for about 5 minutes. Drain well and cut in half lengthwise. Scoop out a good deal of the pulp with a teaspoon, but do leave enough for a solid shell. Chop the pulp (don't blenderize it) and mix with an equal amount of soft bread crumbs, salt and pepper, and a little beef or chicken stock made with a bouillon cube and hot water. Just enough to hold the mixture together nicely. If you like herb flavorings, a pinch of marjoram or thyme is nice. Or you can add a bit of shredded parsley, but neither is necessary. Now pile the mixture back in the boats, sprinkle with plenty of buttered crumbs and then a generous dousing of Parmesan cheese from the shaker. Line the boats up in a shallow pan and bake at around 350 degrees for 30 minutes or so. You can test the squash part for tenderness by poking the outside with a toothpick.

If you like, add Parmesan right in with the stuffing itself. Chopped canned or slightly cooked fresh mushrooms add wonderfully to the stuffing, and I have also eaten them with a little flaked crabmeat mixed in. Any which way, they are just fine. Here are some other ways.

Buttered Zucchini

Sometimes I think this is the best way of all, because the delicate squash flavor is so enjoyable just in itself. Slice the vegetable about ¼ inch thick. Leave skins on unless the zucchini is very mature. Cook in salted water just till tender. Drain, pepper, and butter.

Italian Tomato Zucchini

A large skillet does well here. Sauté some diced onion in butter, margarine, or good olive oil till it is limp and a little yellow. Slice zucchini no less than ¼ inch thick. Add. Cook for 5 minutes, stirring gently. Now add a can of those flavorful Italian plum tomatoes or 1 cup of fresh ones, diced. Add ½ cupful of diced celery, if you like. Cover and simmer till the squash is tender but still retains its shape. Takes about 20 minutes. You may have to add a bit of water or tomato juice from time to time. Pass the Parmesan shaker at the table.

EGGPLANT

Dear Nan: Eggplant is so often overlooked or underrated, although it is a nutritious, low-calorie, versatile vegetable. For a quickie dish, I brown eggplant cubes in a small amount of fat, add a few tablespoons water, cover and let steam until tender. Then simply add a can of stewed tomatoes that already have the proper seasonings of green pepper, onions, etc. Simmer for a few minutes and it's voilà!

—CAMERON, MISSOURI.

B R O C C O L I

Here is a little doozy of a way to dress up broccoli no end!
Or any other green vegetable, for that matter. I have been
known to toss in a few extra shrimp, cut in pieces.

Broccoli with Shrimp Sauce

You can start this quick but glamorous sauce a little ahead of
your frozen broccoli because that is surely one vegetable that
should never be overcooked!

2 to 3 ounces chive cream cheese, softened	1 can condensed frozen cream of shrimp soup, partly thawed
¼ cup milk	2 tablespoons lemon juice

Blend the cheese, milk, and soup. Cook over low heat
until it is smooth and hot. Takes about 15 minutes. Stir in the
lemon juice and cook for another 2 minutes, stirring. So far,
so good.

Cook 2 packages frozen broccoli spears as package directs. Drain well and transfer to a serving platter. Pour the
shrimp sauce over and garnish with chopped almonds. A few
dashes of paprika won't do any harm, either. Looks pretty and
doesn't affect the flavor. Didn't I tell you this was good? *Makes
4 to 6 servings.*

B E E T S

*Dear Nan: What in the world can I do with beets besides
butter them? We're tired of them that way. —*ELKO, NEVADA.

Lots of things. Pour a sweet-sour juice over the beets. Then
thicken with a bit of cornstarch and serve piping hot. Right
away quick, one type of Harvard beets. Or do this with the

beets: Heat them in slightly thickened orange juice, cooking till clear. You might like just a touch of lemon with the orange.

Please tell me why beets shrivel when making buttered beets.
—QUARRYVILLE, PENNSYLVANIA.

If you put diced or sliced cold cooked beets directly into hot butter to cook, they'll shrivel, darken, or both just about every time. If canned, heat them gently in their own liquid, drain, and pour a little melted butter over them. And it's best to wait till then to season them. A little orange juice and a touch of brown sugar mixed into the butter are nice for a change. Fresh beets can be brought back to piping hotness simmered in just a little of their own cooking water before buttering, but don't let them come to a boil.

RED CABBAGE

Dear Nan: I surely do wish I could cook red cabbage the way I've tasted it while traveling through Germany. What you put into it nobody can tell me, beyond a little of this and a little of that. —MADISON, KANSAS.

My grandma Kunz used to make this dish all the time; she never measured anything, but here's an approximate facsimile. Put about 3 tablespoons of cooking oil or bacon drippings into the pot and shred a head of red cabbage into it. Put the lid on and smother slowly for about 1 hour over low heat. Add 1 diced apple, skin and all, 1 sliced-up onion, along with about ½ cup sugar, 4 to 5 tablespoons vinegar (preferably red wine type), 1 teaspoon salt, a bay leaf, and 2 to 3 cups water. Mix 1 or 2 tablespoons of flour in with part of the water and stir in. Let simmer for another ½ hour or more. Add enough water during cooking so it's level with the cabbage. *Makes 4 servings.*

Sometimes grandma sprinkled in some caraway seeds— whatever suited her. Some cooks toss in a handful of raisins.

Others use rendered chicken fat in place of the oil that first goes into the pot. Or if you want to make an all-in-one meal out of this, do the whole thing in a large heavy casserole and add about 4 medium-sized ham knuckles. I remember this being served at home with pot roast. Any which way, it all smells great while it's cooking!

GREEN BEANS

Dear Nan: Last summer we journeyed through the Missouri Ozarks and several eating places along the way served the most delicious green beans we've ever eaten, so they must be typical of that part of the country. They were well flavored with ham or maybe bacon drippings but they tasted sweet, too, and the pot liquor had been cooked way down so it was just this side of syrupy. I have experimented but can't come up with the same thing. Would you have any idea how this is done? —SAGINAW, MICHIGAN.

Ozark Green Beans

Now, I know good and well you should never cook the daylights out of any vegetable, but if you want something that simply tastes great, this is it. These beans might never pass muster at "better restaurants," but they go big a lot of other places.

It takes fresh green beans to do this dish best. Home-canned green beans are next best. Commercially canned or frozen beans just don't seem to absorb the flavor as well, although they're not bad, either.

I can't give you an absolute so-much-of-this-and-that recipe any more than those Ozark cooks could. On a rough guess, I would say I add 1 tablespoon or more bacon drippings per 1 pound of beans, plus about ⅓ cup brown sugar. Or you can use partly fried salt pork bits or ham scraps or—when I have been in a hurry—the chopped salt pork or bacon added raw. The big trick is in the long, slow simmering till that pot liquor gets cooked way down. Doesn't matter if they get done ahead of time. You can always reheat them later. Pretty good next day, too, if there are any left.

Green Bean Casserole

Remember back a few years when the favorite vegetable for brides to serve—and a lot of us not bridey—was baked green beans with cream of mushroom soup and fried onion rings? Here's a newer version with just a little lemony flavor.

Thaw two 10-ounce packs of frozen green beans. Heat about ¼ cup vegetable oil in a skillet. When it's hot add the green beans, 3 tablespoons chopped onion. Cook, stirring constantly, for just 1 minute. Cover and cook for an additional minute. What you're after here is to keep the bright greenness of the beans and a crisp, crunchy texture.

Now, stir in 1 teaspoon flour, 1 tablespoon water, and just a teeny bit of grated lemon rind. About ¼ teaspoon. Add a tablespoon chopped parsley and ½ cup sour cream, but don't boil this or the cream curdles. Line a 1½-quart casserole with a 1-inch layer of potato chips broken up so they're no larger than a quarter in size. Takes about 2 cups. Pour the bean mixture on top of the chips, sprinkle with another layer of chips. Top with anywhere from ¼ to ½ cup grated Cheddar cheese. Bake in a 350-degree oven for 30 minutes. *Makes 4 to 6 servings.*

LETTUCE

Dear Nan: I'd like to make a suggestion about using those outer leaves of lettuce and romaine you might ordinarily throw away. Wash them and store them in a plastic bag in the refrigerator. Then, when cooking cabbage, cauliflower, or brussels sprouts, place said lettuce leaves over and around the strong-smelling vegetables. Believe it or not, that does away with those cooking odors. Other vegetables, like peas and green beans, are delicious cooked under lettuce leaves.

Have the lettuce dripping wet and very little cooking water will be needed. Having cooked for a large family for years, my problem now is cutting down to just the two of us, but I'm learning. —SAN BERNARDINO, CALIFORNIA.

Yes, lettuce does wonders. Cooking raw peas with very little water, generous blobs of butter, and layers of lettuce leaves is a very French touch. You can even do them casseroled in a slow oven that way.

SPINACH

Dear Nan: We have our own garden spinach this year and love it, but no matter how many times I wash it, it is still gritty after it is cooked. —BAKERSFIELD, CALIFORNIA.

Bet I know what you're doing wrong with that washing chore. Probably dunking the spinach in a pan of water, then pouring it off the same way you would drain noodles. That way, you are just pouring the soaked-out sand right back over the leaves. Do this: Lift the spinach from the water and you'll be surprised at how much residue there is left in the bottom of the pan. Do that three times, using plenty of water in the first place. Then you shouldn't have any problem.

Another system is to hold each leaf or segment upside down and let cold tap water pour over it full force. If you have a sink spray for this, it's even better. Even where you do not have sandy soil, hard rains spatter dirt onto the spinach at ground level and that's where it collects.

BROILED TOMATOES

It could be you have never broiled red tomatoes, no matter how many times you've heard about them, and I don't want to be an accomplice in furthering your oversight.

The tomatoes should be firm-ripe. Thoroughly ripe ones,

fine for slicing, are apt to squish to a fare-ye-well with broiling. I have even broiled green tomatoes—not just those special non-acid greens but honest-to-Hannah unripened ones when frost caught me with the vines still loaded. Only I sprinkle greenies like that with a little sugar, too, if they are pretty puckery.

Beautiful Broiled Tomatoes

Cut tomatoes in half and line them up in a shallow pan. Spoon melted butter or margarine over the tops. Sprinkle with salt and pepper. I really like garlic salt or a mixed-seasoning salt for this. Broil the tomatoes until they start to soften and get a little brown. Sprinkle with a decent amount of buttered crumbs, then some grated Parmesan cheese. Or something else you can do in place of the crumbs-cheese stuff: Mix equal parts of dairy-type sour cream and mayonnaise. Broil the rest of the way till the little angels are lightly browned.

You can't use the sour cream by itself because the acid of the tomatoes and the high heat will curdle it.

GREEN PEPPERS

Dear Nan: Is there something you can do with green peppers besides stuff them or use them in soups or stews? Sometimes we get an unusually good pepper crop or I come across a bargain at the store. —ADA, OKLAHOMA.

Here's a side dish I like so well I never fail to check the "distress counter" at produce sections. Sell-'em-quick packs are often still good quality with no real soft spots.

Fried Peppers

Cut the peppers in half, scoop out the seeds and membrane, cover with boiling water, and cook ever so gently for no more than five minutes. You don't want them limp. Take care to drain them well.

Heat about ½ cup of oil in the skillet with maybe 1 clove of garlic, if you like that flavor. Or you can marinate a split garlic clove in the oil for ½ hour before using. Quarter the peppers and cook them in the hot oil just until they begin to brown. Serve them hot with salt and pepper. Fine!

Any time you can pick up sweet red peppers to use with the green, go right ahead. That makes an unusually attractive dish.

COOKED CUCUMBERS

Here is a fine way to cook cucumbers. Cut the cucumber in strips, much as you would for French fries, dip them in very fine bread crumbs or seasoned flour, then in 1 egg diluted with 2 tablespoons of water, then in the crumbs again. Fry in deep hot fat just till the coating turns a deep gold. A good but simple sauce for these is just 3 tablespoons of bottled horseradish blended with ⅓ cup of melted butter or margarine.

10 / Simply super salads

Salads know no seasons, now that fresh and frozen fruits and vegetables are available all year round. I hope you will like this cross section of my favorites.

Here are some tips you may not have thought of.

1. Want really crisp greens? Then park the washed and separated leaves in your freezer unit for 15 minutes before serving. Set a timer so you don't overdo it. These must be served at once, on removal from freezer.

2. If you just can't be that daring, wash the greens the day you intend to use them and place them in a bowl containing ice cubes for half an hour or so. Then fling off as much water as possible, pat dry with paper towels, and store in the crisper bin of your refrigerator.

3. Torn-up greens for a tossed salad won't go limp if you toss them with just a teaspoon or two of salad oil—till they glisten—before adding other vegetables. Helps seal the crispness in and keeps them fresh longer.

4. When using tomatoes for a tossed salad, slice them vertically instead of horizontally. Somehow they retain their juice better and don't "water down" the rest of the salad so quickly. I don't know why it works, but it does.

5. When making gelatin or other salads in molds, you won't have any trouble getting them out intact if you first grease the molds just lightly, with a brushing of salad oil or mayonnaise.

6. If you are counting calories, it pays to use a flavored gelatin low in calories. Costs a bit more but the fruit flavors are so much more true.

7. Do you own a pepper mill? Once you discover what freshly ground black pepper does for even the simplest tossed green salad, you'll never go back to anything else.

8. Try this with a green salad sometime! Add grated raw cauliflower, generous sprinkles of dried Parmesan cheese from the shaker, and freshly ground black pepper to a thinned-down mayonnaise laced with the juice of a garlic bud. Use a press for the garlic. Toss this mixture with the greens. Top with bread crumbs well toasted in butter.

VINEGAR AND OIL DRESSING

Dear Nan: I love vinegar and oil dressing. I would like to know what proportions to use for making it, and also what kind of oil and vinegar. —SCHILLER PARK, ILLINOIS.

The classic "rule" is 1 part vinegar to 3 parts oil—¼ cup vinegar, ¾ cup oil, for example. It may surprise a lot of people but this is a true French dressing, not the red kind we know so well in this country. French green salads use this dressing, one or more types of greens, and nothing more.

Of course, there is no law whatsoever that says you can't change these vinegar-oil proportions to suit your own taste or the salad of the moment. If you like a sharper flavor, try ⅓ cup vinegar to ⅔ cup oil. You can even substitute lemon, grapefruit, or orange juice at times. Same thing with "salt and pepper to taste." Try ½ teaspoon salt and 6 grinds of the pepper mill for a starter.

For superior flavor you just can't beat olive oil, although you may use any vegetable oil you like. There are people who object to olive oil on the grounds that it gets cloudy when refrigerated (as it should be) and rancid if it isn't. Don't worry, it unclouds as soon as it warms up to room temperature. Virgin olive oil is the aristocrat and is known as "first press." Lesser types of olive oil may be used for cooking, with quite passable effect.

A wine vinegar or even an herb vinegar is ideal. Otherwise, use the very best vinegar you can find at the moment. And really, the vinegar and oil mix to best advantage, with small chance of separation, if both ingredients are cold. Shake good and hard in a capped jar till you see just tiny droplets of oil suspended in the vinegar. Or use your blender.

From there on out, you can do all sorts of variations, such as the famous Breslin dressing for which you add 1 tablespoon finely chopped pistachio nuts and ½ tablespoon finely chopped black truffles. Even if you have to substitute chopped black olives for the expensive truffles, you can still smirk, "Oh, just a little something I whipped up on the spur of the moment."

Vinegar

Dear Nan: So many different vinegars on the grocer's shelf! I am quite confused as to which one I should use for vinegar and oil dressings, or for the various other dishes that call for it. —REDDING, CALIFORNIA.

Without getting technical about the whole thing, vinegars fall into three general classifications: cider, distilled white, and wine vinegar. Any one may be used as the base for a whole range of herb-flavored vinegars. Each is suitable for a vinegar and oil dressing, although their personalities are as different as those of all the neighbors on your block. If a recipe does specify a type of vinegar, then use it.

THE COOK'S FAVORITE DRESSINGS

"How do you make really good Roquefort dressing like they serve at our nicest restaurant?" is the question I get over and over again.

Long ago, conferring with top chefs, I learned their personal preference is for just three ingredients, all of top quality: real Roquefort or bleu cheese, thick mayonnaise, plus cream or sour cream to get the consistency you like. There is really no set amount of any of those that will suit every taste. Roquefort has such a distinctive taste, no salt is needed.

Usually, the cheese is softened to room temperature before mashing with a fork. Blend in the mayonnaise and then the cream. A chef friend says, "If you like a bit of color, add a touch of French dressing or paprika. Or flavor with sherry wine." He prefers sour cream to plain cream. Some people like to add a little garlic juice or lemon juice.

If you like dressing very smooth, use your blender or electric mixer. I like to bite into actual chunks of cheese, so I don't do that. My husband, on the other hand, prefers the cheese to be cold when it is grated so it is quite firm, then added to a red French dressing.

A friend of mine uses only buttermilk to blend into the softened cheese, no mayonnaise at all.

Lemon-Honey French Dressing

So nice for just about any fruit salad. If you prefer more honey, don't be bashful.

½ cup lemon juice	1 teaspoon paprika
½ cup salad oil	2 tablespoons honey
½ teaspoon salt	

Combine and shake or blenderize well. *Makes ½ pint.*

Nan's Biltmore French Dressing

Not for weight watchers, but a beautifully deep red, somewhat thick dressing with an unusually good flavor. If I run out of this at our house, I hear about it! Fine for tossed salads, but try it sometime on sliced oranges, sweet onion rings, and green pepper strips on greens.

⅔ cup salad oil	1 teaspoon salt
⅓ cup vinegar	2 teaspoons paprika
2 tablespoons lemon juice	2 tablespoons grated onion
⅓ cup catsup	with juice
⅓ cup brown sugar	1 split garlic clove
⅓ cup white sugar	

Combine in a jar and shake well to dissolve sugar. Let stand 24 hours before using. Then fish out garlic if you like (I just leave mine). Some people add a dash of Worcestershire, others like a teaspoon of celery seed. *Makes about 1 pint.*

HEARTY SALADS

Dear Nan: When I asked a friend of mine for her potato salad recipe because it tasted so much better than mine, she laughed and said it was the same recipe I had given her ten years ago except that she adds celery seeds and a tablespoon of sugar. Celery seeds I can believe, yes, but sugar in potato salad? Do you think she was putting me on?

—CORVALLIS, OREGON.

Not at all. Sugar perks up everything else in the dish and brings out the flavor as much as salt does. For an even better potato salad, blend in 1 tablespoon of white corn syrup. Use this to thin your mayonnaise so the salad won't be soupy. Or, if you use shredded onions, mix those with the sugar and let stand for ½ hour before adding. Or you can mix the chopped onion with the sugar and let it stand until it makes its own syrup. The flavor distributes so well when it is mixed in. (You can use this for macaroni salad, too.) Some cubed canned pineapple will add even more zest to your potato salad.

German Potato Salad

I must have been twelve years old before I knew potato salad was made any other way. I had to go visiting before I tasted the mayonnaise variety. My grandma never measured anything, but this Milwaukee version comes about as close to hers as I can get. Supposed to be served at room temperature, but we used to fight over any refrigerated leftover.

2 pounds cooked red potatoes	1 teaspoon salt
3 slices bacon, diced	⅛ teaspoon pepper (about)
⅓ cup bacon drippings	½ cup cider vinegar
¼ cup sugar	½ cup water
1½ tablespoons flour	2 green onions sliced or 1 small onion diced

Boil potatoes till just tender, not overdone. Cool, peel, and slice thin. You should have about 6 cups or so. Fry diced bacon till medium brown. Remove from drippings. Blend sugar, flour, salt, and pepper. Stir into drippings to make a smooth paste. Blend in vinegar and water. Boil about 2 minutes, stirring constantly. Mix in potatoes and onions right in the skillet. Turn off heat and let stand at room temperature for an hour or so till potatoes absorb all the flavor. You can sprinkle the crisp bacon bits over the top at serving time or mix them right in with the salad. Recipe may be doubled. *Makes 4 to 6 servings.*

Texas Caviar
(Pickled Black-eyed Peas)

You might not call this a salad, but it is served as such, on shredded greens, at a pretty fancy price at some top Texas hotels. You can make it quite inexpensively. Men love it. A make-ahead.

2 cans cooked dried black-eyed peas	1 clove garlic, split
½ cup salad oil (preferably olive)	¼ to ½ cup thinly sliced onion
¼ cup vinegar	½ teaspoon salt
	Freshly ground pepper to taste

Drain peas well. Put in bowl. Add rest of mixture, stir well. Pour into glass jars to refrigerate. At end of first day remove garlic if desired. Or you may mince the garlic fine in the first place and just leave it if you favor the flavor (I do!). Let age another 2 days before using. *Makes 4 to 6 servings.*

Nan's Old-Fashioned Macaroni Salad

Don't let the sugar in this one scare you! It's what perks up the flavor no end. Substitute boiled potatoes for the macaroni, and you have an excellent potato salad.

4 cups cooked elbow or shell macaroni (½ pound uncooked)	1 cup mayonnaise
1½ cups sliced celery	2 teaspoons prepared mustard
½ cup cut-up green onions	1 tablespoon vinegar
¼ cup sliced radishes	1 teaspoon celery seed
2 tablespoons snipped parsley	1½ to 2 teaspoons salt
1 cup slivered American cheese	⅛ teaspoon pepper (or more)
	3 to 4 teaspoons sugar

Combine all ingredients several hours before serving and refrigerate. Heap in a lettuce-lined bowl or platter. Garnish with tomato or hard-cooked egg wedges, sliced olives, grated carrots or pickles. *Makes 4 to 6 servings.*

INDIVIDUAL STYLE: Press into greased custard cups to refrigerate. Using a curved grapefruit knife, unmold each cupful onto a thick tomato slice.

Putsch's Famous Fresh Spinach Salad

A specialty concocted by this outstanding Kansas City, Missouri, restaurant.

½ pound fresh spinach leaves, stems removed	2 chopped hard-cooked eggs
½ cup finely chopped celery	½ teaspoon salt
½ cup chopped onion	½ teaspoon Tabasco
1 cup diced processed Cheddar cheese	1½ teaspoons vinegar
	1½ cups blender mayonnaise

To water-chop spinach (which is the way they do it), place half of spinach loosely in blender jar and cover with water. Turn control to high, then off again very quickly. Takes just a few seconds. You do not want this to be mushy. Repeat with rest of leaves. Drain well in colander or sieve. Add salt, Tabasco, and vinegar to mayonnaise. Combine with rest of ingredients. Serve on lettuce and garnish with some grated egg. Good served with small portions of horseradish on the side. *Makes 4 to 6 servings.*

Blender Mayonnaise

1 egg	1 tablespoon vinegar
¾ teaspoon salt	1 tablespoon lemon juice
½ teaspoon dry mustard	1 cup salad oil
¼ teaspoon paprika	

Put egg and seasonings in container. Blend well at high speed. Add lemon juice. Start at high, removing filler cap if you have that type blender. If not, switch to stop and remove whole cap. Very slowly pour in half of salad oil. Add vinegar, then rest of salad oil very slowly. Work ingredients down well into processing with spatula. Spin on high. *Makes 1½ cups.*

DRESSING VARIATION: 1 cup mayonnaise with 4 tablespoons lemon juice and 2 tablespoons horseradish stirred in. Good with many a salad. Any surplus refrigerates well in a capped jar.

Dutch Slaw

Fastest sweet-sour dressing ever! If you have real cream, lucky you. I usually use unsweetened evaporated milk right from the can.

1 cup cream or evaporated milk	2 to 3 tablespoons cider vinegar
2 to 3 tablespoons sugar	1 teaspoon salt
	Dash of pepper

Place cream in a small bowl. Stir in sugar to dissolve. As you add vinegar, keep beating with a fork. It thickens miraculously. If not, add a little more vinegar. Season.

Pour over shredded cabbage that has been crisped in ice water for an hour, but drain cabbage well. A few chopped chives go right well with this. Dressing is fine on sliced tomatoes, too! *Makes 4 servings.*

"Chilly" Con Carne Salad

Honest-to-goodness chili fans may want more chili powder, but wait to taste after refrigerating. That spice can intensify on standing.

1-pound can kidney beans	2 tablespoons chopped green pepper
1 cup diced celery	
¾ cup coarsely diced lunch meat or ham	¼ teaspoon salt and dash pepper
2 tablespoons chopped pimento	½ teaspoon chili powder
	½ cup chopped sweet pickle
¼ cup mayonnaise	1 small onion, grated

Drain beans thoroughly. Add rest of ingredients with more mayonnaise if necessary. Serve very cold. *Makes 4 servings.*

Green Peas Salad

Tired of trying to get that daily green vegetable on the menu? Zipped up with pickle relish and cheese, here's one answer.

1 can baby peas, drained (No. 2 can)	½ cup diced celery
	3 tablespoons pickle relish
1 tablespoon chopped onion	¼ cup grated yellow cheese
2 hard-cooked eggs, diced	Mayonnaise to moisten and hold

All you do is blend, chill, and serve on greens. *Makes 2 to 4 servings.*

GELATIN SALADS

You don't have to be a pro to accomplish these little master-pieces. They also make spectacular conversation points! After I featured this first recipe in a column some time ago, I saw it entered in a professional chef's competition.

Cheese Frosted Melon Surprise

1 package fruit gelatin (3 ounces)	1 medium cantaloupe or honeydew melon
1 cup boiling water	2 to 3 packages (3-ounce size) cream cheese
1 cup drained fruit cocktail	Milk to soften cheese
¾ cup juice from fruit or cold water	

Use any flavor gelatin you like, but this is prettiest if you contrast with color of the melon. Lime green for the golden tones of cantaloupe, red for a honeydew.

Dissolve gelatin in boiling water. Stir well. Add juice or cold water. Chill till quite thick but not set.

While that is taking place, peel the melon, but leave it whole. Cut a small slice from one end but be sure to keep that slice. Scoop out seeds from melon cavity and turn it upside down to drain completely.

Now place melon right side up in a bowl just large enough to hold it there. Mix the fruit in with the thickened gelatin and spoon it into the melon. (Use excess in other molds.) Fasten the cut slice back on with toothpicks. Wrap in clear plastic wrap to prevent drying out while refrigerating till gelatin is firm.

Just before serving, blend the room-temperature cream cheese with milk to make a smooth fluffy mixture but don't get it too thin. Use 2 to 3 tablespoons milk.

Now cut just a thin slice from one side of the melon (not top or bottom, but the long way) so it will stay steady when placed on plate. Spread the cheese all over the melon. Refrigerate for a few minutes so cheese firms a bit. Then surround melon with greens and bring to the table in all its glory. Slice to serve.

A terrific surprise for those not already in the know. *Makes about 6 servings.*

Easy Molded Main-Dish Salad

I don't know where I got this one but it's been a meal-saver more than once.

1 cup condensed cream of mushroom soup	1 whole canned pimento, diced small
1 tablespoon (1 envelope) unflavored gelatin	½ cup cooked salad dressing (not mayonnaise)
¼ cup water	2 cups diced cooked turkey, chicken, veal, ham, or tuna
1 cup diced celery	

Soak gelatin in water. Add the heated condensed soup. Stir to dissolve. Add rest of ingredients. Refrigerate till firm. If you like, you may freeze this one for future use, but no longer than two weeks, so be sure to date the pan. Thaw overnight in refrigerator. *Makes 4 to 6 servings.*

TOMATO ASPIC

Dear Nan: I would like to know why my tomato salad doesn't jell. I used a recipe calling for shredded cabbage, onion, and green pepper in a lemon gelatin base but using tomato juice instead of the regular amount of water. It was soupy! —FLAGSTAFF, ARIZONA.

Anytime I add various vegetables or fruits to a gelatin salad, I always cut the liquid down by at least ¼ cup, no matter what the recipe says, and especially with tomato aspic. Sometimes, when a salad is pretty thick with vegetables, I may cut ½ cup of the liquid. There is some moisture in all fruits and vegetables —in some more than others—so that alone is bound to turn out a not-so-solid mold. I drain canned fruits very well indeed, using a colander and then pressing down a bit to get rid of excess syrup. I trust you know better than to add fresh pineapple to a gelatin base. It won't jell at all. Use canned pineapple.

ARTICHOKE HEARTS

Dear Nan: Can you tell me something to do with canned artichoke hearts? Someone gave me several cans of the things. I know they are supposed to be a delicacy but they really taste so blah I just haven't learned to appreciate them.
—MONTGOMERY, ALABAMA.

Like avocados, they can be an acquired taste. Once you're hooked on them, you can go broke buying them. Try marinating the hearts in a vinegar and oil dressing with a touch of garlic to it. Give them a couple of hours or even overnight to soak up the flavor. Icy cold, they are wonderful.

Here is a fancier artichoke salad: Marinate the cooked or canned artichoke hearts in a French dressing. Then arrange about 3 of them on shredded lettuce and top each one with a little ball of cream cheese. If you are an anchovy paste addict, mix a little of that into the cream cheese before rolling. Arrange some mandarin orange or grapefruit sections in between the artichoke and pass more of the dressing.

PEPPERS MARINADE

Dear Nan: Out on the West Coast we were served whole green peppers at a picnic. They were cooked and marinated in something and were considered a picnic salad. I would like to know what the marinade might have been composed of.
—GREEN BAY, WISCONSIN.

Here is a recipe for a cooked marinated pepper salad: Choose your favorite red-type French dressing or, better still, a good zesty Italian kind. I would like a marinade on the garlic-y side, so if yours doesn't have that potency, add 1 or 2 cloves of garlic, split. You can use the long green peppers with part of the stem left on, but the deal can work with not-too-large peppers of any shape. The yellow banana peppers would be good, too.

To start, cut gashes in peppers from top to bottom, but not all the way through—just so you can scoop out seeds and membrane from one side. And remember, leave those tops on. Then drop peppers in boiling water and cook until just barely tender! That doesn't take more than 3 to 5 minutes. If you overcook them, they'll fall apart. After these are drained, marinate them overnight, turning them now and then. You may serve the peppers, dressing and all, on crisp greens. Or you can put them in a help-yourself bowl with no greens at all.

There is really only one satisfactory way to eat these peppers: Hold them by the stem and start eating from the bottom. Better supply bibs as they so wisely do in the finest spaghetti restaurants.

LETTUCE LEAVES

Dear Nan: We are always told that the best vitamins are in the outer deep green leaves of head lettuce, but so often those leaves are ragged or just won't crisp enough for a salad, so what do you do with them? —CHARLOTTE, NORTH CAROLINA.

They make excellent wilted lettuce, using the same sweet-sour dressing you would use for the leaf lettuce variety. For that matter, you can do this with the whole head if you shred it thin enough. It's a nice change when leaf lettuce isn't available. I also toss extra lettuce leaves into the soup pot.

Here's a simple little recipe for making the dressing, and it's just about as good as any. Fry 6 bacon slices, drain them on paper toweling, and crumble. Pour off the bacon fat and return just 2 tablespoons of it to the pan. Heat that with ¼ cup vinegar, 1 to 2 teaspoons sugar, salt and pepper to taste. Pour at once over the prepared lettuce and sprinkle the bacon bits on top. Thinly sliced onion or green tops cut up over the lettuce are pretty nice, too. This salad should be served at once.

TOSSED SALAD

Now and then we all get stuck with the problem of trying to toss a large amount of salad when it has suddenly occurred to us the mixing bowl we'd planned on using is busy elsewhere.

A large crystal punch bowl is ideal for those times when you are showing off by tossing the salad right at the table for your guests. Or it looks quite something in one of those outsize brandy snifter affairs, but for that one you had better toss the salad in the kitchen in something else and then transfer. And you will need a good big pair of salad-server tongs to get it from the snifter gracefully.

Otherwise, anything goes—from a giant mixing bowl to a big pottery casserole dish. For barbecue parties I have often used a dishpan or an old enameled roaster, one of those blue and white speckled things. They seem to fit the occasion better than anything more formal.

11 / The staff of life: breads, biscuits, pancakes

Since the day man first learned how to light a fire that would heat a flat rock, there has been bread of some sort. Thin, unleavened breads at first, yes, but still bread.

What else did Marie Antoinette's starving subjects demand except bread? Whatever would our early pioneers and prospectors have done without their sourdough breads?

The bread section in any sizable grocery still takes up major shelf space. Sad to say, nine-tenths of those loaves are a pretty poor excuse for bread as it used to be. Hold a slice of it up to the light and you can read through it. And that, my friends, is why home bread baking is back in fashion. Even some pretty busy people are buying bread recipe books like mad, once again trying their hand at what used to be an everyday art.

Biscuits and pancakes just have to come under the "staff of life" heading. They have never waned in popularity.

HOME-BAKED BREAD

Dear Nan: I finally got up courage enough to try my own hand at bread baking. That first loaf wasn't perfect by any means. It was a little coarse and dry and the center crust was cracked. What did I do wrong? —BANGOR, MAINE.

Probably what you didn't do. There just isn't any one single thing more essential to turning out beautiful bread than that first kneading. Nothing makes up for the lack of it. When I say "knead," I mean you really get in and slug that dough. Little love pats won't do it. Punch it, lift it, turn it till it feels absolutely smooth and satiny. You'll know when you've hit it.

Another thing to watch: not too much flour. That causes coarseness. Spread no more on the breadboard than you absolutely need to keep the dough from sticking during the kneading process. It's even a good idea to save 1 cup of the flour called for in a recipe; use that for the board technique. It gets rolled in and absorbed that way without any surplus that can toughen the crust.

A cracked crust usually means you filled the pans too full. Knowing when the dough has risen enough is something that comes with practice.

There is such a resurgence of interest in bread baking today that it is now a status symbol to produce homemade bread.

How do you get the 80-to-85-degree temperature you are supposed to have for the rising of bread dough? In today's air-conditioned homes, or if your kitchen is as cool as mine in the winter, that's pretty hard to come by. Is there any answer to the problem? —HOLLAND, MICHIGAN.

There are several answers. Ada Lou Roberts, the author of books on bread, told me about a solution from one of her male readers who bakes bread as a hobby. When an electric heating pad had reached the point where it no longer gave maximum performance, he found it just perfect for the dough-rising process. He simply covered the bowl of dough with the heating pad and set it on low heat.

Another suggestion from Mrs. Roberts is to set the dough bowl on a plate over, not in, a pan of warm water. You might have to replenish the water from time to time to keep the temperature constant. She also recommends placing the dough at the back of the gas range, just beyond the pilot light. It would be wise to test the area with a thermometer, so you'll know just what you have. Too hot a spot could be disastrous.

If you have an electric range you can switch your oven to preheat for 1 minute, then switch off entirely before placing the dough inside. Again, I would test with a thermometer. Some people use their electric skillets at the lowest setting.

The bowl of dough set over the pan of warm water, though, is what I would consider safest and easiest to use.

> *I am just learning to bake bread. I think my biggest problem is in knowing when the dough has doubled in bulk like it's supposed to. Isn't there some way to tell beyond guessing?*
> —KNOXVILLE, TENNESSEE.

When you think it has doubled, poke the dough gently with your finger. If a slight indentation remains, that's it. You can also tell when the dough in the pans is ready for the oven. Heft those pans on the palm of your hand. They should feel as light as "cloud nine"—hardly any weight at all.

MOLDING OF HOMEMADE BREAD

> *Dear Nan: Can you tell me how to keep homemade bread from molding? I let it cool thoroughly and then wrap it in waxed paper. I usually make two or three small loaves at a time, but the last one usually gets a little mold on it before we use it.* —PIERRE, SOUTH DAKOTA.

The only sure way to beat that is to store it in refrigerator or freezer. Be proud your bread does mold eventually. It shows it's the real stuff.

BREAD FLOUR

> *Dear Nan: What is bread flour? I have a recipe calling for it, but grocers don't know what I am talking about. They say it is just all-purpose flour.* —INDIANAPOLIS, INDIANA.

Real bread flour has a higher gluten content than all-purpose flour. You don't find it on grocers' shelves very often. Your best bet would be to locate a small neighborhood bakery willing to sell you some. All-purpose flour is a blend of hard and soft wheat flours, and that's what makes it so versatile.

FROZEN BREAD DOUGH

Dear Nan: I would like to try my hand at some of the frozen bread dough you get at groceries, but I have never baked a loaf of any kind of bread and I can't believe these little old things would ever bake up into a good fat loaf.

—LITTLE FALLS, NEW YORK.

That frozen dough doesn't turn out as great a loaf as starting from scratch, but it still beats most of what you pluck off the shelf. It is cheaper in the long run, and, oh, the lovely aroma of baking bread to fill the house!

If you've never baked your own bread, this is a great way to catch on to at least a few of the rudiments. You'll have some idea of what the dough should look like when it is ready for the oven, and how to judge when a loaf is done.

The package I had was pretty sketchy in saying, "Let rise in a warm cozy place"—I knew it should be at 80 to 85 degrees.

You can hasten rising of frozen dough by letting it thaw in the refrigerator overnight, but if you do that grease the inside of the sack, or the dough sticks next morning when you try to get it out.

SCONES

The frying of bread dough is something of a touchy subject with me. I will never forget the to-do I raised when I answered in print this next question. The whole thing came to be known as the Great Scone Caper.

Dear Nan: Can you tell me the do's and don'ts of deep-fried scones? I am using a plain roll dough recipe but the scones turn out tough and heavy. Have tried to find other recipes but no one seems to know what I am talking about.

—BOISE, IDAHO.

I replied that I had never heard of fried scones. True scones are a griddle-baked Scottish favorite. Then I really got my ears rapped. Mail flooded in from all directions.

My mother fried bread dough for scones and the grease had to be hot, hot, hot. Also, don't pinch the dough very much after it has risen high. Just snip off pieces ever so gently, fry in the hot fat till golden brown. Roll in sugar, and yum-yum! Lighter than a raised doughnut.

—LAKEVILLE, MINNESOTA.

I make mine from a regular yeast roll recipe. Sounds like the lady is using too much flour or she isn't having the fat hot enough. Just take pieces of the dough, shape into fairly flat squares with the hands, drop into deep hot fat till golden. Extra good if you sift powdered sugar over them while still warm. —WISCASSET, MAINE.

Toughness and heaviness is usually due to too stiff a dough, cooking too fast. Dough should be soft but not sticky. I use a 325-degree temperature for mine. —PAYSON, UTAH.

I don't have any do's or don'ts, but just don't deep fry! Scones wouldn't be scones if they were fried. They should be baked on a hot griddle (even a large-size skillet is great), but be sure not to grease it. Leave perfectly dry. Use your favorite biscuit recipe. Mine uses buttermilk. Scones should be griddled about 5 minutes, turning only once to brown nicely on both sides. —CAMDEN, MISSOURI.

Yes, the soda-buttermilk mixture and procedure are typically Scottish, but some of my Scottish friends pat their dough into a circle ½ inch thick, then bake in a hot oven for 10 to 15 minutes before cutting into wedges to serve with butter or jam.

GARLIC BREAD

Dear Nan: Back in 1945 my husband ate in a Seattle cafe where he raved about the garlic bread. It was in small individual loaves that, when broken open, filled the air with garlic aroma and were simply delicious. I have tried repeatedly to duplicate this bread, but, when sliced or broken, mine tastes flat. —KANSAS CITY, MISSOURI.

Bet you'll have better luck if you'll use dehydrated garlic chips, grinding them in a mill or mortar for more even distribution in the bread. They aren't all the same, even when they look to be, so get the finest spice line available. For large or small loaves, pat the dough ½ inch thick, brush with melted butter and garlic flavoring, roll up, seal, and let rise.

SEED STICK

Dear Nan: I enjoy baking my own bread but have been unable to discover the secret of making sesame or poppy seeds adhere to the crust. Brushing with beaten egg white, shortening, and milk have all failed me. After baking the bread, the slightest jar causes the majority of the seeds to fall from their perch. What's the answer? —FLINT, MICHIGAN.

When you bake those hard-crusted breads where seeds are used, always start with a pan of boiling water on the floor of the oven. The steam affects the gluten in the bread, literally pastes the seeds to the crust.

Have you tried a cornstarch glaze for this sort of bread? For this one I am indebted to Ada Lou Roberts, oft-quoted bread baking authority. Here's what she does: Make a smooth paste of 1 teaspoon water and 1 teaspoon cornstarch. Slowly add ½ cup boiling water. Cook till clear. Cool before using. Then brush that on the loaves as soon as they are shaped, and again a second time (after rising) just before placing the loaves in the oven. At this point sprinkle them with seeds.

There are two important rules for seed-coated bread: Don't grease the tops of the loaves or breadsticks after shaping, nor the pans used for baking. If you aren't using nonstick pans, sprinkle the pans lightly with cornmeal. Turn the loaves upside down and roll in flour to coat. Turn right side up, ever so gently so as not to dislodge the flour.

MELBA TOAST

Dear Nan: Can melba toast be made at home? Is there a special cutter that slices the bread so thin? If so, where can I buy one? —HOLLAND, MICHIGAN.

Bread and meat slicers for home use can now be bought at most houseware departments of any size or at an electrical appliance center. If you don't want to go to that expense, your best bet would be to buy the bread at a bakery where it is sold in the whole loaf and have it sliced to your instructions on the spot. For melba toast ask that it be sliced "as thin as possible." Day-old bread works best for melba toast. Remove the crusts and spread the slices out in an oven that is barely warm. Let them stay there until crisp and slightly browned.

ENGLISH MUFFINS

English muffins have become tremendously popular. Now that you can find them in just about any grocery store, there is no reason not to indulge yourself now and then. Do you know there are other things you can do with them besides just splitting them apart, buttering, and oven toasting?

A long time ago a nun passed along to me a recipe that really gilds the lily. She calls them Teatime English Muffins. Break muffins apart (with a fork, of course, never a knife), then break each half in two. Drizzle with cream, brush with melted butter, place under the broiler to toast. Top with orange marmalade or preserves, then with whipped cream or well-softened cream cheese. Oh, glug, are those good!

Of course, sprinkling with freshly grated cheese for toasting isn't a bit bad, either. Another suggestion is Eggs Benedict. You use halves of the toasted muffins for each serving, cover with thin slices of ham, then a poached egg topped off with Hollandaise sauce or even a good, buttery cream sauce. You can also sneak a thick slice of broiled tomato between the ham and egg if you like.

SUGGESTIONS FOR BLUE RIBBON BISCUITS

Dear Nan: What's the matter with my biscuits? They turn out tough. No matter what recipe I've used, they are never as high as I would like them to be. —DOVER, NEW JERSEY.

When it comes to biscuits, most of the secret in turning out the float-off-the-plate kind is not so much in any particular recipe, but in the way they are put together. It is always quick mixing, fast stirring together, speedy kneading, if any. The light touch from start to finish.

Maybe your biscuits aren't as tall as you would like them to be because you roll them too hard and too thin. For the puffy kind, the cut-out rounds should be about ½ inch thick. If you like a crisper kind—more crust than usual—roll to ¼ inch thick. Make that 1 inch for shortcakes.

Few people use lard anymore but, as with pie crust, it can do something wonderful. And buttermilk always makes for a light and lovely biscuit, even in the canned types. I like them so much better.

With any biscuit making, here are some tips to keep in mind:

Don't add the liquid all at once. Just about ⅔ of it at first. Flours can differ and don't absorb to the same degree. Too much milk makes a sticky dough, too little makes for stiffness. That's when you get tough, dry biscuits.

The shortening should be cold. If the whole mixture is warm, the fat melts. That alone makes for a less tender result.

Cut down into the flour as lightly as you can, using a scooping motion. Don't mash down!

Avoid too much flour on the board as you would a gossipy neighbor.

Once the dough is clinging together in a light mass, mound it up on the board and give it a little kneading but don't overdo it. Pounding the dough too much develops the gluten in the flour and causes toughness and flatness. About 12 to 15 light, quick punches are enough, even with turning the dough 2 or 3 times in the process.

Patting the dough with floured hands is even better than rolling it. Remember—at least ½ inch thick unless you prefer the thin kind.

Biscuits nestled close together on the baking sheet always seem to rise higher, but don't brown on the sides as they do if placed 1 inch apart.

As mentioned, I favor buttermilk types, so have a go at this recipe.

Old South Buttermilk Biscuits

2 cups sifted all-purpose flour
½ teaspoon salt
2 teaspoons sugar
3 teaspoons double action baking powder
½ teaspoon cream of tartar
½ cup shortening
1 cup buttermilk

Sift dry ingredients. Cut in shortening until like coarse cornmeal. Add milk gradually as you stir dough with a fork.

You may not need that much milk. Roll or pat dough ½ inch thick on a lightly floured board. Bake on an ungreased cookie sheet at 450 degrees for about 15 minutes. Makes about 15 biscuits using a 2-inch cutter. Do not use larger cutter or biscuits may be soggy.

If you like soft tops to your biscuits, brush them with melted butter the second they come out of the oven. Many cooks insist butter makes the ideal biscuit shortening. It does give a flavor and richness all its own. If you are using a biscuit mix and it doesn't make biscuits as rich as you like them, add ¼ cup soft shortening or butter, or 3 tablespoons vegetable oil, to the mixture before you add the milk.

I have a friend whose child is allergic to milk, so she makes her biscuits with water and gets lighter biscuits than ever before.

Here are some ways to vary biscuits; do try them.

Herb Biscuits: Just great for a meat shortcake or chicken pot pie. For these, add ½ teaspoon dried rosemary or mixed herbs (generally sold as *fines herbes*) to the dry ingredients. Brush the tops of the biscuits with a bit of slightly beaten egg white and sprinkle with poppy seeds before baking.

Raisin Biscuits: Add ½ cup chopped seedless raisins to the dry ingredients.

Tomato Biscuits: Nice with salads! Substitute tomato juice for the milk.

Cheese Biscuits: Add ½ cup grated cheese to the flour-and-shortening blend before adding the milk.

Caraway Biscuits: You'll like these with a sauerkraut dish for sure. Spread half the unbaked rounds with softened or whipped butter. Sprinkle lightly with caraway seeds. Top with the rest of the rounds.

Honey Biscuits: Ladies' luncheon special. Split hot biscuits in half. Spread bottom half with honey butter and put back together again. Honey butter is made by beating and blending equal amounts of softened butter and honey.

Shrimp Biscuits: Try these with cocktails! Roll the dough out just ¼ inch thick. Cut out with no more than a half-size cutter. Put 1 small spoon of chopped seasoned shrimp on half the rounds. Cover with the rest. Bake as usual.

SODA CRACKER BISCUITS

Dear Nan: When I was a little girl, I adored my neighbor's older daughter who made "original soda cracker biscuits." All I can remember is that she rolled dough thin, cut it in exact squares, and made tiny holes in those. Then we all waited patiently for them to come out of that huge iron oven. Can you help? —HAWKESBURY, ONTARIO, CANADA.

Neither my editor nor I had much hope of digging up that one, but I tossed it to our readers. To our amazement the mail poured in by the sackful. Almost all the recipes were identical.

With a pastry blender mix together 5 cups of unsifted flour, ½ cup lard, ½ teaspoon soda, and ½ teaspoon salt. Add enough water to knead to a stiff dough but go easy, add that water very gradually. You don't want a sticky mass or the dough won't roll easily. Now—and in the old days this was supposed to be important—beat with a rolling pin for 20 minutes! Roll very thin, cut in squares, prick plentifully with a fork, and bake in a 350-degree oven until barely beige.

I have serious doubts that very many people today are going to stand there whaling away at that dough for the specified 20 minutes. But I know people who just give the dough a thorough kneading and the soda biscuits are fine.

There is another very old version that is more like a butter cracker. That one calls for 6 beaten eggs, 12 tablespoons milk, 6 tablespoons butter, and ½ teaspoon soda mixed with "enough flour to make a stiff dough." Bake as above.

CANNED BISCUITS

Here are some ways to use a can of biscuits.

Miniature Fried Fruit Pies: Tiny versions of those old-time favorites. Dust rolling pin and board with flour very lightly. Just barely. Work with no more than 3 biscuits at a time.

Roll each into very thin oval or circle about ⅛ inch thick. Center with 1 teaspoon thick jam. Peach or apricot is especially good. Moisten biscuit edges with water. Fold over to half-moon shape. Crimp edge with floured fork. Turn over with spatula. Crimp other side.

Fry in deep hot fat at doughnut temperature, about 370 degrees. Turn to brown both sides well. Drain on paper towels. Dust with powdered sugar if desired.

No, these will not be soggy if you roll biscuits thin. Nor will they pop open in frying if you fork-crimp both sides.

Appetizer Fried Pies: Prepare as for Fried Fruit Pies but substitute cheese, ham, or lunch meat cubes or sliced frankfurter rounds. Sprinkle rolled-out biscuits lightly with seasoning salt if desired. Have cheese or meat cubes about ¼ inch thick, ½ to 1 inch wide.

Baked Miniature Fruit Pies: Lifesavers when unexpected company pops in, no dessert planned! Prepare as for Fried Pies but place on cookie sheet, brush tops with melted butter. Bake at 450 degrees till browned, about 10 minutes.

Baked Appetizer Pies: Same procedure as for Baked Miniature Fruit Pies. Your guests will bless you when you serve 'em hot!

Sandwiches for Soups, Salads, Snacks: Bake biscuits and split while hot. Fill with tuna or salmon salad, or with deviled ham spread, or with egg salad topped with tomato slice, or with bacon and tomato. You'll think of lots more!

Hearty Filled Biscuits for a Whole-Meal Lunch: They'll never recognize that leftover ham, roast, or chicken. Grind or shred meat to get at least 1 cup, depending on how many of these you want. You can always piece out with a finely chopped hard-cooked egg, a touch of grated onion, plus drained pickle relish or chopped pickles or olives to suit. Bind mixture with just enough thick gravy or undiluted canned soup (cream of mushroom or celery is good) to hold together.

Roll biscuits fairly thin, a little less than ¼ inch. Place spoonful of filling in center. Moisten biscuit edge, top with another. Crimp together with floured fork. Brush with melted butter. Prick tops with fork. Place on baking sheet.

Bake at 475 degrees till browned. Serve with cheese sauce, canned chicken or beef gravy, or slightly diluted canned golden mushroom soup.

"Little Pillows": Press 2 biscuits together. Roll out very thin. Cut into 1½-inch squares. Don't worry about the scraps. They fry up fine, too! Drop a few pieces at a time into hot fat, 370 to 400 degrees. At first turn over 3 or 4 times, quickly, to make them puff evenly. Should be golden brown.

May be served as a hot bread with soups or salads or dusted with cinnamon sugar as a sweet.

Sunday Breakfast Bowknots: Stretch biscuits gently till about 6 inches long, or easy to tie in bowknots. Or spiral-twist and pinch ends together. Deep fry, serve with maple or berry syrup.

Parmesan Pickups: Terrific with any beverage, so quickly made, such a wonderful aroma! Roll biscuits to 3-inch ovals. Spread with melted butter, finely grated dried Parmesan cheese plus a little garlic or onion salt, a dusting of paprika. Bake at 425 degrees for 12 to 15 minutes. Serve as is or cut in half for big-bite size.

VARIATION: Brush with melted butter, pizza sauce, sprinkle with cheese.

Fast Caramel Coffee Cake: This one calls for 2 cans biscuits but you won't regret it. Start melting about ½ cup butter or margarine. Grease a 9-inch-round cake pan. Sprinkle with 3 level tablespoons sugar. Cover with ½ cup chopped or broken nuts. Pour on ¾ cup commercial caramel sauce.

Dip each biscuit in melted butter or margarine. Arrange 15 in slightly overlapping circles around edge of pan. Use rest for inner circle.

Bake at 425 degrees for 20 minutes. Cover with serving plate, invert to serve. Comes out easy! Let stand a few minutes before serving.

Little Pigs in Blankets: For cocktail set or lollipop set, they're popular all the way. Expensive canned sausages not needed!

Cut regulation frankfurters in half crosswise. Roll canned biscuit just large enough to fit around frank. Place seam side down on baking sheet or shallow pan. Brush with melted butter. Bake at 475 degrees till browned. Serve with catsup, mustard, or favorite relish.

Cheese Cheers: Rough-grate pasteurized processed pimento cheese chunk right from the refrigerator. It's easier. Place biscuits apart on cookie sheet or close together in round pan. Brush with melted butter, sprinkle generously with grated cheese. Or let a 3-ounce package pimento cream cheese soften to room temperature. Add about 1 tablespoon well-drained canned pimento, mashed with a fork and spread on biscuits. Bake at 450 degrees for about 15 minutes.

Barbecue Biscuits: Wonderful with those barbecued ribs! Roll biscuits to ¼ inch thick. Brush with melted butter, sprinkle lightly with hickory smoked salt or powdered poultry seasoning or any mixed-seasoning salt. Bake at 475 degrees. Pass more butter and keep the seasoning shakers handy.

Honey-Raisin-Pecan Upside Downs: Mix ½ cup honey with ½ teaspoon cinnamon. In each of 10 muffin cups place ½ teaspoon melted butter. Sprinkle with broken nutmeats and a few raisins. Divide honey mixture equally into cups. Top with a biscuit.

Bake 15 minutes at 475 degrees. Remove from oven, let stand about 2 minutes to set. Invert pan quickly onto waxed paper. Let stand 5 minutes, lift off pan, serve at once. (Cold ones seldom go begging, though.)

Quick Buttery Onion Rolls: Melt 1 stick butter or margarine (½ cup). Stir in ¼ to ⅓ cup dry onion soup mix. (Larger amount soup mix gives saltier biscuits.) Let stand 5 minutes for butter to somewhat absorb mix.

Spoon half the mixture into an 8-inch ungreased round pan, taking care to spread onion evenly. Arrange 1 can separated biscuits on top. Spoon rest of mixture over all. Bake in 400-degree oven for 12 to 14 minutes or till nicely browned. Serve at once.

Double Delight Figure Eights: Breakfast baiters! Flatten biscuits. Holding in both hands, stretch slightly, twist once to make figure eight. Place on ungreased baking sheet, work deep hollow into each end by pressing dough down with thumb. Fill depressions with contrasting jams—red on one side, golden on the other. Brush with melted butter. Bake in 425-degree oven about 10 minutes.

BROWN-AND-SERVE ROLLS

Dear Nan: Is there some way I could use my present refrigerator roll recipe to make rolls similar to the brown-and-serve kind you buy? I get along fine with my recipe, but would like to make these ahead of time, just to the final baking stage. —DAVIS, CALIFORNIA.

Yes, you can make your own brown-and-serves, but they might not turn out as nicely as your freshly baked ones do at present. They don't seem to taste quite the same, although a lot of people make them and find them nice enough.

You can use either a plain or sweet roll dough. Shape them and put in greased muffin cups. Let rise but not till doubled, just about ¾ of the way. Bake in a 300-degree oven about 40 minutes. You may have to do a little experimenting with this. They should be done in the center but not brown on top yet. Take them from the oven and let stand right in the pans for 20 minutes. Then remove, cool the rest of the way, wrap, and pack for freezing. They store pretty well for about

2 months. To use, thaw at room temperature. Brown in a 400-degree oven for 5 to 7 minutes.

PARKER HOUSE ROLLS

Dear Nan: When I make Parker House rolls some of them pop open way big. If I pinch them shut again they look like a funny bun. —MILBANK, SOUTH DAKOTA.

Perhaps you are not rolling the dough thin enough for your rolls, but more likely your problem is in the fold-over technique. Roll the readied dough just about ¼ inch thick and use a floured biscuit cutter that is large enough—about 3 inches. Many recipes will tell you to use a floured knife handle to make a deep crease right across the center, then fold and pinch. The knife handle is okay as far as it goes (I sometimes like the handle of a wooden spoon better), but make the crease to one side of center. Then roll the knife or spoon handle toward the edge, slightly flattening just half the roll. Brush with melted butter as usual, but then fold the thicker half over the thinner one to pinch closed. So many cooks do just the opposite, and that's usually when the roll pops open. Bake the rolls 1 inch apart on a greased cookie sheet.

PANCAKES

Dear Nan: How can I get my pancakes to look like the ones they do at restaurants? Those are always so evenly brown and smooth. Mine always turn out with sort of crusty, humpy edges no one in the family likes. —LINCOLN, NEBRASKA.

You are undoubtedly using too much fat on the griddle or in the pan. It takes just a soupçon of that greasing, if any. And what is a soupçon? Somewhere between a smidgen and not one darned bit!

Have you ever sat at a drugstore counter and watched

the flapjack artist at work? Take a good look at that griddle. Most likely no grease on it. A good heavy griddle seldom needs greasing. Or perhaps just barely. The cook may give a swipe with a pastry brush now and then, but not often. Pancakes are meant to be baked, not fried. Once you grease a griddle you are probably going to have to do that forever after, unless you have one with a nonstick finish.

A simple way to grease the griddle or pan, when needed, is with a folded piece of raw bacon so you get the merest film. Or you can wipe it with a cloth dipped lightly in oil or melted shortening, but don't have it dripping. I have heard of using a cut piece of raw turnip, too, but who has turnips handy all the time? Then there is the old salt-bag trick if you want to go to the trouble of hunting up some cheesecloth. Just put 2 table-spoons of salt in 1 square of cheesecloth and rub it briskly over the griddle. That's a good way to clean up the thing between fryings, too.

Few people are going to tell you exactly how hot your griddle should be for pancakes. Even thermostatically con-trolled grills don't always act the same with every kind of bat-ter. Best way is to have it medium to fairly hot, but not geared way up. You'll know when it's right, if you'll do what old-timers always did. Flip a few drops of water on the griddle. When they bounce around like somebody with a hotfoot, that's it.

When bubbles appear on the pancake's surface and the edges look dry—and with the right heat that shouldn't take more than 1 minute or so—it's time to flip the cake. Just once. If you go flipping it over and over, you'll have a great substitute for an innersole.

Pouring the batter from a small pitcher or a spouted measuring cup can turn out rounder, more uniform cakes than using a spoon. You just have to learn to "say when" on the amount. That comes with a couple of practice tries.

It's a good idea to do a test cake first. Only you know whether you like them thick or thin. Too thick a batter? Add a little milk. Too thin? Add a little flour.

Have you ever heard of oven pancakes? I would surely like to know how to do them because I hate standing at the range doing skillet after skillet till my family gets filled up. By that time I don't care if I never see another hot cake, and what's more I don't like to eat alone, staring at a mess of syrupy plates. —MENTOR, OHIO.

A blind lady told me about these years ago. Aided by her compensating sense of smell and touch, she could make pancakes safely this way and no other.

You stir up a batter using 2 cups of a mix, the way it tells you on the package, or an equal amount of your own recipe. Oil a 15-by-10 jelly roll pan good and proper. Pour in all the batter at once so it is even and slide it into a preheated 425-degree oven. When the all-in-one oblong is lightly browned it is done. Takes about 15 to 20 minutes. For a smaller recipe use just a cup of the mix and pour into a greased square cake pan.

Just to make sure about doneness you might give it the center test. Cut into squares to serve. I can't say these are exactly like regular hot cakes you would fry, but they are very light, more cakelike, not a bit greasy. It is an easy way to have a whole lot of piping hot cakes all at once. *Makes 6 servings.*

Any time you have a mob-scene breakfast, you can do more than one pan at a time. The one on the lower rack will brown faster—at least mine will. You can keep extra cakes warm by turning off the oven and leaving the door ajar for 1 or 2 minutes.

Teen-agers can have a ball making these oven deals for after-the-game fill-ups and there won't be nearly as much kitchen mess. Just for a change you might like to add a few thin raw apple slices. Not too many or the pan won't hold the amount. Don't chop the fruit or it might make for soggy cakes. A little canned whole-grain corn does fine, too, but it must be very well drained.

One of those large electric griddles you can plug in right at the table would be another solution for you. That way you can cook, eat, be sociable with the family all at once.

FRENCH TOAST

Dear Nan: When I was a boy one of the thrills of my life was to ride a Pullman train and eat in the diner. The French toast they served was out of this world, and I remember it being very fluffy with a real vanilla flavor. My French toast turns out flat. No matter how much vanilla I use, it isn't the same. —FOREST PARK, ILLINOIS.

No, it's not all nostalgia. You get fluffy French toast by beating the egg yolks and whites separately and dipping the bread quickly, so it doesn't have a chance to get soggy. They never used thin-sliced sandwich bread for that toast; the bread was better textured. It was fried in real butter.

I can't say for sure, but vanilla sugar might have produced the special vanilla flavor. That is made by mashing about a 1-inch piece of vanilla bean, split and pounded up with an equal amount of sugar. Then stir that into 2 cups of sugar and store in an airtight can. In whatever dessert or dish sugar is called for, use this and omit the vanilla extract. The flavor will be far superior.

Meanwhile, back at the French toast. Whether you use vanilla bean or extract, do this: Add 1 tablespoon sugar, ¼ cup milk, and a dash of salt for every 2 eggs used. But, whatever else, beat those yolks and whites separately. Fold the whipped whites in at the very last, dip the bread at once. That's the secret.

DOUGHNUTS

Dear Nan: I like to make fried doughnuts but they always crack before they brown completely, and then they are greasy inside. —OLEAN, NEW YORK.

The temperature of your frying fat is probably too hot. Try it at around 370 degrees. This is pretty hard to guess at, so unless your fryer has a thermostatic control, you would be smart to invest in a cooking thermometer.

Do you know that if you let your cut-out doughnuts rest for at least 20 minutes before frying they will almost always be much better? They won't absorb nearly so much fat. I hope you are not using an ordinary fork for turning them in the fat. It is so easy to prick them accidentally and that is one way of getting those annoying cracks. Use a two-tined fork placed through the doughnut hole. A pancake turner will do the trick, too.

It has long been an axiom that you turn doughnuts just once in the frying. I have found, though, that if I brown just lightly on one side, the same thing for the other side, and then one more turning, I have better luck. Then drain them on plenty of paper toweling.

Sometimes when I am in a flying hurry or just too lazy to dig out the doughnut cutter, I cut the dough in strips with a floured knife, pinch the ends together, and let 'er rip. They may not be as even, but they taste just as good.

Anytime you have stale doughnuts hanging around the house try splitting them, toasting, putting back together sandwich-style with honey or jam. A bit messy but good!

My family simply loves glazed raised doughnuts and I make them often, but the glaze is always sticky. Would you please give me correct proportions and dipping procedure so it won't be? —EDMONTON, ALBERTA, CANADA.

Sometimes, when the weather is humid or there is a lot of moisture in the house, any glaze will stay sticky. Do you dip the doughnuts while they are still warm? You should.

Here is a very simple glaze. Gradually add about ⅓ cup boiling water to 1 cup sifted confectioners' sugar. Stir well, then dip. Or boil 1 cup of water and 2 cups of granulated sugar together for about 5 minutes. If you will cover the pan for the first 2 minutes, you'll get away from crystals forming around the sides of it. Those crystals can ruin any glaze. Dip the warm doughnuts quickly. Setting the glaze mixture in a pan of very hot water helps keep it the right consistency until the job is finished. In either case, drain the coated doughnuts on racks to dry thoroughly.

CORNMEAL DUMPLINGS

Dear Nan: My husband remembers, as a child, his mother making cornmeal dumplings. Do you have a recipe for them? And what should they be served with? —SMYRNA, TENNESSEE.

There are about as many ways of making cornmeal dumplings as there are religious sects, but those made with cornmeal all the way tend to be heavy. They come out lighter if you use part flour, part meal. And you can use buttermilk in place of sweet milk if you're of a mind to. Just so you get a rather soft dough that slides off the spoon and into the simmering liquid easily. When you get to that point, keep 1 cup of water handy so you can dip the spoon into it before each spooning up of more dumpling liquid. Then they really slip off fine; you don't have to push or poke them with your finger. That sometimes ruins dumplings. I like yellow cornmeal because it looks richer, but it really makes no great difference. Here's the recipe.

Cornmeal Dumplings

Beat ¾ cup milk and 1 egg together in a fairly large mixing bowl. Mix in 2 teaspoons finely grated onion. Stir 1 cup sifted flour and 1 cup cornmeal together. Add 3 teaspoons baking powder and ½ teaspoon salt. Stir in the milk-egg mixture. Last of all stir in 1 tablespoon melted bacon drippings or butter. The bacon does give an awfully nice flavor without being overpowering.

Drop large spoonfuls into whatever simmering liquid you are using. It's best to have at least 5 cups broth so the dumplings can sort of float. Don't crowd them. Cover the pan tightly for about 10 minutes. Don't peek! A heatproof glass pie plate makes a good cover because you can watch the dumplings' progress without the lifting that is so fatal to lighthearted dumplings. Sometimes, though, that glass plate isn't large enough to cover the size of pan you need to use. It is more important to watch that bit about not crowding the tender things. If your liquid is deep enough, just simmering, they'll turn out fine on the timing given. What makes dumplings soggy is lifting them out too soon.

These cornmeal dumplings are good when dropped into pot liquor in which ham hock, corned beef, chicken, or turnip greens have been cooked. They do well in some soups and stews, if there aren't too many vegetables to crowd them. *Makes 4 servings.*

POPOVERS

Dear Nan: Please discuss a workable recipe and method for turning out beautiful high popovers that do not get too brown before the end of baking time but will still slip out of the pan without sticking. I have tried everything with poor results. —MINNEAPOLIS, MINNESOTA.

Do you happen to be using one of those fine old cast-iron pans? They can do a terrific job, but after just so long they can need reseasoning to prevent sticking. Do that by greasing with unsalted shortening and placing in a 200-degree oven for a couple of hours. Then wipe out, don't scour. Same goes for iron skillets. Otherwise, popovers slip out of anything "just like that." They really are supposed to be a rather rich, crusty brown, glossy on the bottom, hollow inside.

The commonest cause of failure is too much flour. Whatever kind, sift twice to measure and spoon very gently into the measuring cup. Use a knife to level off. Even so, with eggs being different sizes, you may need a bit more milk. Batter should be just heavy-cream consistency. Pans need to be at least 1½ inches deep. Fill about ½ full for glassware, close to ⅔ for anything else. I have fine luck with thick glass custard cups; a measuring cup showed my cups held 6 ounces, so now I make sure I fill with 3 ounces of batter.

The battle still rages on old and new techniques. You just have to find the one that works best for you. What works fine in one part of the country won't do at all in another. Nature, in the form of humidity, prevailing winds, altitude, still holds the whip hand.

The time-honored method is to preheat the pans before greasing and filling, then to bake at a high temperature, lowering it halfway through. Newer ways insist that cold pans or cups do just as well, with the same temperature all the way. I still get a better "pop" if I preheat the pans. I do find a consistent 425-degree oven for 40 minutes does well for me, if cups are set on a cookie sheet. If that one temperature doesn't dry out the popover interiors as much as it should, I prick each one with a toothpick several times, about 5 minutes before baking time is up. One authority calls for doing popovers at 500 degrees for 15 minutes, then swinging to 250 degrees for another 15 minutes, but my popovers scorch every time that way. Others recommend 450 degrees for 30 minutes, 350 degrees for the rest of the usual 40 to 45 minutes. Tin or very thin aluminum pans do not do anywhere near as well as heavier types, whether they be glass, iron, cast aluminum or a nonstick coating over aluminum.

12 / Pickling, preserving, freezing, and such

Few kitchen jobs are more rewarding than doing up your own pickles, preserves, and relishes! It's such fun to stand back and admire those well-filled shelves, knowing you did that yourself. Make up a few extras. They're perfect for later-on gifting when nothing else seems quite right.

Do your canning and preserving in small lots. It's easier; you won't get so hot and tired as from an all-day job.

Be sure you have everything needed before you start. Buy a fresh supply of spices. Last year's leftovers may have lost their true strength.

Use fresh paraffin, not some you've saved from last year's jars. It may not make a perfect seal. Always melt paraffin over hot water. Over direct heat it can catch fire. It is easy to get a perfect seal if you transfer the melted liquid to an old coffee pot or some such for pouring. Keep the utensil for just that purpose.

Don't paraffin too thick. It can press down, cause seepage. About ⅛ inch is usually enough.

Try a fragrant geranium leaf in the bottom of jelly glasses, especially for apple jell. Tantalizing flavor.

Always use a rack in pan bottom when canning by the boiling water bath or you may have jar breakage. Place finished jars upright on folded towels or a rack till cool, again to avoid breakage from contact with cool surfaces.

When using pressure canners, don't fail to hunt up manufacturer's directions. Don't trust to memory! Pressure gauges should be checked at least once a year. County demonstration agents or utilities companies can tell you where.

"Adjust lids" means according to type you are using. They are not all the same. Follow manufacturer's directions.

In many instances it is next to impossible to estimate how many jars will be needed for any one canning or preserving recipe. Size and condition of fruit or vegetables, as well as water content, vary widely. Some will cook down much more than others. For example, size of cucumbers used for pickles would determine how many to the jar. Too, standard weight of bushel, lug, or box is not the same in all areas, and not the same for all fruits and vegetables.

The number of jars needed for the Brandied Peaches would depend very much on size of fruit, as would the tiny ears of pickled corn. The *Ball Blue Book of Canning* never gives "how many jars of what size" for anything. It simply uses an overall "approximate" chart at the back of the book—how many pounds of what might make a quart—but few women have a kitchen scale. It would be impractical to provide such a chart for this chapter.

CORNCOB JELLY

Dear Nan: Several years ago you gave directions for making jelly and table syrup from dried corncobs and I thought it was just about the craziest thing I ever heard of, but recently a friend gave me a small jar of it and it's delicious! I'll eat crow if you'll just find it in your heart to let us doubters have that one again. —TULSA, OKLAHOMA.

Never mind the crow, just eat the jelly and enjoy it. You are really supposed to have red cobs for this, but you can add a few drops of food coloring if you use the white ones. Otherwise it looks like a big bunch of nothing but it tastes fine.

Assemble 12 dried corncobs (red, if possible), 3 pints of water, 1 package powdered pectin, 3 cups sugar, and 1 tablespoon lemon juice. That last is optional but it does something nice.

What you need is dried corn on the cob, such as many farmers store in cribs, then shell and use just the cobs. Rinse the cobs well to get rid of any chaff. Break them in half. Boil them rather gently for about 30 minutes (they fit best in my big old roaster) and then strain the juice through a wet cloth. A dry one absorbs too much valuable sap. Measure to get 3 cups. If you must, add water to get that amount. These dry cobs do soak up liquid.

Now add the powdered pectin and bring to a full rolling boil. Add the sugar and heat to dissolve. Bring to a boil again, boil for about 1 full minute, or until the mixture starts to jell when you lift some on the spoon. Might take another minute or so. Skim, pour into sterile glasses, and seal. *Makes approximately ten 4-ounce jars.*

I would like to try that corncob jelly but what does it taste like? —HANOVER, CONNECTICUT.

Like an unusually good apple jelly, with maybe a hint of peach. Completely delicious and perfectly beautiful. Even the smallest jar of this jell makes a novel gift, especially for city slickers. The cobs may give off an odd aroma while cooking but don't let that bother you. It doesn't show up in the flavor.

PICKLED CORN

Dear Nan: While in West Palm Beach, Florida, last winter we ate at a buffet supper where there was a dish of tiny, pickled corn ears. They were just about two inches overall. They were delicious! Could you tell me where to get midget ears like that and how to pickle them? If not, where can they be purchased? —MARENGO, ILLINOIS.

The first time I saw those itty-bitty ears some years ago I thought, "Good heavens! Who would want to work to get that little bit of corn off a cob?" until I found that you ate cob and all.

Pickled Corn Ears

You need immature popcorn ears for these, not more than 2 or 3 inches long. You'll either have to grow your own or wangle some from an obliging farmer well before harvest-time to get the ears small enough. I wouldn't try to work with too many ears at a time. Drop them into boiling salted water. Add 1 tablespoon salt to each quart of water. Drop the corn in, let stand for 3 minutes. Drain and pack tightly in small sterile jars to stand upright.

Make a hot syrup of 1 quart vinegar, 1 tablespoon sugar, 2 tablespoons mixed pickling spices tied in a cloth sack. Pour that over the hot packed corn. Then add ¼ pod of hot dried red pepper to each jar and seal. They'll be ready in about two weeks. I know that sounds like a lot of vinegar, but it is necessary to pickle the corn, and by the time you pack the ears in the jar there really isn't much space for the solution. After you try your first batch, you might want to add more sugar next time.

GOMA'S OWN CHILI SAUCE

If I didn't can anything else, I would still make chili sauce. I have yet to see store-bought that tastes like homemade. The hot chili peppers make this a little on the zippy side. Sissies may omit them, torrid tongues may add more. Use fully ripe tomatoes for any chili sauce.

3 quarts peeled ripe tomatoes, cut up	2½ tablespoons salt
⅔ cup chopped green pepper (about)	2 hot chili peppers (maybe 3)
2 onions, chopped fine	2 teaspoons allspice
4½ cups vinegar	2 teaspoons cinnamon
½ cup sugar	2½ teaspoons cloves

Combine all. Gradually heat to boiling point. Simmer for at least 1 hour, more if you like it thicker. Depends on natural moisture in tomatoes. Pour into hot sterilized jars. Seal at once. *Makes about 3 pints.*

AUNT EMMA'S CUCUMBER PICKLES

So easy! We've been making these at our house for years. They were my daughter's very first canning effort; she did just fine. These pickles have fine keeping qualities.

4 quarts medium cucumber slices, ⅛ inch thick	1 tablespoon celery seed
7 tablespoons salt	2 tablespoons mustard seed
1½ quarts vinegar	4 cups sugar

Sprinkle unpeeled cucumber slices with salt. Cover with cold water. (I use my large enameled roaster for this.) Let stand overnight. Then drain off brine, wash slices in several waters. Bring vinegar and rest of ingredients to a boil. Add cucumbers. Heat 4 minutes, stirring constantly but gently. Do not let the mixture come to a boil. Pour at once into hot sterilized jars. Seal immediately as manufacturer directs for your jars and caps. *Makes about 5 pints.*

BEET RELISH

Anytime you have a surplus of cooked beets, from wine making or anything else, it's a snap to make an easy relish you keep in the refrigerator till serving time. All you need is 2½ cups finely chopped cooked beets (even canned ones will do), 5 tablespoons horseradish, 5 teaspoons vinegar, and 5 teaspoons sugar.

Combine all that and season to taste with salt and pepper, plus a dash of cayenne pepper if the notion strikes you. If that turns out a little too zingy to suit you, just add another ½ cup of chopped beets. We like this especially well with ham or pork roast. *Makes 2½ cups.*

CUCUMBER-CARROT RELISH

Dear Nan: I make a cucumber-carrot relish I thought you might like to pass along. My family loves it on hot dogs or just to eat with any meal. It's so easy to make.

Put 4 to 6 cucumbers through the food chopper on coarse grind. Enough to make 3½ cups. Do the same thing with 6 medium carrots, enough to make 1½ cups, and enough onions to make 1 cup. Combine the vegetables and stir in 2 tablespoons salt. Let stand 3 hours, then drain. Now combine 2½ cups sugar, 1½ cups vinegar, 1½ teaspoons celery seed, and 1½ teaspoons mustard seed. Bring to a boil, add the vegetables, simmer uncovered for 20 minutes. Seal at once in hot sterilized jars. This makes 2½ pints. I always chill it before serving. —PARADISE, PENNSYLVANIA.

Pennsylvanians surely do know good eating when they find it! While this little gem can be made any time of year, it is best when you find cucumbers at a moderate price.

TOMATO BUTTER

Dear Nan: I don't know if you hear from a lot of men or not, but as cooking is a great hobby of mine I read every one of your columns and have saved quite a few. What I want to know is, do you have a recipe for good old-fashioned tomato butter? —MONTCLAIR, CALIFORNIA.

I hear from lots of men! It would take an awfully hard heart to resist a plea like yours. How does this recipe strike you?

You'll have to get together 12 cups raw tomato pulp, 7

cups sugar, about ⅓ cup lemon juice, ½ teaspoon ginger, 1 teaspoon cinnamon, and ¼ teaspoon powdered cloves. You might just want to increase those spices a bit, but better wait till you've cooked the stuff for a while, then taste and use your own judgment. You could substitute 1 cup chopped onion or 2 cups chopped apple for part of the tomato. I don't know how many tomatoes you'll need to get the pulp—depends on variety —but they should be firm-ripe.

Cook them till they're soft, then press through a food mill or sieve. Drain off all the juice (I would save that for soup, stew, or vegetable flavoring). Mix the pulp with the other items and boil till thick. Make sure it's good and hot when you pour into jars. Process in a boiling water bath for 10 minutes to be totally on the safe side.

CHUTNEY

Dear Nan: I would dearly love to know how to make a good homemade chutney! We like it so much but it gets rather expensive if you buy a lot of it. —LITTLE FALLS, NEW YORK.

This is one of the best I ever tasted, homemade or otherwise. We call it Olga's Chutney for the dear friend who gave it to me.

Olga's Homemade Chutney

1 lemon, seeded and chopped	3 ounces (¾ cup) crystallized ginger, chopped
1 clove garlic, chopped	
5 cups peeled chopped apples	1½ teaspoons salt
1 pound brown sugar	¼ teaspoon cayenne
1 pound seeded raisins	2 cups red wine vinegar

Combine all ingredients and cook till fruit is tender. You may substitute pears and mangoes for part of the apple, but take care that the fruit is firm and slightly underripe. *Makes approximately 3 quarts.*

ADELAIDE'S BRANDIED PEACHES

It's nice to have southern friends! They'll sometimes part with treasured old family recipes. You should have no trouble in figuring the liquid for this one. When in doubt add more spirits!

8 pounds peaches, not too large
5 pounds sugar
1 pint water

1 quart pure grain alcohol (obtainable at liquor stores) or 1 quart good brandy

You can peel the fruit outright, but the easiest way is to plunge the peaches into boiling water 2 or 3 at a time, rather quickly in and out so they don't mush. Skin as you go, popping each into a pan of cold water at once so they don't discolor.

In the meantime, combine sugar and water over low heat, stirring to dissolve. When that makes a fairly thick syrup, put peaches to float in whatever pan will hold them without crowding. (If syrup gets too thick toward last add a little more water.) Cook gently till tender enough to be pierced with a straw. Lift out with slotted spoon, place in colander over a bowl to drain further. Keep doing this till all the peaches are cooked. Pour the syrup that was drained from fruit back in with the sugar syrup.

Pack peaches in sterilized jars. Using 1 measure of syrup to ½ measure of alcohol or brandy, fill the jars and seal. Each day, for three days, shake each jar. After that they will keep indefinitely—if you hide them.

FROZEN PEACHES

Dear Nan: I just can't let another fresh peach season pass into history without letting you know about the keenest way yet to freeze peaches!

Take a peach—1, ½ dozen, or a bushel. Wash, dry, place in a plastic bag. Suck out the air with a straw. Secure

with a rubber band and place in the freezer. To use, drop the peach into a bowl of water. In a few minutes the skin will slip off easily just as though it had been scalded. Cut up while only partially thawed. Peaches like that add a lot to a fruit salad.

Anytime I come across an especially nice peach it is likely to wind up in the freezer this way for later use. I put two or three in one bag, or sometimes just one if the peach is large. A larger quantity could be flash-frozen. That is, freeze them on a tray until they are solid, then put into the sacks.

When I first heard of this some years ago I thought a step must have been omitted. I phoned the local extension office and was assured that no blanching or any other preparation was necessary. Of course these peaches may be used in any way that calls for fresh peaches. Pies, cobblers, or whatever. —HUTCHINSON, KANSAS.

FROZEN POTATO CHIPS

Dear Nan: Here is my "saver" hint. You save money when you buy the large sacks of potato chips, but our family doesn't always use them up quickly. They go stale, so I tried freezing them. You can't put them in sacks, of course, because they would crush easily if anything happened to get piled on top of them. They do fine, though, in tightly covered plastic containers. —WAUKEGAN, ILLINOIS.

FROZEN VEGETABLE SHORTENING

Dear Nan: Is it all right to freeze vegetable shortenings? Since my family has dwindled I don't bake a lot. I find my large can of shortening has a strong odor when I get to the last of it. Would it be okay to put part of it in plastic bags for freezing? —PAWHUSKA, OKLAHOMA.

General consensus of expert opinion is that freezing is perfectly permissible.

FREEZER GREEN BEANS

Dear Nan: I grew Kentucky Wonder beans last year, put them in the freezer the same day I picked them. I was in a hurry so I didn't blanch them the way I always have before. As we used them through the winter we decided they tasted ever so much better than with blanching. So I did the same thing with the same kind of beans this year. I have just used the first pack and they taste terrible! I just hate to throw them away. Is there any way I can take care of this problem for the rest of them? —LITTLE ROCK, ARKANSAS.

Oh, dear, this happens all the time when people take the kind of shortcut you did. Your trouble stems from—you guessed it—skipping that brief blanching. Those beans have what is often termed "straw flavor." There isn't one thing I can tell you to do with those beans, and I'm not going to rub it in because I think you have learned your lesson. Here you spent seeds, time, labor, freezing preparation (all except that one bit), and took up freezer space all this time, only to have it all go for nothing.

You were right to rush your beans to freezing as soon as they were picked. The sooner the better. But just 3½ minutes of blanching, plus the follow-up chilling, would have prevented that dreadful off-flavor. Not only that, but blanching guards against any toughening, helps keep the garden flavor, and increases storage time.

13 / Cakes, cookies, and candy capers

With such a wide variety of mixes on the market, most of them not at all bad, I am pleasantly amazed at the number of women who still prefer to concoct their own cake and cookies. My cake file of recipes-questions-answers is just about the fattest one in the lot and it grows daily, even with the fast-paced-save-time life most of us lead these days.

There just doesn't seem to be any form of cookery that is more soul satisfying to a home cook than turning out a cake that is totally her creation. But, mixes or from scratch, problems do arise.

OLD RECIPES

Dear Nan: Some time ago I came across eleven recipes in my great grandmother's handwriting scribbled on the back of a letter dated 1848. I would very much like to try some of these, but there is one drawback. For heaven's sake, what is saleratus? It seems to be a leavening agent, but do you know if I could substitute soda, baking powder, or what?
—KANSAS CITY, MISSOURI.

The saleratus referred to in old cookbooks is what we call baking soda. Substituting the soda in those recipes would probably work out just fine. Remember, some old recipes may not turn out so well today because there is such a difference in shortenings, flours, and even eggs. However, I would surely give your heirloom recipes a whirl, even though instructions are probably pretty sketchy, such as "butter the size of a walnut" or "a teacupful of flour." Some of us have figured out the teacup measure at about 6 ounces.

CAKE FLOUR

Dear Nan: When I have a recipe that calls for cake flour, can regular flour be substituted with success? And can cake flour be used when regular flour is called for? I use cake flour so seldom the box is apt to spoil before I get around to the rest of it. —LA VERNE, CALIFORNIA.

One cup of sifted all-purpose flour equals 1 cup plus 2 tablespoons of sifted cake flour. Or, where 1 cup of cake flour is called for, use ⅞ cup of sifted all-purpose. That is, 1 cup minus 2 level tablespoonfuls. You might lose a little in the translation with some things, but it works passably well. I don't think, though, I would care to try all-purpose flour for an angel or sponge cake.

I wonder if you could tell me how to use self-rising flour. —POMONA, CALIFORNIA.

Self-rising is an all-purpose flour with salt and baking powder added. In recipes not calling for this flour, just omit the salt and the leavening. It will work out all right in most cases.

BAKING POWDER

Dear Nan: Will you please print the proper time to add baking powder to a recipe? —FORT SCOTT, KANSAS.

General procedure is to sift the baking powder with the other dry ingredients before adding to the rest. It is about the only way you can make sure of equal distribution.

BAKING SODA

Dear Nan: There are a few cooking items I have always wondered about. What is the difference between baking soda and cream of tartar? —POUCH COVE, NEWFOUNDLAND.

Baking soda is a by-product of common washing or sal soda, also known as bicarbonate of soda. Cream of tartar is made from the argol deposit of grape juice after it has fermented. For generations it has been a part of some baking powders. All clear?

CREAMING THE SHORTENING

Dear Nan: When a recipe says to cream butter or margarine, wouldn't it be all right just to melt it? Sometimes it is so hard as it comes from the refrigerator. —ROME, NEW YORK.

Melting the shortening wouldn't be the same thing as creaming at all. Here and there it might work, but in most baked items it could make a whale of a lot of difference in texture and overall results. Write yourself a note and tape it to your refrigerator door as a reminder to remove the shortening in time.

Who of us hasn't forgotten to take butter or margarine out of the refrigerator early enough to cream it easily? I find if I grate the hard cube of butter I can use it immediately or, better still, in 20 minutes or so. Either way, it gets the cook out of hot water. —OGDEN, UTAH.

Right you are.

FOLD-IN PROBLEM

Dear Nan: Recipes say to fold in beaten egg whites. When all the ingredients have been mixed with an electric mixer anyway, why can't the beaten egg whites be added in the same fashion? It seems to me I knock more air out of them with my inept folding-in than I would by using my mixer at low speed. —PRAIRIE VILLAGE, KANSAS.

I am afraid using an electric mixer for blending in your whipped egg whites, even at low speed, would knock even more air out of them than your "inept" hand. You can't be that much of a powerful Katrinka. Just use a gentle folding motion (a wooden spoon helps) and take your time.

ROUNDED LAYERS

Dear Nan: I have tried every suggestion I can get and still my cakes rise higher in the middle than on the sides. Round, square, or loaf pan, it is all the same. I want to decorate cakes but can't if I keep getting those "towers."
—BOULDER, COLORADO.

Mostly it is normal for butter cakes to have some slight rounding, and I can't say that displeases me. If cakes actually hump on top, the trouble just almost has to be one of four things:

1. Too hot an oven at the start of baking.
2. Wrong size pan.
3. Too much flour or not the kind called for.
4. Not enough liquid in a butter cake.

There are other things to watch for with any kind of cake baking. Some glass measuring cups aren't accurate. For dry ingredients, I like my nested metal cups, four to the set. You can fill those to the brim, then level off with a spatula.

It is okay to use both baking racks at once, but place

the pans diagonally, like playing tic-tac-toe. Don't have the pans touching. Allow enough circulation around each one.

Maybe the lady hasn't tried this little trick I learned in cake-decorating class. Cut strips of turkish toweling the width of the cake pan edge. Dampen the strips so they aren't dripping and secure a double layer of that toweling around the cake pan edge with string, clips, or pins. Fill the pans and bake as usual. Baking time may be a little longer but this trick has never failed me. My cakes always come out flat topped.
—CHINO, CALIFORNIA.

Plenty of other professional cake decorators agreed on that one.

STICK PROBLEM

Dear Nan: I have a problem with cakes sticking in the pan, which I always grease. Am I not greasing enough or should cake be completely cooled before trying to get it out? Also, I notice some recipes recommend flouring the pan after it is greased, which I usually do not do. Is this the problem?
—HARTFORD, CONNECTICUT.

Could be, but flour lightly over the greasing or the bottom of the cake may be tough. I usually sift a little flour right into the pan, shake it around for even coating, dump out any excess. Most cake layers do require 10 to 15 minutes of partial cooling before turning them out on a rack to cool. Placing the pan on a thick wet towel for a couple of minutes helps loosen it. I prefer cake pans with removable bottoms or the lever type of loosener.

I never have any trouble getting cakes or any baked goods out of the pan because I always use waxed paper. An easy way to get an exact fit on that paper is to turn the pan upside down and measure off enough paper for two pans. Fold the paper and lay on the pans. Take your fingernail and go around the edge. Makes a light mark, then it's easy to scissor out the two circles together. I grease and flour the sides of the pans, put the waxed paper in the bottoms. After the cake is baked and cooled, loosen with a thin knife. Cakes come out so easily and the paper peels right off.

—HICKSVILLE, OHIO.

How about cutting out a whole lot of those waxed paper liners all at once for pans you use often? They'll be ready for next time. They'll stay flat and clean stored in a file folder or placed in a cake pan with one of the same size nested on top.

You can also make your own handy cake pan coating by mixing together 1¼ cups vegetable shortening, ¼ cup salad oil, and ¼ cup flour till creamy. Store in covered plastic bowl right in the refrig. It keeps just fine for a long time.

Use a pastry brush or your fingers to coat the cake pans. This takes the place of the everlasting instruction to "grease and flour pans well." Even tender cinnamon rolls come out of the pan without tearing.

Rumpot Cake

Dear Nan: My family and friends have talked me into telling you about a fruitcake I make, using fruit from my rumpot. I am the lady who wrote to you several years ago about putting a whole peeled banana into the crock at that time. It is still holding its shape but is much smaller now. I stir carefully just to see how much longer it will last.

—DES MOINES, IOWA.

1 cup mayonnaise (not salad dressing)	1 cup well-drained rumpot fruit (*see* Rumpot, page 189)
1½ cups buttermilk	1 cup chopped walnuts
3 cups sifted flour	1 tablespoon vanilla
1½ cups sugar	2 tablespoons rum
¾ teaspoon soda	
1 teaspoon salt	
Grated rind of an orange	

Blend mayonnaise and buttermilk. Over this sift the flour, sugar, soda, and salt. Add grated orange rind and mix well. Stir in the drained fruit, nuts, vanilla, and rum. Pour into a well greased and floured 9-inch tube pan. Bake at 325 degrees about 2 hours. Let cool slightly before removing from pan.

This cake freezes well. For that I divide the cake into three parts.

NOTE: Do drain the fruit for this cake extremely well or the center is apt to be soggy. Cut larger fruits in small pieces. Rum-pot pineapple is particularly good in the cake.

Brazil Nut Cake

This is especially nice for those who do not care for fruitcakes containing candied fruits. The slices are just beautiful, but do use a very sharp knife so you cut through the nuts without having them pull out.

3 cups shelled Brazil nuts (about 2 pounds in the shell)	¾ cup sugar
	½ teaspoon baking powder
	½ teaspoon salt
1 pound pitted dates	3 eggs
1 cup maraschino cherries	1 teaspoon vanilla
¾ cup sifted all-purpose flour	

If you will freeze the nuts in their shells for at least 24 hours, they will be much easier to dig out. Do not cut them up; leave them in as large pieces as possible. Be sure to drain the cherries extremely well or the cake center could be soggy. I cut cherries in half, drain in a colander, pressing down gently to remove excess juice. The dates are left whole.

Preheat oven to 300 degrees. Grease a 9-by-5-by-3-inch loaf pan. Line with waxed or brown paper. Grease again, but lightly. Sift together flour, sugar, baking powder, and salt. Put shelled nuts, drained cherries, and dates in a large bowl. Sift flour mixture over these. Use hands to mix till everything is well coated. Beat the eggs till foamy, add the vanilla. Stir into the nut mixture thoroughly. Pour into the pan and spread evenly.

Bake 1 hour and 45 minutes (approximately) or until cake tests done in center. Leave in pan and cool on cake rack for about 15 minutes. Then loosen all around the edges with a spatula. Invert on rack and peel off paper. Place back right side up and finish cooling. Wrapped in foil, the cake refrigerates well for about 4 weeks. It also freezes well. This is not only a holiday treat but a staple for year-round enjoyment.

Pound Cake

In baking pound cake, what is the advantage in putting batter in a cold pan in a cold oven to start? Some recipes recommend it. I don't do it. Am I doing wrong?

—PORTLAND, TENNESSEE.

Not if your cake turns out well. I have always done mine in a preheated oven. The only advantage I can see is that starting with a cold oven might prevent overbrowning of the cake. That sometimes happens. Whichever way, if your cake seems to be well browned at the end of 30 minutes (the cake will not be done), cover it with a brown paper sack just laid over the top of the pan. Don't worry if your cake cracks on top. A good pound cake does that.

Mrs. LBJ's Favorite Chocolate Cake

The nicest, moistest chocolate loaf I have ever tasted! Freezes well or may be kept in refrigerator for several days if well wrapped in foil.

1 stick butter or margarine	½ cup buttermilk
2 cups sugar	2 squares unsweetened
2 cups all-purpose flour,	chocolate
sifted	1 cup hot water
2 eggs	1 teaspoon soda
1 tablespoon vanilla	

Melt chocolate in a double boiler first. Cream margarine and sugar well. Add eggs. Sift flour and add alternately with buttermilk. Then add just ½ cup of the hot water to melted chocolate. Put other ½ cup in pan and bring to a boil. This is important. To this, add soda. Immediately add to chocolate mixture. Pour this into batter, add vanilla. (Yes, the tablespoon vanilla called for is correct.) Batter will be quite thin. Bake in a large greased loaf pan at 325 degrees for about 1 hour and 10 minutes. Cake will pull away from sides slightly when done. Do not overbake.

According to the recipe I received directly from the White House, batter is supposed to fit in a 9-by-5-by-3-inch loaf pan filled about ¾ full, but pan measurements are not always accurate. If you have a little leftover batter, it may be baked as cupcakes or in a small layer cake pan. A 13-by-4½-by-2½-inch pan is ideal for holding all the batter. Makes a longer, narrower loaf, ideal for party slicing. May also be baked in a tube pan. Takes about same timing.

The cake really does not need icing, but you may use the following if you wish.

Chocolate Glaze

2 tablespoons cocoa	2 tablespoons plus 1
1 tablespoon vegetable oil	teaspoon water
1 tablespoon white syrup	1 cup powdered sugar

Mix first four items, over low heat, till smooth. Then stir in powdered sugar till smooth and shiny. Pour over cake and let run down sides.

Norma Williams Sour Cream Coffee Cake

This one was served at a series of recent political coffees and the winning candidate swears it was what put him across.

¼ cup butter	1 teaspoon baking powder
1 cup sugar	½ teaspoon salt
2 eggs	1 cup (½ pint) cultured
2 cups sifted flour	sour cream
1 teaspoon soda	1 teaspoon vanilla

Topping: Combine ⅓ cup brown sugar firmly packed,

¼ cup white sugar, 1 teaspoon cinnamon, 1 cup finely chopped pecans.

Preheat oven to 325 degrees. Cream butter and sugar. Add eggs, one at a time. Beat well. Sift dry ingredients and add to creamed mixture alternately with sour cream, beginning and ending with flour. Stir in vanilla. Pour half of batter into greased 9-inch-square pan. Cover with half of nut topping. Pour remaining batter over filling. Top with rest of nut mixture. Bake about 40 minutes.

FROSTING PROBLEM

Dear Nan: It seems that every time I make a boiled frosting where I cook 1 cup sugar with ¼ cup water till it spins a thread, then beat into a beaten egg white, it looks fine at first. But after it has been on the cake awhile, it soaks in and disappears. What would cause this?

—MINNEAPOLIS, MINNESOTA.

You need ½ cup water with those other ingredients you mentioned. Even so, that would just frost 1 layer or possibly a loaf cake. Trying to spread it over 2 layers, using some in between, could be your problem. Are you letting the icing cool a little before placing it on the cooled cake? It is better if you plan to use the cake the same day it is baked. That icing doesn't hold over too well.

You say you let the sugar and water spin a thread, but it should be at least three inches long and look sort of wavy. A candy thermometer would be the only way to make sure you've reached the required 238 degrees. On wet or very humid days you would have to go a few degrees higher.

Quite often, boiled icing starts to harden too fast. A teaspoon of hot water, ⅛ teaspoon cream of tartar, or a few drops of lemon juice for every 2 egg whites at the last beating prevents that.

MOLASSES COOKIES

Dear Nan: Could you please tell me how to bake molasses cookies so they won't get hard when they cool? My husband keeps saying, "Please, honey! Soft molasses cookies, not gingersnaps!"   —RACINE, WISCONSIN.

You aren't the only one with this complaint. One sure way to soften any cookie that has hardened—especially molasses ones —is to cut an apple in half, then quarter the halves, and stash those pieces among the cookies in a tightly capped tin. I find large coffee cans with plastic lids make the best cookie containers, even if they seldom hold a full batch. Outside of that, the general rule is: "Soft cookies, tightly capped; crisp cookies, loosely capped."

Soft Molasses Drop Cookies

Not as dark as some molasses cookies but easy to make, pleasantly spicy, and with a cakelike texture. Store in tightly covered container as soon as they are cool and they'll stay soft.

½ cup shortening	1 teaspoon ginger
⅓ cup sugar	1 teaspoon cinnamon
⅔ cup dark molasses	¼ teaspoon salt
1 egg	2 teaspoons baking soda
2¼ cups sifted all-purpose flour	½ cup milk
	1½ teaspoons vinegar

Cream together shortening, sugar, molasses, and beaten egg. Sift dry ingredients together. Combine milk and vinegar in a cup. Add flour mixture with milk mixture alternately. Drop by heaping tablespoonfuls on greased baking sheets, about 2 inches apart. Bake at 375 degrees for 8 to 10 minutes. Watch carefully for burning around edges. Cookies will be 2½ to 3 inches. *Makes 3 to 4 dozen.*

Old-Fashioned Cartwheel Molasses Cookies

These mellow-flavored favorites are well worth the effort. May be iced if desired.

¾ cup butter or margarine	2 teaspoons soda
5 tablespoons boiling water	1½ teaspoons ginger
1½ cups dark molasses	½ teaspoon cinnamon
4 cups cake flour	¼ teaspoon salt

Have shortening at room temperature. Add boiling water and stir. Add molasses. Mix and sift dry ingredients, add to first mixture. Dough will be way too soft to roll so refrigerate for several hours, preferably overnight.

Sprinkle pastry board or cloth and rolling pin with just enough cake flour to keep from sticking. Work with just ¼ of dough at a time, keeping rest refrigerated. Roll out ¼ inch thick, no less. Use 2½-inch cutter. (A floured glass or cup will do if your cutter is too small.) With fingers dust off any excess flour from cookie bottoms.

Place 2½ inches apart on greased cookie sheets. Just 6 cookies will fit on most pans. Cookies will spread at least another inch. Bake at 350 degrees for about 12 minutes. Do not overbake. Cool pans before placing more cookies. They spread too fast, too far on hot pans. Remove from pans at once. As soon as cookies are cool, pack in tightly capped tins with waxed paper between layers. *Makes 3 to 4 dozen.*

Aunt Alice's Praline Cookies

You just can't beat these for speed and wonderfully caramelized coating. Everyone loves them, including utilities test kitchens when they need a fast demonstration.

Place 20 to 30 graham crackers on an ungreased, rimmed cookie sheet. Blend 1 cup of butter or margarine with 1 cup of brown sugar. When well creamed, add 1 cup of chopped nuts. Put a good spoonful on each cracker. Bake in a 350-degree oven until light brown and bubbly. When cool, break apart.

THIMBLE COOKIES

Dear Nan: How do you make those jelly-filled thumbprint cookies without having the jelly melt and bubble all over the cookies? They taste all right but they don't look very pretty.
—HONEYBROOK, PENNSYLVANIA.

Those vanilla drop cookies are what we used to call "thimble cookies" because a floured thimble makes just the right size depression in the center of each cookie. You won't have any trouble if you do them this way.

2 cups sifted flour	1 egg yolk
1½ teaspoons baking powder	½ teaspoon vanilla
½ teaspoon salt	3 tablespoons milk
¾ cup shortening	1 egg white, slightly beaten
⅔ cup brown sugar (packed)	2 tablespoons water
⅓ cup corn syrup	1½ cups nuts, finely chopped
1 whole egg	Jam or jelly

Sift together flour, baking powder, and salt. Cream shortening. Add sugar gradually and cream till fluffy. Add syrup. Blend well. Add the whole egg plus the 1 egg yolk, beating thoroughly. Stir in vanilla. Add sifted dry ingredients alternately with the milk. Chill the dough.

Roll into about 1-inch balls. Dip in slightly beaten egg white mixed with the 2 tablespoons water. Roll in the finely chopped nuts. Place about 1½ inches apart on ungreased baking sheets. Bake at 375 degrees for just 5 minutes. Remove from the oven. Quickly make a depression with a thimble in the top of each cookie and dot with red or green jelly or very thick peach jam. Return to the oven at once and bake about 10 minutes longer. *Makes 72 cookies.*

MACAROONS

Dear Nan: Can you tell me how to keep my almond macaroons moist and chewy for longer than the day they are baked? I follow the recipe on the can of almond paste. They turn out beautifully and are delicious. I put them in a tightly covered tin box and the next day they are dried out and crunchy. —CAMDEN, NEW JERSEY.

You are probably baking them a little too long or at too high a temperature. It is a great temptation to let them take on a golden tone, but they should just be the color of good cream when finished, or even look like soft mashed potatoes. Next time, cut your timing by 5 minutes. Macaroons made with almond paste usually call for no more than a 300-degree oven. I trust you are baking this type on unglazed paper over the cookie sheet, then placing the paper on a moist cloth when finished, till they are easy to remove without squashing. Those made with sweetened condensed milk and coconut use a temperature of about 250 degrees. This kind may be permitted to brown lightly.

I'd like to add my note for keeping macaroons moist. You are quite right that they should not be overbaked but, in addition, if they are stored in the right box in the refrigerator, they will remain moist and chewy for several days.
—REDDING, CALIFORNIA.

Here is another viewpoint from an obliging male.

May we add our experience with macaroons? We put them in a plastic bag, leaving the top open, and put the bag in the fresh-food part of the refrigerator (vegetable hydrator). They keep luscious and chewy to the last one. —SABETHA, KANSAS.

CREAM PUFFS

Dear Nan: At our house we love homemade cream puffs, but what makes mine stay soggy inside? And sometimes the batter all goes into the puff part, leaving no bottom half at all. I hate to scoop out all the moist part and throw it away. If you could help me with these two problems I would be forever grateful. —EVANSVILLE, INDIANA.

Family history has it that the morning I was born my grandfather brought my mother a dozen of his fresh cream puffs as the nicest gift he could imagine. He was a pastry chef who had learned his art under Parisian masters. The only thing I remember about his particular method is that he refrigerated the dough before baking at high heat. In France that is still done today. Now it is a rare book that even mentions this step.

Recipes are pretty standard, so I doubt if there is anything wrong with the general mixing procedure. I'll bet it is in the baking. Cooking tomes give all manner of time and temperature and one even goes so far as to say, "Scoop out any soft dough from the finished puffs." Ideally, there shouldn't be any. Not as much as you seem to get, anyway.

Recommended baking temperatures vary widely. I have the best luck when I use a 450-degree oven for just 15 minutes, then swing way back to 300 degrees for 30 to 40 minutes, depending on puff size. The first high heat puffs them quickly, especially if you have refrigerated the dough first, and tints them a delicate brown. Then the lower heat bakes them to the proper dryness without making them too brown. Be sure to cool the puffs on a cake rack to guard against bottom sogginess or you'll get that every time.

If you still have trouble do this. About 5 minutes before the puffs are done (when they are nicely puffed and browned) quickly cut a slit in the side of each puff and put right back in the oven for the rest of the time. That lets any built-up steam escape, and you aren't so apt to get those gooey interiors.

Not every time-and-temp works for everyone. You just have to try first one, then another, till you hit the one that works best for you. Too, when you place your puffs for baking, have them at least 2 inches apart so the heat circulates well around each one. Here is the basic recipe.

Cream Puff Paste

1 cup water	¼ teaspoon salt
½ cup butter (or ¼ cup butter plus ¼ cup vegetable shortening)	1 cup sifted all-purpose flour
	4 eggs

Bring the water, shortening, and salt to boiling. Be sure the shortening is completely melted. Then turn the heat back as far as possible without having it off altogether. Add the flour all at once, but don't dillydally at this point. Stir as hard and fast as you can until the mixture forms a ball that clears the side of the pan. The second that happens, don't do another stir.

Take from the heat. Add whole eggs one at a time, beating well after each addition. The finished mixture will be stiff but glossy. NOTE: Eggs should be room temperature.

Scrape rounded tablespoons of the paste onto lightly greased baking sheets at least 2 inches apart. Bake at 425 degrees about 50 minutes, or until no bubbles show on the surface. This makes 12 large puffs. The recipe may be cut in half if you like.

Fill with creamed custard, sweetened fruit, or ice cream, but not until you plan to serve. I often cut a small slice of the top off each puff, fill with vanilla ice cream, top with sweetened crushed strawberries or raspberries. A chocolate or butterscotch sauce is good, too.

CANDY

Here are sumptuous suggestions for candy treats.

Chocolate-Coated Bourbon Fondant Balls

Whether you use semisweet chocolate or the regular bitter cooking chocolate for coating is up to you, but the fondant is so sweet that the bitter chocolate makes a nice contrast. Any which way, it's great! If you like, divide the fondant in half and try some of each kind of coating.

2 pounds powdered sugar, sifted
¼ pound butter
1 cup chopped pecans
¾ cup bourbon

½ pound semisweet or bitter chocolate heated to 80 degrees in the top of a double boiler over hot (not boiling) water

Soak the chopped or ground pecans in the bourbon overnight, using an airtight glass jar. Then drain the bourbon and add it to just 1 pound of the powdered sugar. Cream the other pound of sugar with the butter. Combine the two. Add the nuts. You may have to use your hands to get the conglomeration well mixed. Chill for at least 30 minutes. Form into 1-inch balls. Chill again, uncovered, till slightly crusty. Dip into the melted chocolate, using a pickle fork or something similar. Can't be too large. Shake off excess chocolate. Place on waxed-paper-lined cookie sheets. Set aside to harden.

NOTE: If you have any difficulty getting your chocolate to melt to good dipping consistency, you may add 1 level tablespoon or 2 of shortening but it makes a softer coating. Be careful not to let any moisture from boiler or hands get into chocolate or it may have gray streaks when hardened.

Marshmallow Nuts

Melt a few marshmallows in the top of a double boiler. Dip pecan or walnut halves into marshmallow just halfway, then into pastel green or pink tinted coconut.

To tint coconut: Blend 1 teaspoon water with just 1 drop or 2 of food coloring. Add 1½ cups shredded coconut. Toss with fork to blend. (If too dark, add more coconut. Excess stores well in capped jars.) Spread on waxed paper to dry before using.

Apricot Coconut Balls

If apricots are too dry you can plump them in a steamer or by placing in top of double boiler over hot water.

1½ cups ground dried apricots	¾ cup sweetened condensed milk (not evaporated)
2⅔ cups flaked coconut	Powdered sugar

Combine ground apricots and coconut in a mixing bowl. Blend in just enough milk so mixture can be formed into 1-inch balls nicely. If you dust your hands with powdered sugar while mixing, it is easier. Roll the balls in more powdered sugar. Place on a baking sheet. Refrigerate till firm.

14 / Pie pointers

Easy as pie!

Sounds great, doesn't it? But many an enraged pie maker would like to shred that breezy platitude to bits right along with the pie dough. Meringues weep, crusts crack, fillings either blow up all over the oven or resemble nothing so much as wallpaper paste. So what to do? Read on.

PIE CRUST

Dear Nan: I do not have good luck with pie crusts no matter what kind I try. They are always tough. Is there a foolproof recipe you could recommend?

—ASHEVILLE, NORTH CAROLINA.

I am convinced it isn't in the recipe, it's in the handling. Any regulation cookbook has a big variety of pie crusts—regulation, egg pastry, oil mixtures, the addition of a bit of vinegar or a half teaspoon of baking powder. Then there are the hot-water crusts and the flour-paste types. Take your pick. What works great for one doesn't work at all for the other. It is so often the handling that makes for success.

For regulation pastry, have your shortening and water cold, even icy. That stops some of the gloppy goo right there. At least one topflight pie expert insists that salt has a toughening effect on flour and should be added to the liquid and dissolved well, not sifted in with dry ingredients. The flour should be sifted into the bowl with any other dry ingredients your recipe might call for. Make sure your measurements are accurate. There has to be a decent balance between flour and shortening, no matter what kind you use. If too much flour, you'll get a shoe leather crust every time. Too much shortening makes the dough fall to pieces when you roll it out—although I'd rather risk that. I have patched more than one crust that baked up beautifully flaky.

Got your pastry blender in hand? Okay. Here we run into two different schools of thought. You can cut the whole shebang of shortening in at once, until it looks like fine cornmeal. I've done it for years and never had any trouble. Or you can use the system some people swear by. Cut just ½ the shortening, then the rest of it until it looks like small peas. So far, so good.

Here we come to a possible hazard: adding the ice water. All the time I hear, "But the amount of liquid in my recipe just isn't enough to make the stuff stick together!" It is almost always enough. Water has to be added little by little, whisking the mixture lightly with a fork as you go. One easy way is to put the water in a large perforated-top shaker and shake in just a few drops at a time. When too much water hits a patch of flour, the dough tends toward toughness. Just keep mixing with the fork till everything starts clinging, like Romeo and Juliet before their nasty folks lowered the boom.

Then gently form the mixture into a ball with your hands. You can roll most doughs out right away or you can refrigerate them for half an hour or so, maybe longer. Some mixtures do better that way. When you roll the dough out, have as little flour on the board as possible, just enough to keep it from sticking. I have seen people dump so much flour onto the board that it looked like the blizzard of 1888. A flour-coated crust just has to wind up tough.

Of course, if you are doing an oil-type pastry, you roll that between sheets of waxed paper, no flour at all. Dampening the surface under the bottom sheet keeps the whole thing from skidding off onto the kitchen floor.

One other possible trouble spot: When you start rolling, don't bear down on the dough as though you were determined to crush your worst enemy to a one-dimensional silhouette. Think pretty thoughts, not mean ones. Use light, quick strokes, handling the dough as little as possible. Shift the dough occasionally, so you aren't rolling in the same direction all the time.

By now you should have a right passable crust ready for the pan. If you don't, console yourself that some people just never can master the situation. If I had to put up with that frustration, I would just go buy the frozen shells at the grocery.

But then there's this next question.

FROZEN PIE CRUST

Dear Nan: I've been having frozen pie crust trouble! I have used several brands, both cheap and expensive, with the same results. That top crust just breaks all over the place. I even had my range checked; I followed all package instructions; and I slit the top crust just like the diagram shows. So what am I doing wrong? —MINNEAPOLIS, MINNESOTA.

Do the wrappers of any of those packaged frozen crusts tell you that top crust should be thawed a bit before positioning? If you first thaw that crust a bit, it is an easy matter to patch any cracks by wetting your finger and pressing the dough back together again. You are supposed to loosen the edge—between crust and disposable pan. If you carefully use just the tip of a paring knife here and there, it helps.

Sometimes those frozen shells get banged around a bit in the freezer case, so watch out for any cracks in the bottom shell, too. Otherwise your filling seeps down under the crust and winds up soggy, or the crust can blow right up through the filling like an erupting Vesuvius.

I trust you are placing your pie on a cookie sheet as per package instructions. It is even a good idea to lift pie pan, cookie sheet, and all out of the oven in one, but the trouble you mention will probably have occurred by that time, anyway.

SOGGY CRUST

Dear Nan: What is the cause of pie crusts becoming soggy when filled with pudding-type fillings? Should the crust be hot or cold when filled? —ANDERSON, INDIANA.

Both the pie shell and precooked-type fillings should be cooled before you introduce them. Hot pudding tends to melt the shortening in the crust. A trick that is generations old is to brush the inside of any bottom crust with slightly beaten white of egg or melted butter before baking to prevent sogginess. Chilling dough well before rolling also helps eliminate all kinds of pie problems. Too low an oven temperature can cause sogginess. Lots of beginners don't realize the oven should be preheated to the exact heat called for before placing the pie inside.

CRUMBLY CRUST

Dear Nan: I can get the bottom crust fitted into the pie pan okay, but I am forever breaking the top crust when I try to get it on in one piece. Then the fruit filling seeps through. —GAINESVILLE, TEXAS.

You may just have a marvelously short crust, but there is an easy way around the problem. Wrap the pastry around your rolling pin. Lay the pin lightly at one end of the rolled-out dough. Then, if you are using a pastry cloth, it's simple to tilt one end of the dough to start it around the pin. Lay it on the pie filling and unroll. Crust is nicely in place.

It can be done without a pastry cloth, but you still have

to be very careful. Use an old tea towel. You can get a good tight fit by safety-pinning it under each corner.

If you are making an oil-type pie crust, then the pie dough must be rolled between sheets of waxed paper or the crust breaks all to pieces.

CRUST SHRINKAGE

Dear Nan: In baking, my pie shells always shrink from the sides. I do not stretch the dough and I prick it well. How can I remedy this? —SPINDALE, NORTH CAROLINA.

Try this: Roll the dough out large enough for some overhang. Fold it in half, fit it gently into the pie plate. Be careful you are not stretching the dough. Then pat gently all over the bottom and sides of the shell with a little ball of saved-back dough. This presses out the air, one of the biggest causes of shrinkage. Air is also what causes the bottom crust to blow up right through pumpkin, custard, and similar fillings. You could do this pressing of the pie shell with your knuckles, but you are less apt to miss spots with the dough ball, and you don't risk toughening the pastry with hand moisture.

Now, before trimming off any excess from the crust edge, let it sit there for about 5 minutes. Helps dispense with the later creepy-crawlies. It won't dry out in that time. Then, instead of trimming it flush with the edge of the pan, leave about a half inch of overhang. Carefully fold this under to get a double edge. Lift it slightly to make a stand-up rim. Then either press lightly with a fork-tine design or flute by placing left fingers on the inside of the rim, using right hand to pinch into fluting. This double-dough deal serves as the best anchor I know of. You can then bake the pie shell at once or refrigerate it for half an hour. The chilling seems to help guard against shrinkage in a good many instances.

Do prick the finished shell well, on the bottom and along the sides about every ¼ inch. Then into a very hot oven, at least 450 degrees. Some use 475 degrees. The high heat sets the pastry before it has a chance to shrink. If the shell puffs during early baking, don't hesitate to fork-prick again.

OLD-FASHIONED RAISIN PIE

Dear Nan: Could you give me a raisin pie recipe? My mother told me she had gotten the original recipe from Kent, England. The filling, I remember, was a clear, thick, chewy, sugary-sweet, vanilla-flavored sauce with plenty of space between the raisins. They weren't packed solid like today's pies, nor was it a raisin custard. It had top and bottom crust and was baked in a square pan. Mighty good served hot.

—EMPORIA, KANSAS.

This cobbler type of pie had me stumped. But if I didn't know, a whole flock of readers did. Here is just one of the many raisin pie recipes now in my file.

This is one of my mom's recipes and I, too, have fond memories of it. I don't believe the shape of the pan makes any difference, just a matter of personal preference. The results will be the same. Pour 1 quart boiling water over 1 pound of raisins. Grate the rind of 1 lemon into 1 cup sugar, 3 teaspoons flour, and a beaten egg. Mix well and stir into the hot raisin-and-water mixture. Add a small piece of butter. I use 2 teaspoons of it. Stir well and pour into unbaked pastry shells, topping with pastry. This makes three 8-inch pies.

Brush the tops with milk and sprinkle with sugar. Bake at 375 degrees till golden brown. This amount will make two deep-dish pies. You can add a little vanilla to the filling if you like. ——KANSAS CITY, MISSOURI.

APPLE PIE

Dear Nan: You once mentioned something about using the juice from apple peelings for the pie filling, but do you thicken the juice before adding to the filling? And exactly how do you cook the peels first? —ROANOKE, VIRGINIA.

Put the peelings in the pan with a very little bit of water—just enough to keep them from scorching. Cover and cook ever so slowly. When you feel they have cooked enough, mash them down and drain off the juice. You can put juice back and allow to cook down some more if there is quite a lot. Add the juice to the apples in the pie shell. It makes the most wonderful natural syrup and adds so much to the flavor.

I'm rather against any thickening for apple pie fillings. It is all right to maybe mix 2 teaspoons cornstarch with the apples and sugar if the fruit is exceptionally juicy. I like brown sugar best for this. One teaspoonful of vanilla sprinkled over the mixture doesn't hurt anything, either.

Good apples do cook down somewhat, so do use plenty, mounding them up in the center so the pie crust won't cave in. I think I would rather have that, though, than the crust humpin' up over a caved-in filling. That can happen when there is too much flour and not enough shortening in the crust.

Applejack Apple Pie

I once ate an extraordinarily good piece of apple pie. It had such an unusual flavor I was sure the apples must be a variety I hadn't met up with before. The chef said no, he had just added about ⅓ cup of applejack, plus 1 tablespoon or 2 of currant jelly to the usual sugar, cinnamon, nutmeg, and generous dotting of butter. Of course, another thing that made that pie so good was a sharp Cheddar cheese mixed right in with the pastry.

After a bit of wheedling and a swap of a spinach salad recipe he'd been wanting, I got the pastry proportions. Three to 4 ounces of the shredded Cheddar cheese blended with 1¾ cups flour and 1 teaspoon salt. (You'll find that much "loose" cheese will fill a standard measuring cup. Don't pack it down.) Then ⅔ cup of lard, sprinkled with just enough ice water to make the stuff hold together. It usually takes around 5 tablespoons more or less. It is enough for a 2-crust pie.

MERINGUES

There is seldom anything wrong with your meringue recipes. There may be slight differences but ingredients are largely standard. It is the know-how that counts.

Making meringues of any kind is not a hurry up, slapdash job. Take your time and turn out really superb ones.

There are times of the year when egg whites are on the watery side. Weather can also be a disturbing factor. Like the gardener with a green thumb for African violets but not roses, there are cooks who have no luck at all unless they use the wire whisk technique, others do fine with a rotary beater, but most of us use our electric mixers. Here are some hints to help you.

The more egg whites you use, the more gloriously statuesque your pie meringues will be. Two egg whites are supposed to be enough for an 8-inch pie, three for a 9-inch or 10-inch pie. You can use as many as 5 egg whites for a large pie so long as you stick to the rule of about 2 tablespoons sugar for each egg white. When you do that, increase the cream of tartar (if your recipe calls for it) from the usual ¼ teaspoon to ½ teaspoon.

The least little bit of grease can cause meringue ruination so make sure every utensil needed is clean and clear as a redbird's whistle on a May morning.

Never use anything but Grade A eggs, preferably large size. It is easier to separate yolks and whites if done the moment you take them from the refrigerator. Just be sure to let the whites reach room temperature before you beat them. Surest way is to let them set, covered, for about an hour. They will beat to much greater volume.

Humid weather can have a ghastly effect on meringues. On a damp day they are apt to turn out icky-sticky.

Prize winning cooks add no more than a teaspoon of sugar at a time to egg whites while beating them. If an electric mixer is used, start whites, salt, cream of tartar, etc., on low speed till frothy, then switch to high speed. Between sugar additions, it pays off to test mixture by rubbing a bit between your fingers. If it feels grainy, that means sugar is not dissolved enough. Either granulated or confectioners' sugar can be used. If the latter, powdered sugar should be sifted thoroughly before mixing. Once all the sugar is added, keep beating till the meringue stands in stiff peaks when beater is withdrawn. The number of egg whites determines the beating time, which can take anywhere from 15 to 30 minutes.

No cream of tartar in the house? A teaspoon of lemon juice or ½ teaspoon vinegar can substitute for each ¼ teaspoon cream of tartar called for.

Once your meringued pie is out of the oven, place it carefully on a rack for cooling. Do not move it for at least an hour in order to let it set. Protect it against air drafts or air conditioner gusts by taking something like a shirt cardboard, folded in half and set on end as a screen around your pie.

Recommended baking temperatures vary for meringue toppings, but those done at higher setting for a shorter length of time have a chance of being more tender. A timing of 4 to 4½ minutes in a 400-to-425-degree oven seems to work best.

"Big Surprise" Meringue Shell

You'll swear this one will never work, but just try it! Makes one of the prettiest 10-inch shells I have ever seen. Only one precaution: Make sure your oven is accurate. I use a good portable thermometer in mine, as a check against my thermostatic control, just to make sure.

3 egg whites beaten till soft peaks form	½ cup sugar, added a little bit at a time
¼ teaspoon cream of tartar	

Beat, at high speed on electric mixer, for 15 minutes or till definite peaks form. Butter a 10-inch pan well. I do mine in ovenproof glass, but use a good aluminum one if you prefer. Preheat oven to 450 degrees. Shape meringue in pan, having hollowed-out center. Place in oven on low or center rack. Turn off heat at once! Leave in oven overnight or from 4 to 6 hours till cooled to room temperature. Wonderfully crisp and golden. Just remember, your oven must be accurate.

Millionaire's Pie

Several versions of this going around. A rich delicacy! You need a 10-inch meringue shell. Works especially well with the preceding "Big Surprise" shell. Or you may wish to use the 6-egg-white version as given below. Just gives more meringue.

6 egg whites	1 can crushed pineapple,
¾ cup sugar	well drained (1 pound,
1 teaspoon cream of tartar	4-ounce size)
1 teaspoon vanilla	1 can cherry pie filling
½ cup chopped nuts	Whipping cream or
(optional)	dessert topping
2 large bananas, not too	Chocolate curls (optional)
ripe	

Beat egg whites and vanilla till frothy. Add sugar very gradually, at high speed, till barely fluffy. Then add cream of tartar. Beat till very stiff peaks are formed. If desired, gently fold in chopped nuts.

Grease a 10-inch pie pan, including the rim. Pour mixture into pan, shape with hollowed-out center (should be about ¼ inch on bottom). Build up sides very high, almost an inch above pan. Preheat oven to 250 degrees. Bake for 1 hour. Turn off heat. Open oven door, let meringue shell remain till well cooled.

Slice bananas into cooled shell. Bananas should not be too ripe or they will ooze. Cover completely with well-drained pineapple. Pour on cherry pie filling. Refrigerate overnight.

At serving time you may cover entire pie with slightly sweetened whipped cream, but the cherry filling against the pale gold meringue is so pretty it is a shame to hide it. I prefer to place a dollop of whipped topping in the center, and spoon the rest around the edge. If desired, decorate topping with chocolate curls.

FRIED PIES

Dear Nan: Do you have a really good fried pie recipe? Mine doesn't seem to work out very well.
—FRAMINGHAM, MASSACHUSETTS.

I used to go along with the idea that any good pie dough recipe would do just fine, but it doesn't always pan out that way. Part of the trick is in rolling the dough thin enough, about ⅛ inch thick, but not so thin that the filling seeps through. It also takes the correct temperature of deep fat to keep the pie from being soggy.

I think the various preferences in fried pies stem from whatever locality you hailed from originally. I have a recipe from Vermont that is supposed to be one of the old originals. It works fine for me. Add 1 tablespoon melted shortening to ½ cup sugar, plus 1 beaten egg. Stir that together thoroughly. Now add ⅓ cup buttermilk alternately with 1½ cups flour, 2 teaspoons baking powder, ½ teaspoon salt, and ½ teaspoon soda sifted together.

You might have to add a mite more flour, depending on the brand. Roll out quite thin on a well-floured board. You can make miniature pies by cutting the dough with a large cookie cutter, but the regulation-size pies call for a saucer laid on the dough as a pattern. Fill the circles with 1 tablespoon or so of thick, well-seasoned applesauce, or dried cooked apricots or prunes, sweetened to taste. Place the filling to one side of the circle. Moisten the edges well; fold over to make a half moon; press the edges together tightly to seal; using an ordinary fork, prick the tops in several places. Fry in deep hot fat (375 degrees) till lightly browned. Drain on paper toweling, and when partly cooled dust with powdered sugar. Nothing better on a cold, wintry day. Even when completely cold, they make good lunch box fare.

15 / Desserts: the sweet windup

"Really, I shouldn't! Well, maybe just a small serving. It does look delicious." How many times have you heard that one? Or said it? No matter how good the previous part of the meal may have been, there are still a lot of us who consider it unfinished business without the topper of something sweet. But with the medical profession constantly shaking a finger at us about weight control, what can we do about all the no-no's?

Try gearing yourself to half portions or even less. Haven't you noticed that it's these first few bites that taste the best anyway?

Then there are all the low-calorie fruit gelatins, whipped toppings, and pudding mixes on the market. Don't ever toss away their boxes, inside envelopes, folders without a fast look first. They give all sorts of tricky little ideas. So do regulation packages.

BANANAS FLAMBÉED

Dear Nan: When we were in Madrid, we were served the most marvelous dessert, bananas flambéed. All I can remember is that the bananas were sautéed for quite awhile, then three different liquors were added along with some sugar. After that came the dramatic flaming of the contents.

—ROCHESTER, NEW YORK.

It's always tricky to try to match dishes prepared in some far-away corner of the world because some of those lads add their own unique touches that make the difference. However, I do know a real Spanish version so maybe we'll come close.

You need 8 small bananas cut in half lengthwise, 1 cup brown sugar, ½ teaspoon cinnamon, a pinch of powdered cloves, a pinch of ginger, about 8 tablespoons butter, 1 small can crushed pineapple, ½ cup dark sweet rum, either Jamaican or Martinique. This is a baked method but it could be adapted to the chafing dish at table. That's probably where most of the 30 minutes went at the Madrid restaurant.

Blend the spices with the sugar. Roll the cut bananas in mixture. Sauté in the butter till just lightly browned and the sugar begins to caramelize. Place in layers in a shallow casserole or decorative skillet nice enough to bring to the table. Sprinkle with more of the sugar mixture between layers, but save back 2 tablespoons of it. Pour the crushed pineapple with its syrup over the bananas. Sprinkle the top with the rest of the sugar.

Put in a 350-degree oven until the dish begins to caramelize. You just have to keep an eye on it because timing never seems to be exactly the same way twice. Remove, pour the slightly heated rum over the bananas, and touch with a match. Carry it flaming to the table. Watch you don't trip! Or you can ignite it right at the table if you like. It's a very sweet dessert but luscious. *Makes 4 servings.*

WATERMELON BOAT

There are numerous versions of this dessert, and after you've made it a time or two you'll know which combination of fruits you like best. Here's one.

You'll need a medium-sized long watermelon. The round melons are all right to use but the whole effect isn't as spectacular. Too, you usually have to cut a small slice from the bottom of the melon to keep it from wobbling on the tray. Along with the watermelon, you should have at least 1 cantaloupe, honeydew, or casaba melon. I like the cantaloupe best for contrasting color and flavor, and I usually use 2. From there on out, you take whatever fresh fruits you can lay hands on at the time. Strawberries (halved), peaches, sliced bananas, seedless grapes, papaya in syrup (canned), blueberries, red raspberries, the dark sweet Bing cherries.

Cut the watermelon in half very carefully so it is even. It's a good idea to measure and stick toothpicks into the outside of the melon to serve as a guideline. Or you can mark the green rind with a sharp knife, if you think you can see that line as you go. Scoop out the red melon meat with a melon baller. If you don't have one, you can cut the melon in bite-size pieces. Do the other melons the same way and combine with the watermelon. Set aside while you combine whatever other fruits you are using, with the exception of the blueberries, red raspberries, or Bing cherries. You add those at the last, right on top.

You will have some juice from the various fruits, so add that to the melon balls and fruit, well mixed together. Now pour over about 1½ cups sweet white wine and refrigerate. If you would rather use ginger ale, that's just fine but don't add it at this point or it loses its fizz. Pour icy cold ginger ale over fruits at serving time.

Clean out the melon shell. Turn the melon shell upside down so it drains while chilling in the refrigerator. That's where your fruits are, too. When you are just about ready to serve, arrange the melon balls and other fruit in the shell. Sprinkle the raspberries, blueberries, or Bing cherries on top. It's possible to use frozen berries, but they should be only partially thawed or they will be mushy. Pour another ½ cup of the white wine or all the ginger ale on top.

It's nice if you have some fresh mint for a garnish, but you can get by without it. Some cooks like to sprinkle grated fresh coconut over the fruits at the last minute, but for me it rather ruins the effect. If you use bananas, just be sure they are well buried under the other fruits while that mélange is chilling, or they may turn brown. It won't hurt a thing if you would rather play it safe by adding those at the last minute.

CHERRIES JUBILEE

Dear Nan: I tried doing cherries jubilee for company and was terribly embarrassed when they refused to flame, even though I heated the brandy well before touching a match to it.   —NEW KENSINGTON, PENNSYLVANIA.

A common mistake is in getting the liquor or even the cherry mixture too hot, in which case the alcoholic content is cooked away before you light it. Then the liquor doesn't flame as scheduled. It does take a good grade of liquor. Opinion is divided on whether cognac, kirsch, or curaçao is best, but cognac is a top favorite, sometimes along with a fillip of kirsch for good measure. Some prefer using preserved cherries, heated, but the simplest way is with 1 large can (No. 2½) of Bing cherries, pitted. There are about as many versions of cherries jubilee as there are cherries on a tree, but the total effect of the flaming cherries poured over vanilla ice cream is pretty much the same.

Drain the cherries and measure out 1 cup of juice. Then heat the cherries and juice together very slowly, making sure they come just to the simmering point, never boiling. When you are ready to serve, put cherries in a large heat-proof bowl. This makes 4 good servings over ice cream, so you will want ¼ cup barely heated cognac or whatever per serving. Some people use only that much for the whole shebang. Pour the liquor on top of the cherries—just floating it on, not mixed in. Touch with the match right away and ladle over individual dishes of ice cream while the sauce is still flaming. If you want extra insurance that the cherry mixture will flame properly, dip a couple of sugar cubes in lemon extract just enough to moisten well but still hold their shape. Lay those gently on top of the cherries just before flaming. If you like a very potent flavor, you can soak the cherries in cognac ahead of time and they will be pretty hat-rocking. *Makes 4 servings.*

PLANTATION RUMPOT

Rumpot! This has surely been one of the most frequent recipe requests year after year. There are newer versions, some even recommending canned fruit all the way, but they never achieve the "zing" you get with this one.

Put 1 pint of rum or brandy in a stone or glass jar (nothing metal). I use a large beanpot; many people use the largest size apothecary jar. Add fresh strawberries, raspberries, peaches, pineapple, blueberries, cherries—any fresh fruit as it comes in season *with the exception of apples, pears, and citrus fruits.* Dried fruit may be used in part, after the pot is well started, but *no canned fruits* may be included except mandarin oranges and maraschino cherries. Raisins, currants, and dried apricots are good if used with the other fruits. For each 2 cups of fruit used add an equal amount of sugar. Wait about a week before adding more fruit and sugar. Stir daily. According to old colonial recipes, this mixture should age 3 months, but it is ready long before then. If you use raisins—and they do seem to help fermentation—*do not use equal sugar.* Use only 1 cup sugar for each 2 cups of raisins, since they have their own natural sweetness.

Cover the jar in which you are making rumpot but do not use a screw-on lid. You cover the jars with several thicknesses of folded cheesecloth held down with strong string or heavy rubber bands. Both beanpots and apothecary jars allow just the right amount of air to aid fermentation. Keep in a fairly cool place. I have mine on a kitchen drainboard away from any heat of the range. My house is air-conditioned.

As you use your rumpot sauce over ice cream, puddings, or plain cake slices, add more fruit and sugar in proportion to what you have taken out. It is not necessary to add more liquor because the original amount plus fermentation of fresh fruits keeps it going.

If you give your rumpot away, keep a cupful as a

"starter"—two cups is better—but fruits and sugar should be added in small quantities for a while. This may be kept going for years. Some people do add more liquor as they go along for a stronger taste.

If you are late getting started with fruits in season you may use frozen fruits. For each regulation pack (about 10 to 12 ounces) add just 1 cup sugar *if fruit is sweetened*. If it is unsweetened, then add cup for cup as with fresh fruits.

TRIFLE

Dear Nan: I added another pint of brandy to my rumpot and it tastes marvelous but now I have an awful lot of juice. We mostly like just the fruit itself poured over ice cream, so is there anything I can do with all that juice?

—LAFAYETTE, INDIANA.

You could use excess juice for the dessert known as trifle. Break sponge cake into pieces in a deep crystal bowl. Pour in enough rumpot liquid to moisten the cake bits well. Then stud the cake pieces with toasted almonds. Refrigerate till serving time. Just before bringing to the table, pour custard sauce over the soaked cake. Pile whipped cream on top.

A variation of this old favorite calls for spreading the cake with good jam before adding the sauce and whipped cream. A raspberry or peach jam is particularly good. Almost any stale cake can be used as the basis for trifle. It doesn't always have to be sponge cake, although that absorbs the liquor or wine best.

If you don't have a recipe for soft custard suitable for trifle, here's one that works well.

Old-Fashioned Boiled Soft Custard

2 eggs, slightly beaten	1 cup milk, scalded
1 tablespoon sugar	½ teaspoon vanilla or ¼
Dash of salt	teaspoon almond extract

Combine eggs, sugar, and salt in a bowl. Add the scalded

milk slowly, beating constantly. Pour into a double boiler over water that is just simmering. Cook, stirring constantly, until the mixture coats the spoon. Cool a little before adding the flavoring.

RUTH HARRIS'S
SWEET POTATO PUDDING

Dear Nan: Here is an antique "receipt," as they used to call it back when this one originated. It's for grated raw sweet potato pudding. I started making it from memory, having watched my mother make it, and she, in turn, had watched her mother-in-law, so who knows how long it has been used by previous members of the family. My grandmother came to Arkansas from Mississippi back in the early 1900s and my dad remembers eating this delicious dish when he was just a boy. I didn't get the recipe before my mother died, so I had to experiment a little to get exact proportions before I could pass it on to anyone else. First time I made it I used cinnamon, but it didn't taste like what I remembered. Now I have finally hit it and I'm glad to share it. I think the secret is in the stirring so often. Makes it rather chewy and really good. Please try using just the spices I did. I think you'll enjoy it.

Pare and grate enough sweet potatoes to get 2 cups. Beat 2 eggs till thick and lemon colored. Gradually add 1 cup sugar and continue beating. Into that mixture stir 3 cups milk and 1 teaspoon each nutmeg and allspice. Lastly, add the grated raw sweets. Pour into a greased casserole, dot generously with butter or margarine, using a full stick. Bake at 350 degrees. After the first 20 minutes, stir well, being careful to scrape down the sides. Thereafter, stir well about every 15 minutes, and keep the potatoes from settling to the bottom. Bake until the mixture looks thick and glazed. Serve warm with plain or whipped cream. Or you might cover with marshmallows and brown lightly. —BELTON, MISSOURI.

Scoops of plain vanilla ice cream melting over the warm pudding are luscious, too! This makes 6 servings. I would make one suggestion. Since sweet potatoes darken rapidly when peeled, it's best to have the egg-sugar-milk mixture all ready before grating the potatoes. Then get them into the liquid as fast as possible.

BAKED CUSTARD

Dear Nan: Some time ago you had a letter from someone whose egg custard always became watery. I, too, had that problem in my early married life until someone gave me a helpful hint that keeps custard perfect. Heat the milk but do not let it boil. Never have the oven set higher than 325 degrees. This turns out perfect custard, whether baked in a pie or custard cups.

I put home-canned peaches in the bottom of the cups, then set them in a pan of water for baking.

—CAMPBELLTOWN, PENNSYLVANIA.

OZARK PUDDING

Dear Nan: Several times I have tried to bake Mrs. Harry S Truman's popular Ozark pudding, but it always falls way down in the center after I take it out of the oven. Why does it? —FAYETTE, ALABAMA.

In some sections of the country, this happens with such frequency it has led one book to comment, "It's supposed to." Not really. Many people, myself included, have baked that pielike pudding with never a fall-in. A difference in apples can account for this happening. Some apples cook down mushier than others. A good Jonathan usually does okay, but even this variety isn't the same everywhere. Then there is that egg. It should be a large one, not overbeaten. If you use an electric beater, keep it at low speed and use briefly. I just wallop the egg briskly with a fork, stir in the sugar, give it a chance to dissolve well before another fork walloping, then blend the rest of the simple ingredients. Pecans are traditional for this, but the inexpensive chopped mixed nuts are almost as good.

The pudding might fall a little when you cut it into wedges but not much. Even if it does cave in to a larger extent, all is not lost. The recommended topping of whipped cream or vanilla ice cream will cover that up. It still tastes rich and wonderful. At any rate, it is a splendid easily-whipped-together refreshment finale for that bridge game, and you don't need another thing with it but coffee or tea.

Mrs. Harry S Truman's Ozark Pudding

1 large egg	¾ cup sugar
1 to 1½ teaspoons baking powder	2 tablespoons flour
½ cup chopped nuts	⅓ teaspoon salt
1 teaspoon vanilla	½ cup chopped raw apple

Beat the egg to medium. Add sugar gradually. Then beat till smooth, making sure sugar is well dissolved. Mix flour, baking powder, and salt. Stir into sugar mixture. Add apples, nuts, and vanilla. Bake in a 9-inch well-greased pie pan in a medium oven (350 degrees) for 35 minutes. Serve with whipped cream or ice cream. A little rum flavoring might be added if desired, or ¼ teaspoon almond extract along with the vanilla. *Makes 4 to 6 servings.*

WINE JELLY

Dear Nan: Do you know anything about an old-time dessert called wine jelly? This isn't the kind of jelly you spread on toast. My maiden aunt used to make it for us to tempt our appetites when any of us kids were getting over an illness. It was supposed to be strengthening. I don't know about that, but it surely is good with cream or a thin custard sauce poured over. —MURFREESBORO, KENTUCKY.

I don't know why this dessert isn't made in home kitchens so much anymore. Perhaps we have too many packaged quick-mix things on the grocer's shelves now. There is really nothing difficult about this recipe, and it makes a really delightful dessert for anyone who likes the flavor of wine.

1 tablespoon (or 1 envelope) unflavored gelatin	½ cup hot water
¼ cup cold water	¼ cup orange juice
½ cup sugar	1 tablespoon lemon juice
⅛ teaspoon salt	¾ cup wine (sweet sherry, port, or Madeira)

Soften the gelatin in the cold water. Add sugar, salt, and hot water. Stir to dissolve over hot water. Add the combined fruit juices and the wine. Turn into individual molds. If you wet them first, the jelly is easier to unmold. *Makes 4 to 6 servings.*

You can do something else with wine jelly. Press it through a ricer as an unusual topping for vanilla ice cream. Or you can cut out the center of a sponge cake. Leave the bottom and sides thick enough to hold the jelly when, partly thickened in the refrigerator, it is turned into the shell. Chill this well and serve topped with whipped cream.

CAKE AND . . .

Dear Nan: I so enjoy making little cakes. On Valentine's Day I made a sheet cake, then cut it into individual heart shapes. I tinted the batter pink, same shade pink icing, had a slightly darker candy rosebud on each. That was fine, but in the future I need recipes to help me use leftover cake scraps. Can you help? —NEWCASTLE, INDIANA.

Delighted to. Those cakes of yours would be darling at bridal showers, too. But we can't have those scraps of yours going begging. Not when you can make such nice desserts from them. Whip 1 cup heavy cream for about every 2 cups of cake bits and toss together with a fork. Add whatever amount of chopped nuts you like. Pour into refrigerator trays and freeze. You can add cut-up maraschino cherries or other well-drained fruits, such as sweetened fresh peaches. Sort of a mock biscuit tortoni.

You can skip any fruits in the cake-cream mixture. Just slice it and top with a fruit sauce or almost-thawed frozen fruit, still icy cold. Instead of nuts or fruit, you might try crushed peanut brittle, topped with butterscotch sauce for serving. Or what's the matter with crushed peppermint sticks mixed in and a chocolate sauce over all?

But let's say you don't want to fool with freezing. Here's where parfait glasses with alternate layers of cake, whipped cream, and jam get into the act. Or, again in parfait glasses, use layers of pour-type custard alternating with cake pieces and thawed frozen raspberries.

NESSELRODE SAUCE

Dear Nan: Could you please tell me how to make Nesselrode sauce? At least that's what a caterer in town calls it but, when I asked, she said it was a restaurant item, not available in stores. She didn't mention all the contents, just pineapple, but whatever else was added was like cut-up candied fruit. One time I tasted it, it was like a conserve, the next time like a sauce, but it didn't run. —LONGVIEW, WASHINGTON.

I can't blame any caterer for trying to keep an actual specialty to herself. It isn't special when everyone else makes it. Nesselrode has been around for a long time. You can buy it at some select food shops, if you want to pay the price. Or you can make it yourself without too much trouble.

There are various versions, but the one I like calls for a 6- or 8-ounce bottle of maraschino cherries, ½ the cherry juice, 3 to 4 ounces candied pineapple, 1 cup orange marmalade, 1 cup nutmeats. That's the basic. You can substitute other candied fruits for the pineapple if you like. Some use citron, but I would hate to skip the pineapple altogether. This recipe calls for ½ cup candied ginger in addition. If you do not like that flavor, make up the difference with one of the other ingredients.

Any which way, when you get it all mixed together add

½ cup rum—maybe more if the sauce is too thick to suit you, but too much rum can be overpowering. The nuts can be pecans, English walnuts, or unsalted pistachios. Originally chestnuts were used, but not so much anymore. It takes two weeks for the sauce to be at its best, so seal it in screw-lid jars and put it out of temptation's way. I always save the rest of the maraschino juice in case I think the sauce needs it. Even if it isn't needed, it is still usable in a great big way for so many other dessert flavorings. Maraschino juice is nice for any pudding sauce. It's even good, as is, poured over vanilla ice cream. *Makes about 1 pint.*

DARK SECRET

For me, this chapter would not be complete without the beautiful memory of a long-ago dessert my mother made for very special occasions, including my birthday. I never cared whether I had a birthday cake or not—my grandmother probably took care of that—as long as there was Dark Secret for my party. The neighborhood kids didn't seem to care, either. After all, their mothers never made Dark Secret. That was my status symbol.

I have never seen this precise dessert in any book. I really thought it was lost forever until I came across it in my mother's unmistakable handwriting scribbled in the back of an old *Chicago Daily News* cookbook. It is somewhat like a date bar concoction and I suppose you could get by with that as the basis, but you will notice mom's "secret" takes less flour than date bars and is more chewy. Here it is.

3 beaten eggs mixed with 1 cup sugar	1 heaping teaspoon baking powder
1 cup pecans	3 tablespoons flour
1 cup dates, cut fine	

Mix together and bake in a greased shallow pan, 9 by 13, in a slow oven, 300 to 325 degrees, for 40 minutes. Watch carefully. Cool before breaking into pieces. Place in stemmed sherbet glasses. Top with diced oranges or canned mandarin oranges and sliced bananas. Takes about three of each. Sugar those. Cover all with vanilla-flavored sweetened whipped cream. Whipped cream may sound strange on top of oranges, but with the rest of the stuff it's awfully good! *Makes 6 to 8 servings.*

16 / Snack snappers and quick-fix sandwiches

For better or worse, we are a generation of snackers around the clock: the midmorning kaffeeklatsch, the after-school sandwich, the TV-time potato chips and popcorn, the cocktail hour, the midnight refrigerator raid, the endless array of sour-cream dips, cheese spreads, corn chips, and crackers we buy.

As a kid I was such a sandwich addict that my grandma used to say I would make a sandwich out of soup if I could only figure how. Maybe heredity has something to do with it. Somewhere back in the clan there was a great-uncle who insisted on layering his liverwurst sandwich with molasses. My mother used to mention that every time my younger sister spread honey over pimento cheese. The rest of us considered it such a perfectly revolting combination that we never did take June up on her pleas to "Go ahead, try it. It's great!"

So, some years later, what do I see in a magazine but "a new and delicious tea sandwich." What else but pimento and honey. You just never know. I am not about to destroy any of your Dagwood-type creativity but every now and then it's nice to happen onto a few tricks that might be new to you. Like maybe here?

GARLIC CARROTS

Dear Nan: Maybe you can tell me how to fix garlic carrot sticks the way we ate them in San Francisco. I can't figure how they picked up the flavor because there wasn't a shred of garlic showing. They weren't cooked and they hadn't been marinated in anything. —DENTON, TEXAS.

Garlic carrot sticks are at their best when you use young, tender, long carrots. Slice them in half lengthwise, or in smaller sticks if you prefer. Soak them for ½ hour in lightly salted water— 1 teaspoon salt to 1 quart water with plenty of ice cubes in it. Then drain well and wrap them in a wet towel with some coarsely chopped garlic. Park them in the refrigerator for a few hours. Then shake all the garlic away and serve before they have a chance to uncrisp.

I suppose you could use the dehydrated bottled garlic chips, but I can't promise the flavor will be the same. The carrots make a great little cocktail snack item. You can't use mature carrots for these because they usually have some woody center to them; they just aren't as snappy.

GARLIC OLIVES

Dear Nan: I just love those black olives in an oil and garlic dressing but sometimes they are pretty expensive. I think I would like a little stronger garlic flavor, too. Could I make them at home? —LOGANSPORT, INDIANA.

Why not? Shred 1 or 2 garlic cloves and mix them with a cup of the best olive oil you can find. Drain the juice from a can of ripe olives and pour the garlic oil over them. I like to let these marinate at least overnight. Don't throw the garlic oil away when you've eaten all the olives. You can save the oil for a start on your next batch, or it's fine for a vinegar and oil salad dressing.

OLIVE CHEESE PUFFS

Dear Nan: We ate something awfully good at a party one evening. The hostess said she wouldn't mind giving me the recipe, but we both forgot. Now she has moved away. These snacks were some sort of cheese mixture wrapped around stuffed olives and baked. Could you help?
                                                —SAN ANGELO, TEXAS.

How nice that those should happen to be one of my favorites, too! You need 2 cups grated sharp American cheese, ½ teaspoon salt, ½ cup room-temperature butter, 1 cup sifted all-purpose flour, 1 teaspoon paprika, and about 48 small stuffed olives, well drained.

Blend the butter and cheese together. Add the dry ingredients. Wrap about 1 tablespoon of the mixture around each olive. Arrange these on a cookie sheet and bake at 400 degrees for 10 to 15 minutes. The cheese-butter mixture can burn easily, so keep a sharp eye on the baking. *Makes 48.*

AMERICAN BEAUTY EGGS

Everybody knows about deviled eggs, but have you ever tried American Beauty Eggs? A platter of these is a real eye-catcher at a party when you place them on any sort of greens, especially parsley or watercress.

Place whole hard-cooked eggs in pickled beet juice till tinted, at least overnight. Here's how to make that pickled beet juice if you don't have any handy. Drain the juice from a large can of beets. Boil ½ cup of the juice and ½ cup of vinegar together. (Use that ratio for whatever beet liquid you are able to scrounge from the can.) Add and heat to boiling 2 or 3 teaspoons sugar, 3 whole cloves, ½ teaspoon salt, and 3 whole peppercorns. I like perhaps ¼ of a bay leaf and a small sliced onion here, too. *Makes enough liquid for 6 to 8 eggs.*

Dry the eggs, cut in half and remove the yolks. The original recipe calls for filling the halved whites with caviar and a sprinkle of combined lemon and orange juice. The yolks get grated over the top with a final dusting of paprika!

Very plush, I admit, but that caviar is a bit much for most of us. However, even a small can of caviar goes a long way and domestic varieties are quite good. I also use this mixture as a filling for those tinted eggs: Mash the yolks just as you would for deviled eggs, add some chopped shrimp or even sardines, soften the whole thing to the desired texture with mayonnaise and maybe a bit of cream. Then comes the paprika.

FRENCH FRIED ONION RINGS

Dear Nan: How do you freeze French fried onion rings without having the coating come off? That always happens, either when I fry them the first time or when I take them out of the freezer for refrying. How do they do those at the drive-ins? They always taste so good.

—SPOKANE, WASHINGTON.

They all do well if you observe a few simple rules. There is nothing tricky about it and doing your own is a big money-saver. Here is my daughter's method, which couldn't be more simple. She always triples the batch because it's a slightly messy job and she figures she might as well get it over with all at once. Doesn't take much more time.

Jayne's French Fried Onion Rings

They even freeze well.

6 medium onions sliced about ¼ inch thick	3 eggs
2 cups milk	Flour and salt

Separate onion slices into rings. Combine milk and eggs,

beat thoroughly, and pour into shallow pan. Drop rings into pan. With your fingers, swish rings around till well coated all over! Lift onions out, shake over pan to drain. Then drop them into a pan of flour, a few rings at a time, again coating well. Place in a wire French fry basket. (Don't fill more than ¼ full for each frying.) Shake off excess flour by giving basket a sharp slap. Fry in deep hot fat (375 degrees), stirring once to separate if necessary. (Use fork gently through the center or you will knock the batter off.) When onions are golden brown, drain on paper towels. Sprinkle with salt and serve hot. Makes 4 to 6 servings depending on onion eaters.

To Freeze: Double or triple batch if you wish. They keep well and the work is all done at once. When onion rings are drained after frying, let cool. Spread individual rings out on a cookie sheet and pop into freezer, unwrapped, till they are hard and set. Then place them in freezer containers (boxes) for longtime holding. To serve later, empty into shallow pan and reheat in oven at about 350 degrees.

NOTE: A common complaint is, "The coating always falls off my onion rings." It seldom will if you: (1) Coat well! Hot fat hitting bare spots can pop coating right now. (2) Slice onions thick enough. (3) Do not have fat too hot. A thermostatic deep fryer is best for this. (4) Do not crowd rings in fryer. Wait for heat to regain temperature before frying next batch or the rings may be soggy.

LORA'S DELICATE CHEESE STICKS

Almost half a century ago my mother-in-law was serving these crisply puffed specialties at her bridge club luncheons as a salad accompaniment. I have never tasted any better! Terrific snack item with any beverage.

1 cup freshly grated yellow cheese
½ cup butter or margarine
¼ teaspoon baking powder
¾ cup sifted flour
½ teaspoon salt
½ teaspoon dry mustard or chili powder (optional)
4 teaspoons ice water

Blend room-temperature shortening with grated cheese. Sift dry ingredients together. Blend into cheese mixture alternately with the water, 1 teaspoon at a time. Chill well. Roll out like pie dough. Cut into strips 6 inches by ¼ inch. Bake at 350 degrees on an ungreased cookie sheet till just light brown, about 8 to 10 minutes, but watch carefully after first 5 minutes. So rich they burn easily. Use a broad spatula for transferring on and off cookie sheet. *Makes 18 to 24.*

TARTARE SANDWICH

Dear Nan: A number of years ago my husband had a "cannibal sandwich" made out of raw ground meat. Did you ever hear of anything like that? If so, what would the recipe be? Is it safe to eat uncooked meat? —UTICA, NEW YORK.

I have not only heard of these sandwiches, but I have eaten some in the past. I have always known them as "tartares"—a derivation from the wild Tartar tribes of Asia.

The ingredients are simple: the very best lean ground beef you can buy, seasoned with plenty of salt and pepper and chopped onion. Then spread mixture on moist rye bread. Or sometimes the ground beef is spread, plain, right on the bread. Then comes the salt and pepper and a large slice of raw onion, or a dash of Worcestershire goes on the meat.

There is also a German version that calls for a little sweet pickle juice mixed into the meat with chopped onion. This gets formed into thick patties with a pretty good depression made in the center of each one into which a raw egg yolk is dropped. The trick here is to refrigerate them for at least an hour before shifting them onto rye bread. In fact, any "cannibal sandwich" should be quite cold.

I have known the egg yolk to be mixed right into the meat, too. With green onions and pickles on the side—and a stein of German brew—you'd swear you were right back in Munich.

There is also a blender version of tartare that gets

spread on crackers. A pretty hot cocktail item in some circles. For that one you put about ½ pound good ground beef in the blender, along with 1 or 2 of those tiny hot red peppers Mexicans love so well, 2 teaspoons Worcestershire, ½ an onion, and at least ¼ teaspoon black pepper. Salt to taste. Try ½ teaspoon first, but you may want to add more. These things have to be well seasoned or they aren't good. Spin mixture to a good spreading consistency. I like to add a little finely chopped green pepper after that (not blenderized) because it looks so much more appetizing.

In making any of these, I wouldn't settle for ready-packaged ground beef, no matter how lean it looked. I would select my own piece of beef, hand it to the butcher, and pay for personal grinding. A USDA inspection stamp should be on the original beef piece.

HASH PIZZABURGERS

Dear Nan: My youngsters say that when they were visiting a friend's school cafeteria in another state they ate something called "hash pizzaburgers," and they were just crazy about them. I know they are made with canned corned beef hash but I can't seem to duplicate them to suit. Would you know what they could be? —ALBUQUERQUE, NEW MEXICO.

They are a school rage with all sorts of variations. Really are good, too! All you have to do is toast split hamburger buns, spread them with a good layer of canned corned beef hash, and top that generously with shredded yellow cheese and a generous blob of pizza sauce. On top of that goes chopped green pepper, onion, or olives. Then a good sprinkling of grated Parmesan cheese from the shaker. Cover with the top bun. Put them in a 400-degree oven until they are hot all the way through. Takes about 10 minutes. If you will lay a sheet of foil over the top of the pan, just loosely, it keeps the buns from drying out too much.

BRAIN SANDWICHES

Dear Nan: After diligent search and various means of trying to get a recipe for brain sandwiches as fixed in restaurants, I am turning to you as a last resort. We are all so fond of these sandwiches that my nieces and nephews, sons and daughters-in-law, head for the restaurants here that serve them as soon as they come to town. Do you suppose any of your readers know how to fix brain sandwiches? What mixture is added, how to prepare them for eating, all the rest of it.

If you can tell us, three generations will be made very happy. There is no generation gap in this department!

—EVANSVILLE, INDIANA.

Calf, lamb, or pork brain sandwiches are real soul food all the way. Many restaurants do feature them. Readers contributed a variety of recipes but they are basically the same.

Soak 1 pound of brains in 1 quart of water, with 1 tablespoon salt added. Drain after 15 minutes, rinse well in clear water, remove membrane. Drop into a colander to drain completely. Mash brains with a potato masher or use your hands. Beat 2 whole eggs. In another bowl mix 1 cup of flour, 1 teaspoon baking powder, salt and pepper to suit. Beat this into the egg mixture. Add brains to the batter. If mixture is not thick enough to plop nicely from a tablespoon, add a little more flour. Fry in plenty of hot shortening but only over medium heat so they get done through. Brown on both sides and drain on paper toweling but serve while piping hot.

ORANGE BUTTER

Dear Nan: How about a recipe for orange butter? I've eaten it in Florida at a restaurant near Lake Wales and it's delicious. I have never seen it in any of the stores.

—ESCONDIDO, CALIFORNIA.

Nor have I. Recipes for this type of butter—not an orange butter frosting or the sauce that uses melted butter—are conspicuous by their absence, but I managed to track down just one. Whether it is exactly like what you tasted is a moot question, but it should be close.

Cream ½ pound real butter with 2 tablespoons powdered sugar. When well creamed, blend in grated rind of 1 medium-sized orange and 1 lemon, plus a dash of salt and the juice of ½ orange. After your first try, you may want to use the juice from a whole orange. They don't all have the same juice yield. Store, covered, in the refrigerator. *Makes ½ pound.*

The use of sugar in the recipe may sound strange, but it's needed to offset the pungency of the grated rinds. Any which way, it is a great spread for hot biscuits or toast.

ALMOND BUTTER

Dear Nan: Here is one I have made for many years with many compliments. Cream ½ pound sweet butter with ½ pound sugar. Add a dozen blanched almonds, finely chopped, ½ dozen macaroons dried and chopped (optional), the grated peel of 2 oranges, and 1 ounce brandy or Cointreau. I use the latter. Blend to a smooth paste.

—SAN DIEGO, CALIFORNIA.

EGG BUTTER

Dear Nan: My great-aunt used to make something she called "egg butter" and we kids loved it on hot biscuits or even plain bread as an after-school treat. All I can remember is that it had a lot of molasses in it but no actual butter at all.

—RALEIGH, NORTH CAROLINA.

I had to reach way back into an old 1897 cookbook for this one and directions are pretty sketchy, but I'm sure this is what you are looking for: "To 3 well-beaten eggs add 1 pint of molasses, orleans or sorghum. Boil till thick. Excellent." If you would like to experiment with a lesser amount, add 2 small eggs or 1 large egg to just ½ pint (8 ounces) molasses. Refrigerate.

A California lady once asked for this egg butter, too, remembering it as quite delicious, but she also recalled that spices had been used in it—cinnamon, cloves, or nutmeg. Maybe a bit of all 3. Nothing said about spices in the recipe I've unearthed, but then, I imagine every woman had her own variation to suit family tastes—probably a few shakes of this and that.

17 / A bevy of beverages

A frequent question directed to me is: "Why can't I make a good cup of coffee? It doesn't taste nearly as good as what I get at drugstore counters!"

Far be it from me to tell anybody what brand or how much to use. Tastes differ too much. Some like it strong enough to walk on; others brew it just a shade stronger than tea. I'm an in-betweener. But once you hit a brand you like, give it the help it needs.

An awful lot of trouble—and some awful coffee—can come from the kind of pot you use. Glass coffee makers do a superb job. I know some topflight chefs who won't have anything else for their home use. They admit the breakage rate can be high but feel it's worth it. Porcelain and stainless steel also do good jobs. Aluminum—and that's what many a percolator is made of—reacts chemically to coffee, and often produces a yukky taste. Then there is a thing about thermostatically controlled perkers. The first cup may be great, but as the liquid cools down that thermostat starts it perking again. Keeps it hot but it can get pretty whammy.

Another point in flavor trouble is not keeping the pot absolutely clean day in and day out. It's so easy just to rinse the thing, but if you do that for several days in a row, those well-known coffee oils build up a residue even if it isn't visible to the naked eye. Do that long enough and you'll eventually get a sourish off-flavor for sure. If you've skipped scouring the pot for some time, it's a good idea to fill it with cold water, toss in 2 teaspoons of baking soda, and let it set awhile. Soda is a great freshener. In all these years, no one has come up with anything to beat it. And it's hard to match a good sunshine-and-wind airing for your coffeepot.

Still another trouble spot can be the water in a given area. Much of our tap water is now chemically treated. That does make a difference. The alternative is to use distilled water, and that can run into money.

A while back, I laughed like crazy when I read that the Coffee Brewing Institute was still searching for a way to make "the perfect cup." It admitted coffee still didn't taste as good as what grandma used to make, even with constant testing and researching.

My grandma used a blue granite pot lined in white. It was a plain old pot, not a percolator or a drip type. She even tossed the loose coffee into the boiling water and took it from the heat right away to "let it settle." At the same time she tossed in a couple of eggshells—uncooked ones. That made the clearest coffee you ever saw, with little golden beads floating on it. She also ground her own coffee, fresh for each potful, in a thing-umajig with a glass jar that hung on the wall and was turned with a side-winder. Many coffee fanatics still do grind their own, but usually in a blender with a powerful enough motor to handle the load.

You can do the next best thing. Keep your ready-ground fresh. The minute you open that vacuum-sealed can, empty the contents into a glass jar with a screw-type lid. The minute that vacuum seal is broken, the best of coffees start to deteriorate, even with those fetching plastic snap-on lids—coffee oils, you know. Refrigerate the glass jar.

PUNCH

Dear Nan: Could you give us a good nonalcoholic party punch that doesn't take an awful lot of expense or items? We need this one for a high school prom.

—GREEN BAY, WISCONSIN.

I don't know of a better one than this! The flavor is fine without being too sweet and you'll find everything at any grocery. Combine 1 large can pineapple juice, 1 large can apricot nectar, and 1 quart of ginger ale—all well chilled beforehand. Pour over a block of ice in a punch bowl. This fills about 32 punch cups, but remember that people will be coming back for refills. Even the pineapple and ginger ale make a nice combo without the apricot. Most stores in a community will make an agreement with you to take back any unused items when they know it's a school affair.

APPLEJACK

Dear Nan: Please settle an argument. Is there a difference between apple cider and applejack?
—ELMHURST, ILLINOIS.

And how! Applejack may start out being cider but, either through distilling or freezing, can wind up so potent that an injudicious amount can have you running through the snow barefoot searching for violets. Some farm friends of mine with a big apple orchard tell me they do their applejack this way: They make their own homemade cider and then, when they're sure they are in for a considerable cold spell, they put the barrel outside to freeze. When it is solid, or appears to be, they poke a sturdy pole or ax handle into the center and hit liquid. The part that hasn't frozen gets siphoned off; it is practically pure alcohol.

There is an applejack brandy or liquor, too. It has a very smooth, pleasing flavor.

FROZEN DAIQUIRIS

Dear Nan: Have you ever heard of making a sort of frozen daiquiri with the pink lemonade frozen concentrate? A friend of mine tells me you don't even need a blender.
—COSTA MESA, CALIFORNIA.

Ah, yes, I know all about that one. There was that sudden 1967 Chicago blizzard—thirty inches of snow yet, with drifts over your head—and I was trapped out in the suburbs. I didn't have a prayer of getting a cab so I could make a plane or train back home. Nothing was running. With no place to go and no way to go and no way to get there, the neighbors decided we might as well enjoy the whole thing, and pool what we had by way of food and drink for a real bang-up indoor picnic. I had never tasted this beverage before, but it was the hit of the evening. Watch it, though. It's sneaky. Tastes as innocent as pop.

The most popular version is a 1-2-3 count: 1 can undiluted frozen pink lemonade concentrate, 2 cans vodka, 3 cans water. Mix that all together and pour into shallow freezer trays. The vodka keeps it from freezing solid. When you're ready to use it, break the mixture into chunks with a fork. If you have a blender, that's the easy way for the next step. Just give it a brief buzz, so the stuff pours into glasses like slush. Otherwise you have to wait a couple of minutes before whipping it with a fork or an electric beater. Use a good big bowl if you do that, so you won't get any splash-up.

There are people who sniff at the 1-2-3 proportion as being on the sissy side, so they reverse the amount of vodka and water: 1 can concentrate, 2 cans water, and 3 cans vodka.

You can make this thing with rum, too. A lot of people like it that way. Yes, you can use other frozen fruit concentrates—something like orange or a lemon-orange mixture—but nothing as sweet as grape.

WINE

I had no idea what I was getting into when I first hunted up an asked-for recipe for homemade dandelion wine. My Swiss grandfather had always made it, but all I could remember was that it was a beautiful golden color—just like liquid sunshine. I had no sooner printed an answer to the first wine request than the others came flocking in. For grape, elderberry, rhubarb, heaven knows what all. Some were from ministers in rural areas with good grapes. I can only trust they were used purely for sacramental purposes.

Grape Wine

20 pounds grapes　　　　　　　10 cups sugar
5 quarts boiling water

Wash and pick over grapes. Mash them thoroughly in a stone crock. Add boiling water and let stand 3 days and 3 nights. Strain through a bag made of cheesecloth or thin old towel or sheeting. Put juice back in crock. Now add sugar and cover crock again. Let stand till fermentation has stopped (when it quits bubbling and "singing"). Skim off scum, strain juice, bottle tightly with corks or closures recommended by suppliers of homemade wine gadgets. If you use corks, seal bottles well with sealing wax.

Currant, Blackberry, or Elderberry Wine

Same procedure as Grape Wine.

Dandelion Wine

2 quarts dandelion blooms,　　1 yeast cake
   all stem stripped away　　　 1 lemon (small) cut into
2 quarts cold water　　　　　　　 pieces
2 pounds sugar

Put flowers in a large crock and pour cold water over them. Let stand 3 days and 3 nights. Strain through cloth. Add sugar, yeast, and lemon. Let stand 4 days and 4 nights. Strain again and bottle. This should be made in a cool place to prevent too-fast fermentation.

Rhubarb Wine

Bruise or press 5 pounds of rhubarb stalks. Add 1 gallon of water and let stand 3 days. Pour off liquid. For every 4 quarts juice, add 3 pounds sugar. In 3 or 4 days, fermentation will have stopped. Pour off liquid into a cask and let stand 11 to 12 months. Then it should be "racked off" and more sugar added if it is not sweet enough. The lady who gave me this recipe couldn't say how much—just pretty well according to taste, depending on whether you want a dry or an extrasweet wine.

Rhubarb wine is best made in the spring when stalks are fresh and new. Of course, if you have such rhubarb in the freezer and it is unsweetened, you could start with that.

Then I got into "balloon wine." I had never heard of it until a pert little neighbor told me about it and brought me a generous sample. It really is a fun thing to try, and it does make a nice little wine.

Betty Smith's Frozen Grape Juice or Balloon Wine

Absolute simplicity from start to finish. No special equipment needed unless you count the balloon. It turns out a perfectly gorgeous ruby shade.

2 6-ounce cans frozen grape juice	¼ cup lukewarm water
5 cups sugar	1 strong balloon—ten-cent variety
¼ teaspoon granulated yeast	1 gallon jug

Mix the yeast with the ¼ cup lukewarm water. Thaw the frozen grape juice and empty into a large bowl. Add the sugar. Stir frequently to dissolve well. Add the yeast mixture. Using a funnel, pour it into a small-necked gallon jug. A vinegar container is ideal. Fill the jug the rest of the way with just lukewarm water to within 1 inch of the neck of the jug. Now comes the balloon. You do not blow it up. Just fasten it to the opening as a cap. Set in a dark and fairly cool place for 5 weeks. A fairly cool corner of the house is okay. As the wine matures, the balloon fills with air. When all the air leaves the balloon, your wine is ready.

At least the balloon is supposed to go down, but people from various areas began writing, "My wine was started weeks ago and the balloon hasn't gone down a bit! Is it ruined? What did I do wrong?"

I went back to my little neighbor for a fast conference. She had made separate jugs of wine over a long period of time, so she could assure me, "Sometimes the balloon inflates all the way, sometimes it doesn't. No worry. If it doesn't deflate in 5 or 6 weeks' time, un-balloon the jug and cap it. The wine is ready." If your first jug took longer than that for the balloon to deflate, it is not ruined.

When that recipe first hit print, the mail came flooding in from all over the country from people who had questions. We printed up extra copies by the thousands. Stores were puzzled as to the sudden run on frozen grape juice, balloons, and vinegar in gallon sizes only. Since then I have suggested you can get empty gallon jugs, for free, from root beer stands or drugstores that still have a soda fountain.

Then came more questions.

The balloon on my wine is so big I am afraid it is going to burst. What do I do if it does?

I have never known a balloon to burst except in one instance where a four-year-old helped matters along with a pin.

My balloon never inflated at all. What did I do wrong?

Undoubtedly used too hot water for dissolving the yeast. That kills the action at once, same as it would in bread making. The water should be barely lukewarm.

My wine looks ready but there is some sediment in the bottom of the jug. Will that hurt anything?

No. Some sediment is normal. Gently pour or siphon the wine off into smaller containers without disturbing the sediment. Wash the jug well before using again.

Now that my wine is in the making, I am worried that the alcoholic content might be too high. Is there any way I can tell?

Only with the use of a hydrometer. You can buy these from wine-making equipment supply houses.

Chianti-Type Wine

Dear Nan: You've given me so many good hints that by way of some exchange I am sending in a very simple, inexpensive recipe for a Chianti-type wine that also has a lovely rose color, not as deep red as real Chianti but excellent with meats and Italian foods.

Mix 2 cups Welch's unsweetened grape juice with 4 cups sugar in a wide-mouthed gallon jar. Add 1 whole package dry yeast (3 teaspoons or ¼ ounce), and fill the jar with cool tap water to within 1 inch of the top. Cover with a layer of cheesecloth and several thicknesses of newspaper. Allow to stand in a cool, dark place for 5 weeks, or until the wine is clear. Siphon clear wine into quart bottles and cap.

—MURRAY, KENTUCKY.

Beet Wine

Dear Nan: By any chance, do you have a recipe for beet wine? I lost mine and now can't remember proportions. You boiled beets, used the liquid, put it in a crock, spread toast with yeast, put this on top of the liquid, and let it stand awhile. Then you added raisins and sugar. It is a pretty ruby color but turns a beautiful amber as it ages.

—HALVERSON, MINNESOTA.

Never having made any, I had to do some digging, and chose a recipe I feel is reliable and complete.

Cook 5 pounds of beets in a gallon of water till tender. Strain the liquid and add enough boiling water to again make a gallon. Pour into a stone crock. Add 1 pound seedless raisins and 3 pounds sugar, stirring to dissolve. Cool to lukewarm. Spread 1 cake yeast on a slice of toast and float in the crock. Let set 8 days. Strain, let set 4 days. Strain again and bottle. Let set with caps loose till the wine suits your taste, then tighten the corks. Makes 4 bottles (⅘ quart) plus a partially filled bottle for tasting and checking.

I had other suggestions from makers of beet wine. Several people add about ¼ teaspoon black pepper to the mixture. Others call for the addition of three sliced oranges. One lady always spreads the yeast on rye bread, makes sure to turn the bread yeast side down. Grinding the raisins can be a good idea.

Many makers of homemade wines agree that the wine is perfectly drinkable in just a few weeks or months, but it will always taste better after it has aged 2 years. One caution: Do not cork bottles tightly until all signs of fermentation or fizzing have stopped.

NOTE: Federal regulations state that up to 200 gallons of wine per year may be made by "the head of the household" only, served to the family only, not sold or given away. The only requirement is that you fill out Form 1541 and send that to the Alcohol Tax Unit of your local Bureau of Internal Revenue. You may obtain the forms from them. As far as the federal government is concerned, there is no cost involved, but some states have individual rulings requiring a small license fee.

The liquid measure used in any of the wine recipes here is American Standard; 128 ounces comprises the gallon stateside. Readers from Canada, where the Imperial gallon measure is used, take note.

18 / Tips for the time and money saver mob

If you've gone back to an outside job now that the children are in school, don't expect smooth sailing until you get some sort of routine established.

You can't expect to keep the house in apple-pie order, as it was when you were home every day. You are not going to have as much time for home-baked items and elaborate casseroles. When the kids come down with something just at the time the work load at the office is heaviest, make sure you have planned for this ahead of time. Have someone reliable to take over at home during those situations.

Taking on two jobs takes planning and the willing help of every member of the family, or you will be like the frantic lady who wrote:

> Dear Nan: I went back to work three months ago and at first it was fun but this past month has been terrible. The house is a mess, I'm too tired to cook decently, the kids are wild, and I am so tired and cranky I snap at them. Unless I can find some better way of organizing my time and energy, I am afraid I am going to have to give up my job. How do other women manage so nicely? Do you or your readers have any suggestions? —BILLINGS, MONTANA.

That letter made such an impact, readers rushed to give all sorts of helpful advice such as the following, which could serve as a practical blueprint for any homemaker, working away from home or not.

My family is going to remember a fairly clean house and a happy mother. So work out a plan for your own situation and set your standards where you want them. I don't have an outside job now but I have a nine-room house, plus three bathrooms, two teen-agers, lots of out-of-town company, and two demanding hobbies. I set my own standards and schedule and I seldom deviate from either. Everything has to take its turn.

My best helper is the heaviest electric broom I could buy. It does kitchen floors, halls, bathrooms, and carpeting if something is spilled. Another big helper is my blender. I really use it. I made myself learn to do almost everything with it. Then there is my freezer. I bake two of everything. Pies, cakes, casseroles. I freeze one of these.

I make a couple of short trips to the store each week, list and menu plans in hand. I also have an emergency shelf with a master list worked out for my family's likes and dislikes. My "shelf" is actually a cardboard box hidden from me in a closet so I won't use it unless absolutely necessary. It has five separate sacks with complete directions for five dinners. Then, if I am sick or delayed somewhere, one of them is used. Even my husband can and has produced a decent and nourishing meal.

I also serve three simple-to-prepare dinners on the same basis every week. And I never go to the kitchen to do a big job without also thinking of what could be cooking at the same time, such as simmering a stew or marinating something for next day.

My children help. We have some rules and we all work together for two hours on Saturday as hard and fast as we can. Talking and laughing, room to room, we do more in two hours than I could by myself in eight.

MONEY SAVERS

Dear Nan: You sound so practical, I am wondering what you do to save on the grocery bill, or don't you have to?
—HACKENSACK, NEW JERSEY.

Who doesn't? I take it you have learned to shop with list in hand to cut down impulse buying, and sail right past expensive out-of-season produce.

Never send a husband to the store all by himself. Men go hog-wild on things like bottled nuts, the newest snack cracker, or a whole ham when all you wanted was just part of one.

Casserole Pie

Here are my money-saving ideas. Line a casserole with regular pie dough. Put in fresh or frozen corn (uncooked) or canned corn. Add sliced hard-cooked eggs and about ⅓ as much diced raw potatoes as corn. Salt and pepper, add dabs of butter and enough milk so it's about ⅔ of the way to the casserole top.

Put pie dough on top, with steam vents cut through as you would for berry pie. Bake at 425 degrees for about 12 minutes. Then turn the heat back to 350 degrees for another 40 minutes. I serve either fresh green limas or home-baked beans with this. Make full use of the oven by baking a hot dessert at the same time.
—CAMPBELLTOWN, PENNSYLVANIA.

Easy Bean Soup

I do a lot of Pennsylvania Dutch cooking, some of which won't be found in any book. Here is an old one but a good one for homemade bean soup the easy way. Boil a nice piece of beef till well done and cut in small pieces. Remove any excess fat, but there should be a good bit of broth left. Add a couple of cans of boiled white navy beans and 1 can of corn, plus the beef. Let it come to a full rolling boil. Then make rivvels *by mixing 1 cup of flour with 1 beaten egg. Sprinkle into the broth by handfuls. Add salt, pepper, and celery salt to taste, and you have a good hearty soup.*

—HUMMELSTOWN, PENNSYLVANIA.

In case you live where you've never heard of *rivvels,* the literal translation in Pennsylvania Dutch is "lumps" or "flakes." They are used for thickening. You simply run the mixture through your hands or a sieve right over the soup pot so it falls in flakes. I doubt if any two people make them exactly the same way but the principle is the same. Just be sure you simmer the soup long enough so the *rivvels* are cooked through.

Sausage and Hominy Omelet

That's really a rib sticker. Put about 1 pound pork sausage links in a big skillet, add a little water, and simmer, covered, for 10 minutes. Then remove the cover and brown the sausages, after pouring off any remaining water. When sausages are browned, pour off all but about ¼ cup of the drippings. Add 1 large can drained hominy, 1 teaspoon salt, and a good sprinkling of pepper. While that heats through good and proper, beat 3 or 4 eggs with around 6 tablespoons milk. Add that to the hominy and cook very slowly till the eggs are set. Turn the whole thing out on a platter with the sausage links arranged on it any way you please. *Makes 4 servings.*

Leftovers

I am always surprised at the number of women who throw away leftover meat loaf and roast beef! They say warming up a second serving always dries out the meat. Well, I pour 1 or 2 cups of boiling water over the remains of the meat loaf before putting it in a 350-degree oven. After 15 minutes, I may pour in more water. The meat is ready to serve 10 minutes later, nice and moist.

Now, after serving beef roast, I put all the leftovers (potatoes, carrots, and fat) in a bowl to refrigerate. Next day I cut up the vegetables, put them in a skillet with the meat, and slice onion rings over the top. If you have already used the drippings to make gravy the first time, you can use 1 tablespoon each of beef gravy base and margarine in place of it. Add 1 cup pale dry sherry, the juice from 1 can mushrooms, and 1 can steak mushroom sauce or any favorite meat sauce. Simmer till the onions are limp; add water as the sauce gets thick. Take out the meat and onions. Add 1 teaspoon salt and the same amount of herb seasoning. Stir. Add the separately sautéed mushrooms. Serve over the meat. P.S. Omitting the sherry will be a disaster! It won't taste the same. —MINNEAPOLIS, MINNESOTA.

Hamburger and Potato Bake

I think you might enjoy one of my favorite budget beaters, a meat and potato dish, since it is also so easy and a little different. Peel several potatoes, then either cut them in half or in thinner slices, as you prefer. Season hamburger meat to taste, make thick patties either large or small. Salt and pepper the potatoes, put them between 2 of the hamburger patties, wrap in foil, and bake about 30 minutes, according to size. They are so tasty and the juice from the meat is still in the foil and through the potatoes.

—FORT WAYNE, INDIANA.

The lady forgot to mention oven temperature, so I tried at about 350 degrees and it did fine. I sliced my potatoes lengthwise, about ½ inch thick. Or you could slice them quite thin and use more than 1 layer. Then they'd surely get done through. It's always a simple matter to check up on what's happening by opening one foil-wrapped pack for a look. It is best to use heavy-duty foil for this so it won't accidentally pierce and let the juice run out. More than once I have washed such foil, patted it dry, and reused it for something else another time.

Fried Bologna and Potatoes

Dear Nan: Would you believe—frying thick bologna slices that have been dipped in fritter batter or breading mixture seals in the juice and makes fine eating? My mother used to do this forty years ago and I still do. She used to batter-fry thick slices of raw potato at the same time and it makes a great meal. —LOS ANGELES, CALIFORNIA.

HOW TO REDUCE GROCERY BILLS

Here are my ways to beat the grocery bill and still eat well. If you ever find yourself with leftover hot dogs, cut them into diagonal slices, then put them in a double boiler with a can of cream of celery soup, undiluted. Add any leftover vegetables, the more the merrier, with a little pickle relish and its juice for some zip. Serve hot over toast.

Leftover cooked dried beans need never go begging. Mash them down, add 1 beaten egg, freshly ground pepper, and enough soft bread crumbs to hold the mixture together. Form into patties, coat with dry crumbs. Fry in a small amount of bacon drippings. Very good with eggs or a cold meat platter.

Never before have I passed out our family dressing recipe, but here goes. I use equal parts of stale white bread, corn bread, and biscuits. (Never, never put sugar in corn bread; it ruins it.) For every 3 quarts of the combined breads, use 1 large onion, 1 beaten egg, sage to taste, chopped celery leaves, and parsley with enough broth to moisten. Any kind of broth will do. Fowl is generally our favorite, but we like pork and beef broth, too. Venison broth is delicious if you are lucky enough to get it. When I make this dressing, I do a 15-quart container full to the brim. After it is divided and baked in separate pans, I freeze it. This assures me of dressing ready for any occasion. —LIBERTY, MISSOURI.

Now there is a lady who is just full of bright ideas for making prosaic foods taste great! The idea of 3 kinds of bread in the dressing is excellent. It makes for an entirely different flavor than you would get from just 1. Those celery leaves do what even celery itself couldn't do for flavor.

Stretching the Dollar

I will always treasure this next letter.

I have never written a newspaper before but I couldn't refrain from answering your piece on stretching the dollar. I raised seven children through a depression, and we didn't live off the county either.

Did you ever hear of salmon soup? Make it just as you would oyster soup and it tastes like it. I use the pink salmon. Also learn to bake your own bread and you save plenty. You know how much bread seven kids can do away with. Even working, I always managed to do that at night or on weekends. Cook your own potatoes. They're cheaper. Buy chicken wings and backs to cook with your own homemade noodles. With slaw, that makes a good meal even children love. As you say, making your own soup from what would otherwise be tossed out beats any other kind.

I am seventy-six years young and still work as a clerk every day. I am healthy and so are my grown children—no tooth or eye trouble—so eating plain, home-cooked food didn't hurt any of us.

My other "savers" include not washing until I have a full load, taking care to turn off lights as I leave a room, making sure the faucet doesn't drip. From one who knows how to stretch a dollar. —HOPKINS, MINNESOTA.

I have found these ideas work successfully:

Corned beef: No one should destroy the broth after simmering this meat. Start with cabbage wedges, plus the leftover meat that maybe isn't enough for a full meal. Add carrots, diced potatoes, and onions for a quick New England dinner.

Sausage: Browned ground sausage mixed with cans of pork-and-beans and beans-in-chili-sauce makes a hearty dish. The sausage gives a different flavor from that of ground beef and the two colors of beans go nicely together.

Stew meat: I purchase a few cents' worth of beef chunks, simmered till very tender, the broth then thickened for gravy. This is excellent with noodles.

Also, I use a pressure canner all summer. I have used bits from a very meaty ham bone, cooked them up with a big pot of navy beans, then pressure-canned them into pints. This way, I have only a pint of beans at a time without having a huge mess left over.

If a meal seems to be short of protein, I add a slice or so of cheese to the top of mashed potatoes, or a cheese sauce for diced cooked potatoes. Deviled eggs help on protein. Put sliced hard-cooked eggs on top of macaroni and cheese, replace the cover, and let the eggs heat through.

There are many vegetables, such as scalloped cabbage, that can go high protein with cheese. Maybe you have seen all these ideas, but they work for me and might for others trying to keep their heads above water.

—INDEPENDENCE, MISSOURI.

Good girl! Know or not, we all need reminders.

Stuffed Peppers

We hadn't had stuffed peppers at our house for ever so long, much as we love them. Then my husband brought in a whole sackful of green peppers he'd bought at a bargain. So I had to use them up.

I didn't have time to fiddle with an honest-to-gosh recipe. I just remembered how many requests I get for "stuffed peppers without any rice or macaroni in them!"

So I dragged out a chunk of ground beef from the freezer —about a pound or maybe a little more—put it in my biggest skillet with the lid on, and set the heat on low. That way, it cooks and thaws gradually without sticking or too much fast browning, and I can pour off any excess fat as I go. Then I added some chopped onion and a small can of tomato paste along with a little water. It has to be paste, not soup or sauce, for this one, or it will be too runny to make good pepper stuffing.

I really hadn't made up my mind till then what other seasonings I would use. I seldom do a dish exactly the same way twice in a row. My eye lit on a package of dry spaghetti sauce seasoning in the cupboard—about 1 ounce—and it struck me that should work just fine. In it went.

When the mixture had simmered down to a good thickness, I cut the peppers in half lengthwise, simmered them in water to cover for just 5 minutes. This gets them soft enough to cut with a fork, but they still hold their shape nicely and are not loppy to the taste. Line them up in a shallow pan just big enough to hold them steady. Fill with the hamburger goo, and slice some yellow cheese over the top. I stuck mine under the broiler then, just till the cheese had melted. *Fills about 6 pepper halves.*

Kansas Chowder

I notice your readers keep asking for casseroles or one-dish meals that don't cost too much. Here is a dish I devised and I am happy to share it with everyone.

We usually make a large electric skilletful and sometimes—just sometimes—some is left. That warms up well. We had no name for it, so we call it Kansas chowder. Our small grandson, while eating it one day, remarked, "Well, Kansas has its bird and its sunflower and now it has its own chowder."

You can vary it by adding other things in the refrigerator, but this is the basic recipe I concocted. Also, you can add more of some of the ingredients.

Just lightly brown 1 pound hamburger in the skillet. I pour off excess fat. In another kettle I cook 3 diced potatoes, 3 diced carrots (not too fine), 3 stalks celery, and 1 onion. I cook those for about 10 minutes in not too much water. Season the meat with a good dash of garlic salt and onion salt. Add the vegetables, cooking water and all. Now add a can of Cheddar cheese soup.

Cover and simmer on low for ½ hour or more. This holds well when a meal is delayed. Just before serving, it is nice to lay several slices of American cheese on top. Makes 4 servings. With fruit or a salad, this is a satisfying meal.

—RICHMOND, KANSAS.

Fried Cornmeal Mush

How come you've never mentioned cornmeal mush in your discussion of economical foods? I know there are people who say they just can't get it well browned when they fry the slices unless they flour it, dip it in egg, or something. I have found a way around that difficulty.

I reasoned that, when refrigerated mush is placed in hot fat, condensation occurs and the mush won't brown until moisture is evaporated. I also remembered that when my grandmother prepared the fried mush we ate with butter and syrup for breakfast, she would cook the mush in the evening. Then she poured it into a loaf pan to get cold and set. The pan would stand on the kitchen table overnight and would be room temperature the next morning when it was fried. There was never any trouble with browning or spattering.

Now I occasionally buy a "block" of mush at the grocer's and keep it in the refrigerator until the night before I plan to fry it. I then place it on the kitchen counter. The next morning it is room temperature all the way through. I open the wrapper, remove the mush, blot the block dry with paper toweling. I then fry it in hot fat. It is nicely browned on both sides in about 10 minutes.

My mother-in-law used to prepare a similar dish by the unglamorous name of scrapple. I don't remember her proportions of cornmeal and the broth she used. She simmered neck and backbones—I am sure those were pork—for several hours, then removed the meat from the bones, leaving meat bits in the broth. She combined that with cornmeal and salt until it cooked to a thick mush. Then she poured it into an oblong pan to cool and set. When sliced and fried, it was very tasty. We ate it plain or buttered.

—KANSAS CITY, KANSAS.

That is also known as pannhaas or Philadelphia scrapple. If you can find anything more "staff of life" than that, I have yet to see it. And what a budget stretcher without making you feel the least bit deprived.

Philadelphia Scrapple

Use about 4 cups of the pot liquor plus 2 cups cornmeal and the meat scraps. If you'll add a good dash of pepper and about ½ teaspoon powdered sage, all the better.

19 / Low-calorie and sneezer-wheezer crowd

With the get-skinny-quick cult so prevalent in the land, it's no wonder people fall for many of the trick diet fads sweeping the country. They never end. A lot of them make the most glowing—if completely impossible—promises that "this is the way!"

It has long been my contention that not all diets work the same for all people. There is the matter of individual metabolism, activity, digestion, and general makeup. But there are some do's and don'ts that work for us all.

DIET DELIGHTS

Dear Nan: I have heard that anyone on a low-fat, low-cholesterol diet should strip all the skin from chicken pieces before cooking. Is this true? If so, how do you get the skin off without tearing into the chicken meat? Does it take some sort of special knife or gadget? —BURLINGTON, VERMONT.

Not at all. When the chicken is cut up, just grab hold of the skin and peel back. The chicken breasts and thighs are easiest to handle; drumsticks can be a little contrary. You may have to split the skin on one side and at the base of the leg, but you do get rid of quite a sizable amount of fat with skin removal. If you freeze chicken pieces, leave the skin intact until you are ready to use because it keeps the white meat of the bird from drying out during storage.

Elaine's Terrific Chicken Casserole

You will need 2 whole chicken breasts, 4 chicken thighs, 1 package frozen broccoli spears, 1 package frozen asparagus spears (whole or cut), 2 cans cream of mushroom or cream of chicken soup, 4 ounces mayonnaise, 1 to 2 teaspoons curry powder, 4 to 5 slices whole wheat bread, a good pinch of rubbed sage, and some canned grated Parmesan cheese.

Thaw the frozen vegetables. Oven-dry the bread slices. Then tear or crush them into small bits. Skin the chicken pieces and halve the breasts. Place a layer of the two vegetables in a deep casserole and a layer of chicken on top. Then add a second layer of vegetables and the rest of the chicken. Heat the soup, undiluted. Stir in the mayonnaise, curry, and sage. (The amounts of curry and sage can vary widely according to individual tastes.) Pour the soup mixture over casserole contents, cover with bread crumbs, and sprinkle with grated cheese. Bake at 400 degrees for not less than 45 minutes or until chicken is tender. Fruit salad goes well with this. *Makes 4 servings.*

If you prefer, you may substitute frozen spinach for all or part of the other vegetables. If you don't care for sage flavor, use a mixed poultry seasoning.

Low-Calorie Hamburgers

About the only meat I ever fry is hamburgers, but the way I do them they really aren't fried at all. I start the patties in a cold skillet over low heat. No fat is needed. That's something a lot of people just don't understand. After all, the drive-ins use only barely greased grills for theirs. As the fat of the meat slowly cooks out, I pour it off before it has a chance to soak back in. The patties eventually brown enough. With very thick patties, I may put the lid on for a few minutes to get them done through.

Low-Calorie Fried Potatoes

Here is how I more or less first kidded my spouse into thinking he was getting something akin to real fried potatoes. No, they aren't exactly like real fries, but good enough. Slice cold boiled potatoes about ¼ inch thick and line them up in a shallow oblong baking pan with the slices slightly overlapping. Pour in just a little milk to keep them from sticking and brush the slices ever so lightly with melted margarine, salt, and pepper. Put the whole thing under the broiler quite close to the heat. They brown just beautifully. If you want them brown on both sides, you have to turn them, one by one, but I seldom bother. We liked these so well the first time we began doing our potatoes that way quite often.

MOCK SOUR CREAM

Some of my readers have asked how to make diet-type sour cream out of cottage cheese for use as a low-calorie dip for fresh vegetables, relish, or pickle snacks.

It may surprise you to discover that there isn't much difference in calories between the cream-style cottage cheese and the dairy-type sour cream. Four tablespoons of sour cream is approximately 104 calories. The same amount of cream-style cottage cheeses rates at 87 calories. In some areas there is a diet-type cottage cheese, small curd and dry.

Dear Nan: Being diabetic, I use diet cottage cheese. It whips beautifully. I add dill weed or whatever I like for perfect sour cream. If I want to use it for whipped cream, I add a little vanilla and liquid sweetener and use it on fruit. Delicious! —ATCHISON, KANSAS.

I blenderize ⅔ cup dry-type cottage cheese with just ¼ cup water and 1 teaspoon lemon juice. You can add a little salt if you like. You can do all sorts of variations with that base mixture. For instance, sweeten it with 1 teaspoon granulated

sugar substitute, add 3 tablespoons lemon juice and a dash
of ginger. Mint leaves are a nice addition for a fresh fruit
cup. Another idea is to add chopped or grated cucumbers,
parsley, radishes, and tarragon vinegar in place of the lemon
juice. Serve over tuna fish salad or cold cooked green beans.
                                    —NASHVILLE, TENNESSEE.

I am so pleased because I found in using the cottage cheese
dip that it also makes a good low-calorie, eggless salad dressing. I have one daughter who is unable to eat mayonnaise-
type dressings because they contain egg, and another daughter who cannot eat them because she has to watch her
calories. Trying to use a French-type dressing in place of
mayonnaise just doesn't taste as good in sandwich fillings or
potato salad.

    Today I mixed about ½ cup of the dip with my regular
potato salad (minus egg, of course) and the allergic daughter was delighted. Then I mixed ½ cup of the dip with hard-
boiled eggs and tuna for the other daughter. She enjoyed it
just as much as the high-calorie mixture and at the same
time was eating a high-protein, lower-calorie food.
                          —NORTH KANSAS CITY, MISSOURI.

YOGURT

Dear Nan: I like yogurt and was wondering if that made from
cow's milk is as rich in vitamin B as the yogurt made from
goat milk. A while back someone wrote to tell you how rich
goat yogurt is. Is that true with other milk? I have asked
some dieticians but they don't seem to be able to give me
an answer.

                                        —BONHAM, TEXAS.

I am reliably informed there is no appreciable difference between the vitamin content of the two milks. Butterfat content
can be something else again. It varies with the breed of the goat,
and some are even crossbred to produce higher butterfat content for the making of some excellent cheeses and butters. Goat

milk is considered more easily digestible because the fat globules are smaller and the curd softer, making it excellent for those with tricky digestions as well as infants who cannot tolerate cow's milk. But the commercial-type yogurts we buy now at dairy counters have also been processed for easy digestion. The original yogurt, made by the Turks and the Persians, was undoubtedly the goat type.

ADVICE TO ALLERGY SUFFERERS AND RECIPE SAMPLER

Allergies are like dandelions. They can spring up where they never were before. Then getting meals can drive the cook frantic as she tries to fix something the whole family will enjoy, but that will still keep the allergy sufferer from looking wistful because "you can't have that."

These recipes are favorites of "Let's Ask the Cook" readers because they best allow for all-family enjoyment.

Always consult your doctor on recipes and products used. Individual tolerance can differ greatly.

Common allergens are chocolate, wheat, milk, eggs, and corn. The last named may preclude the use of oils, candies, syrups, and spreads containing corn. Specialists differ in opinion but there are those who forbid anything but water-pack canned foods.

Severe corn or egg allergies may preclude the use of some brands of baking powder where cornstarch or egg white may be present. Always read labels for content. You may make your own leavening, free of both, by mixing 1⅛ teaspoons cream of tartar with ½ teaspoon baking soda for each teaspoon baking powder called for in the recipe. It should be mixed fresh each time, not in quantity for storage.

Those who are allergic to cow's milk may find they can tolerate dried or evaporated milk. It is possible to find canned goat's milk, as well as fresh, in many areas. There also are excellent milk substitutes, made from vegetable substances, at most markets. They work as well for cooking as for drinking. Milk allergy people may also find that while butter is a dairy product, it may still bring forth no annoying symptoms or illness.

Again, check with your doctor.

Many cakes, biscuits, and other baked items do almost as well with water in place of the milk called for.

Where rice flour or cornmeal is used in baked products, either will usually give a smoother texture if mixed with the liquid called for, brought to a boil, and then cooled before adding to other recipe ingredients.

Cornflake Pie Crust
(Wheat-Milk-Egg Free)

1 cup packaged cornflake crumbs
1 tablespoon granulated sugar

2 tablespoons melted margarine

Start heating oven to 350 to 375 degrees. Toss together cornflake crumbs, sugar, and margarine till evenly mixed. Use your hands for mixing if necessary. Press mixture evenly and firmly into bottom and up sides of an 8-inch pie plate. Will "stay put" better if you grease inner sides of pie pan first. Bake about 8 minutes.

Poor Man's Cake
(Egg and Milk Free)

1½ cups water, wine, or fruit juice
1 cup sugar
½ to 1 cup raisins
½ cup shortening
2 teaspoons cinnamon
½ teaspoon cloves

½ teaspoon nutmeg
½ teaspoon salt
1 teaspoon soda dissolved in 1 teaspoon warm water
2 cups sifted flour
1 teaspoon baking powder
½ cup nuts

Combine water, wine, or fruit juice with sugar, raisins, shortening, spices, and salt in a saucepan. Bring to boil. Let boil 5 minutes. Cool. Then add soda dissolved in warm water. Beat in sifted-together flour and baking powder. Add nuts. Pour into

9-by-12-by-2-inch pan or a tube pan. Bake at 350 degrees for about 30 minutes or until cake center-tests done.

Despite its title this is a rich-tasting cake, very quick and easy to put together.

Cherry Tapioca

Dear Nan: When my son was on an allergy diet, I still made a dessert he enjoyed. He could not have corn, wheat, yeast, eggs, and a number of other foods, but I did give him minute tapioca. I used the water-packed canned cherries (there is no corn syrup in water-packed fruits), drained the juice from them, and then added enough water to make 2½ cups, ¼ cup of the quick-cooking tapioca, and sugar to taste—all prepared by regular box instructions. After cooling this some, I added the drained cherries. I used quite a bit of beet sugar with it, since there are so few sweets a corn-allergic person can have. Makes 2 servings.

—KANSAS CITY, MISSOURI.

Pineapple-Pork Chop-Rice Casserole
(Wheat-Corn-Egg-Milk Free)

6 slices dietetic water-pack pineapple	1 cup raw rice
Whole cloves	2½ cups dietetic canned bouillon or turtle consommé
4 to 5 pork chops, 1 inch thick	1 teaspoon dextrose-free salt
2 tablespoons safflower or cottonseed oil, depending on allergy	Pinch of dried thyme (optional)
½ large green pepper, diced	Brown sugar, if allowed
1 large onion, chopped	Butter, if allowed
3 ribs celery, diced	

Drain pineapple, stud with cloves. Place in dish with about 3 tablespoons of the juice. Cover, let stand to absorb clove flavor. Season chops with salt and pepper. Brown in hot oil in large skillet. Remove chops. Add a little more oil to pan drippings, if necessary, to cook vegetables till soft. Then add raw rice and toss till golden color. Stir in bouillon, salt called for in recipe, thyme if used. Bring to boil. Pour into 2-quart oiled casserole. Lay browned chops on top. Cover tightly. Bake for 1 hour at 350 degrees.

Lay reserved pineapple over chops and drizzle with the juice and a light sprinkling of brown sugar, if allowed. Dot with butter and cook uncovered a few minutes longer till fruit is heated through and glazed. *Makes 4 to 5 servings.*

Family Favorite Swiss Steak
(Corn-Egg-Milk Free. Can Also Be Wheat Free)

About 2 pounds boneless chuck or round steak
4 to 5 tablespoons wheat or potato starch flour
2 tablespoons safflower or cottonseed oil
1 large onion, chopped
1 cup chopped celery
4-ounce can salt-free dietetic tomato paste with 12 ounces water added
2 teaspoons dextrose-free salt
1 teaspoon or more beet sugar
¼ teaspoon marjoram
¼ teaspoon pepper

Rub steak with chosen flour to coat well. Brown in oil on both sides. Remove steak and set aside. Sauté onion and celery in same pan just till soft, not browned. Mix tomato paste and water with seasonings and stir into pan contents. Return steak to pan and cover. Simmer very slowly for 2 hours or till meat is really tender. Remove to heated platter. Let gravy stand in pan till fat rises to top. Skim fat. Reheat gravy to boiling. Cut steak across the grain in ¼-inch slices. *Makes 6 servings.*

Nice with baked or mashed potatoes.

CITRUS

Dear Nan: Do you sometimes feel the food people are ganging up on you? I do! I have learned to live with allergies, but the hardest one to cope with is being allergic to citrus.

There are very few drinks one can buy that do not say "vitamin C added" or "citric acid added." All this must be a gimmick to sell products, because vitamin C isn't all that hard to come by. I know a lot of people would appreciate a word from you concerning citric acid.

—CLARKSVILLE, TENNESSEE.

I can appreciate your frustration. To clarify the subject, I wrote to Ellanora M. Valle, nutritionist for General Foods Kitchens. Here is her reply, which should surely go a long way toward clearing up the confusion.

From letters we've received from consumers, we believe there is confusion concerning citric acid, ascorbic acid, and vitamin C. Ascorbic acid is another word for vitamin C. Citric acid is a completely different compound, although it is present in many fruits, especially "citrus fruits," which are good sources of vitamin C. Possibly, because of this, the confusion of citric acid with ascorbic acid has resulted.

Although citric acid occurs naturally in many fruits, the citric acid used commercially in food products is normally made by a special fermentation process from sugar—generally cane or beet. During the process the citric acid is so refined it normally loses any identity of the original substance. Therefore, a person allergic to "citrus fruits" would not necessarily be allergic to the citric acid in food products.

It is possible for humans to become allergic to almost anything, and it is best to check with your doctor if you are in doubt. Only a trained allergist can test to make sure you could be allergic to citrus fruits without any allergy at all to citric acid.

Citrus Drink

Here's a delicious drink for citrus-allergic people. When my family was home, I used to make some every year. This "fruit concentrate" calls for 7 pounds of cherries or grapes, 7 pounds sugar, and 3 ounces tartaric acid. Stem fruits and seed cherries. Put in a stone jar with the tartaric. Crush fruit slightly and mix well. Next morning bring fruit to a boil and cook till soft. Strain juice through a jelly bag. Put juice back into stone jar, add sugar. Stir every day for 1 week, then put in sterilized jars without heating. Makes about 4 quarts of syrup. To serve, add a tablespoon or two to a glass of plain or carbonated water. By adding sugar to the discarded cherries and cooking slowly till thickened, you will have a nice preserve. —OTTAWA, KANSAS.

MILK

I have found that pineapple juice makes a wonderful substitute for either fresh milk or buttermilk in baking for those allergic to milk. The pineapple juice makes a slightly thicker batter than fresh milk, so you usually use a little less flour. That is a help, too, when you have to use expensive things like rice or barley flour. When you substitute water in place of the milk called for in many recipes, the result does not brown at all.

20 / Odds and ends

Sometimes questions and answers defy any category. That's how come this chapter. I have tried to put together some informative pointers and helpful hints in response to some oft-asked questions.

> *Dear Nan: Why don't husbands understand that wives can't always have dinner ready the minute they walk in the door! This attitude burns me up. Sometimes I am busy with the children at the last minute, or I've had to attend a meeting. Any suggestions? At least I feel better for having written this.* —ROCHESTER, NEW YORK.

My mother-in-law once told me that when she was a little girl on the farm and the main meal was at noon, her busy mother would sometimes look out the window and hastily turn to say, "Set the table fast, Lorie! The men are coming in from the fields!" She did this even if dinner wasn't ready at all.

Somehow the sight of a set table reassures a man that food can't be long in coming. Or try handing him a mug of hot bouillon in the living room while you get with it in the kitchen. Tell him you just read somewhere that husbands live longer if they settle down a bit with something like that before hitting solid vittles. You won't be fibbing. You just did read it—here. Never let him catch you gassing on the phone at dinnertime. And never ask him to run to the store for something you forgot.

Dear Nan: At a party the other night, we got to talking about our pet peeves and really came up with some lulus. A lot of them were about food. Do you have any along that line? —KNOXVILLE, TENNESSEE.

You have just unleashed the floodgates. If this was simply unburdening my own mind I would skip it, but I know a lot of you feel as I do and don't know what to do about it. If we pool our justifiable peeves with concerted action, who knows what we might accomplish? Never underestimate the power of the shopper. So here we go.

When it comes to prepackaged fruits and vegetables, they may have their place, but I refuse to shop where I am not also given a choice of by the pound or by the item. If I want just one lone cucumber, I don't want to be forced to buy four.

I also want a scale right by the produce department, not where I must walk halfway across the store to weigh an item. I once picked up some ready-sacked potatoes advertised as ten pounds, only to find the actual weight nearer eight. That may not happen very often but, regrettably, sometimes it does. When this happens, I make very loud noises.

Too, I wish there was a law requiring that the price of all packaged grocery items—like cereals and crackers—be stamped on the top or the front of the box, not on the bottom one time and on the side the next. Or the price might appear on such a dark background that it is almost impossible to read anyway.

These are some of my pet peeves.

Some old notions just never seem to die out. Fiction about foods gets passed from generation to generation. Here's one.

Dear Nan: My mother claims all foods should be cooled completely and without any covering before refrigerating or they will spoil. I have always done this with chicken, but is it necessary with everything?

—CHARLOTTE, NORTH CAROLINA.

Not even with chicken. That idea dates back to the days of the old-fashioned icebox, when the iceman and his horse-drawn cart might not show up every day and you hoarded that chunk of ice anxiously to make it last. Otherwise, you were in trouble unless you lived on a farm with a deep, cool well.

It doesn't hurt to let food cool down a little bit, loosely protected with waxed papers. Otherwise, get it into refrigeration as fast as possible, or you may be in for a bad case of the galloping collywobbles.

Dear Nan: Just what is meant by gourmet cooking? If it's what I take it to be, why is so much said about it when so few of us can afford it? —CORPUS CHRISTI, TEXAS.

Believe me, it isn't all truffles and champagne, rare passion fruit, and flaming shish kebabs. Sometimes I get so fed up with the term—as well as what is palmed off as "gourmet"—I vow never to use it again. Originally, a gourmet was an expert taster of wines. Then the word came to mean "one who appreciates fine foods, the delicacies of the table."

What is fine food? It can be any food prepared with care, love, and imagination. I have seen priceless ingredients so carelessly handled they wound up as a mess. Then I have known humble foods—my grandmother's crock-baked beans and white bread done in a coal range—fit for royalty.

Dear Nan: A year or so ago, we had a speaker from a national meat producer who said women are no longer interested in recipes, only in ready-packaged foods, because there is no prestige in cooking. Now, every time I clip a recipe that sounds good, I feel as though I must be something left over from the dark ages —CLEVELAND, OHIO.

No prestige? Maybe not, but it sure beats starvation. Besides, who is the most popular gal at any covered-dish dinner? The one who has brought either the newest casserole dish or an old one with a new twist. Who is the hostess with the mostest? The one who has you licking your chops in anticipation because you know you are going to eat very well indeed. Heaven knows how many job promotions have been decided, how many successful business deals put over, because the boss-guest hadn't tasted home cooking like that in years. And isn't it always safer to spring that bill for the new dress right after papa has complimented you on a marvelous dinner?

Newspapers, magazines, and product packages devote considerable space to cookery. Cookbooks, as a group, are right next to the Bible as best sellers. Housewares departments are cram-jam full of all kinds of new, beautiful cookware and appliances. I'm sure women aren't buying them just to boil water. Nor do women fall in love with the latest in kitchen ranges just to dress up the kitchen. Adult cooking classes and food demonstrations are always filled to overflowing. Good cooking is relished by most people, and it is indeed a prestigious goal to attain.

Every now and then I get a mixed-up feeling after reading my mail. Am I really writing a food column only? Or a speaking-the-public-mind bit? Or a family counseling service? Or what? I seem to get some of everything, a fact I find fascinating. How many family fights do I start when I stick my neck out to answer one of those "Who is right? Me or my sister-in-law?" items?

Maybe it's just that food plays a bigger part in every facet of life than we realize. In my kitchen there hangs this cross-stitch sampler: "We may live without friends, we may live without books, but civilized man cannot live without cooks."

Index